Women at the Center

Women at the Center

Grameen Bank Borrowers
After One Decade

Helen Todd

WestviewPress

A Division of HarperCollins*Publishers*

Copyright © 1996 by Westview Press, Inc., A Division of HarperCollins Publishers, Inc.

Published in 1996 in the United States of America by Westview Press, Inc., 5500 Central Avenue,
Boulder, Colorado 80301-2877, and in the United Kingdom by Westview Press, 12 Hid's Copse
Road, Cumnor Hill, Oxford OX2 9JJ

Library of Congress Cataloging-in-Publication Data
Todd, Helen, 1943–
    Women at the center : Grameen Bank borrowers after one decade / by
Helen Todd.
        p.   cm.
    Includes bibliographical references and index.
    ISBN 0-8133-9000-1
    1. Grameen Bank.   2. Bank loans—Bangladesh.   3. Rural women—
Bangladesh.   4. Poor women—Bangladesh.   I. Title.
HG3290.6.A8G7385   1996
332.1L´095492—dc20   96-12161
                                                                                CIP

The paper used in this publication meets the requirements of the American National Standard for
Permanence of Paper for Printed Library Materials Z39.48-1984.

10   9   8   7   6   5   4   3   2   1

For David

Contents

Tables and Figures

xii

Preface

I visited Grameen Bank in 1985 as a journalist, spending two weeks in Rangpur Zone going to the Bank's Centers in various villages and interviewing borrowers. Since then I have closely followed the replication of the Grameen Bank system in Malaysia — so closely I married one of the replicators and lived for two years amongst the paddy fields where Project Ikhtiar began.

In the 15 years I have worked in Malaysia as a journalist I have become increasingly interested in what could be called development journalism, which meant, to me, getting below the surface of the official rhetoric and the glib statistics to find out who gets what from the spending of the development budget. This work brought two things home to me. One was that the planners and administrators always knew exactly what was best for the poor and always blamed the "backwardness" of the poor when something went wrong with their programs. Second, from the viewpoint of the supposed beneficiaries, the processes of "modernizing" the economy are often not benign, particularly to the rural poor and to women, precisely because they have little power to influence the outcomes or to demand the benefits of development.

In the wake of these experiences, I found the Grameen Bank system, as I saw it working in Bangladesh and Malaysia, very attractive. It politely sidesteps the entire development bureaucracy and the rural power structure that has been the real beneficiary of most development programs, and works directly with poor women. Its work is based on a confidence that women know what is best for themselves; all they need is the efficient delivery of user-friendly credit so that they can get on and do it. By putting money in poor women's hands, it begins, at least, to redress their powerlessness.

There is nothing that the Grameen Bank or the Malaysian project can do to force these women to repay their loans. So the fact they do so with such impressive faithfulness means that they are both making enough money to repay and that they see the benefit of keeping this credit window open so that they can get more loans.

So far, so good. But I knew that there were many controversies surrounding the Grameen Bank. And I had my own doubts about what "income generation" really meant in the lives of poor women. I knew that most borrowers in Bangladesh were using their loans for paddy husking; I had tried to work the heavy wooden *dheki* they used for husking myself. It didn't look much like a weapon of liberation to me. I had been the only woman in a press of men at the weekly *haat* or market — if men sold all the goods their wives produced because women were not allowed in the markets, who got the income that they generated? Did working for income simply increase the burdens on already overworked women and encourage their further exploitation, as some feminists argued?

I knew that the Grameen Bank, like Project Ikhtiar, targeted women for instrumental reasons, at least initially. Women were more faithful with repayment and "better disciplined," which also means easier to discipline. I knew that Grameen Bank was staffed from top to bottom by men. I had seen the women at the center meetings saluting and "Sah"ing. It seemed unlikely that groups like these were about to overturn the patriarchy.

So when David Gibbons, my husband, proposed a one year research project in Bangladesh to test the long-term impact of the Grameen Bank on women borrowers, I was very interested. It was an assignment with two major advantages not usually available to a journalist — time and partnership with a scholar.

David's main concern, from 20 years of research on poverty and six years of replicating the Grameen Bank system through Project Ikhtiar and then Amanah Ikhtiar Malaysia, was with poverty reduction. He wanted to take a systematic and in-depth look at a sample of long-term borrowers in order to research the doubts still so widely expressed by academics about the Grameen Bank. If his study proved that the long-term impact of credit ala Grameen Bank was positive and the operations of both the borrowers and the Bank were sustainable, then it would be possible to generate support for a massive attack on poverty in the rest of Asia through Grameen-type credit programs. This seemed to him to be the one workable chance to liberate large numbers of people from poverty before it reproduced itself manifold into the next generation.

However, we both knew that women are pivotal to the success of Grameen Bank, just as they proved to be pivotal to the very survival of the Grameen replications in other parts of Asia. The day to day processes of how they generate income, what they do with it and how much control they retain over it have been little explored. We were concerned with what it did for them — what benefits the women were getting, not subsumed into the household, but in terms of their own needs, interests and prospects. There has been some work done on how membership of Grameen Bank has affected women's behavior in household decision making and in family planning, but these have been mainly broad statistical surveys which give little in-depth information on the processes or relationships involved.

I have no particular academic qualifications for this task. But I could rely on David to keep the whole project within the bounds of academic respectability, while I used my journalistic skills in the interviewing and the writing. I also had the fanciful idea that being a farmer as well as a journalist in Malaysia and having spent 25 years living in that Islamic environment, I would slip into the Bangladesh village without a ripple of culture shock and avoid the usual Western misperceptions.

I must admit that initially my approach to this assignment was quite lighthearted. I thought it would be an adventure to live in a rural part of Bangladesh for eight months and exercise my mind and pen on a grounds-eye, women's-eye view of the Grameen Bank.

We started work in Tangail, the district where Grameen Bank was refined and institutionalized and where female centers had been in existence for a decade, in January, 1992. By that time I didn't want to be there. Two months earlier, my son Kamal had been killed in Dili, East Timor. He was a second-year university student and an activist on human rights, visiting East Timor to observe a proposed Portugese fact-finding mission. The Portugese mission was cancelled and the resulting climate of frustration and tension erupted at a memorial procession which turned into a demonstration for Timorese independence. Indonesian army units shot Kamal and nearly 300 unarmed, young Timorese as they crowded between the high walls of two cemeteries.

David and I moved into a room in the Area Office and initially each took charge of the data collection in one of our two villages. The village of Ratnogram, where I was responsible for initiating and supervising the basic weekly data collection, is full of small beauties. Water; birds; a patchwork quilt flung over a haystack; a blaze of mustard against a dark and ancient mango tree. Each one speared me with the knowledge of the lifetime robbed from Kamal. For myself, I would gladly have checked out of the whole painful business of going on living. David set the basic research design, the with-without comparisons which are described in Chapter One. At first, I just plodded blindly through it, trying hard to concentrate, to be patient with the frustrations of working through interpreters, suppressing my desire to lie down in the dust and howl.

But little by little the 20 Grameen women and the 12 women in the control group in Ratnogram began to get through to me. They were surprising; they didn't match the lists of grim statistics that wrapped up their situation in the books. They were resourceful. They were funny. They began to emerge as distinct individuals. I began to ask my own questions and pursue my own lines of inquiry.

I mined the weekly data sheets for specific decisions made by the family and used those to jump-start discussions with each woman on how those decisions were made. When I discovered what a drain illness was on the women's assets and prospects, I began to question them more systematically on health issues. I took a scale and a big stick marked off in centimeters into both villages and took the heights and weights of all the younger children, as the easiest measure of the impact of the woman's earning power on those who mattered most to her. I started cross-checking some of the more heroic Grameen stories to get a more accurate picture of how group pressure and support worked in practice. I decided to hold group discussions with small numbers of Grameen women on some of the contentious social issues which had arisen during the year.

I felt too battered myself to make any big judgments on these women. Mostly I listened with growing respect and empathy to the many and varied things they had to say. They are different from each other. They are strikingly different from the image of the South Asian poor woman which permeates the literature — a huddled figure, the end of her *sari* pulled well forward over her head, ageless, youthless, squatting against a dry field, a brown hut, a bare yard; each one of these millions of shadowed faces indistinguishable from the next. I decided that whatever else I did with the huge amount of data we were collecting, I would present the women in Ratnogram and Bonopur as they are — as individuals; as active shapers of their own lives.

Helen Todd

Acknowledgments

My thanks go first to the Grameen Bank, who funded and facilitated the research project from which this book has grown. In particular, Professor Muhammad Yunus, founder and Managing Director, once he accepted our desire to look more thoroughly at the Grameen Bank itself, before doing the research he wanted on the international replications of it, was very open about the issues on which the Bank wanted answers, visited us in the field and made valuable comments on our findings. Before we went to Tangail, at the end of the year of data collection and again when we had analysed the data, we gave seminars to the senior management of Grameen Bank and Grameen Trust, whose reactions gave us important feedback. Whenever we surfaced in Dhaka, Mr Khalid Shams, Deputy Managing Director, and Mr Khondakar Mozammel Haq, General Manager, found time for a stimulating exchange of ideas. Mr Mohammad Mortuza, then Deputy General Manager, Monitoring and Evaluation, was in charge of us, a responsibility he took on with his usual zest and efficiency. He smoothed our path in many ways and shared freely his experiences as Zonal Manager in Tangail during the repayment crisis of the mid-1980s.

In Tangail, all of the Grameen Bank staff were unfailingly helpful, with information, records unearthed from dusty attics and *char*. Our particular thanks go to the Modhupur Area Manager, Mr Md. Fahkrul Islam, and all the staff of the Shajahan and Ghatail Branch Offices. The Zonal Manager, Mr Sheik Liaqhat Ali, added to his already horrendous travelling schedule the task of dropping in to Ghatail, usually carrying my favourite *doy*, and staying to talk about his zone.

Our stay in Ghatail would have been very different without Mr Md. Ahasan Ullah Bhuiyan, the Ghatail Area Manager, and his wife Tanu. They gave us a room in their quarters and Ahasan "managed" our comfort with the same energy and effectiveness that he managed everything else. Ahasan's humanity and humour, and his comittment to the social goals of the Grameen Bank, helped us through several rough patches in the field work, while Tanu's tolerance of David's invasions into her kitchen was admirable.

The research could not have been done at all without the help of our research team: Bilkish Begum and Md. Ahsan Habib, the research investigators for Ratnogram and Bonopur respectively, and Kajal Chowdhury, our chief Research Assistant, who kept the data collection going through monsoon and pregnancy. In the last four months in the field, Nasmunahar joined me as interpreter, adding her tact and language skills, and excellent rapport with the village women, to my efforts to delve into sensitive family issues.

I hope the book itself is sufficient testimony to the respect and affection in which I came to hold the 62 women in our sample. All that remains for me here is to acknowledge how generously they shared with me one of their scarcer resources — their time.

Maheen Sultan, then Area Manager with the Grameen Bank, gave me critical comments on the manuscript at a crucial stage of the writing. Professor Rudolfe de Koninck, of Laval University, who visited us in the field, gave me sound advice about the structure of this book. My daughter, Nadiah, and stepson, James, pointed out the boring bits and the "dung cakes" — references not clear to the average reader.

Without David Gibbons, partner and fellow-researcher, none of this would have happened. He saw the need for an empirical study of the long-term impact of the Bank on its borrowers and invited me to participate. His loving companionship in the field helped me survive a time of great personal pain. Since then we have collaborated in analysing the joint data base and written our separate books side by side.

HT

1

The Bank in the Village

The village of Ratnogram lies one and a half kilometers from the main north-south trunk road which connects the small town of Ghatail to the district capital of Tangail. The main road used to be paved but now is horrendously potholed, a rickshaw driver's despair. Especially on *haat* or market days, it is crowded with briskly walking men, bullock carts, rickshaws and rickshaw vans.[1] Every now and then a bus or lorry roars through this melee at top speed, blasting its horn, scattering a wave of people to the front of it and a cloud of dust to the back.

The small, earthen road to the village is equally potholed, but quieter. Apart from the rickshaws, traffic here is all on foot. It is still mostly men, but there are family groups and occasionally a group of women on the move. Secondary schoolgirls in uniform take the shortcut across the fields to Ghatail, clutching their books protectively against their chests.

On either side of this rural road lie fields of paddy, with occasional patches of mustard, coriander or wheat. Depending on the season, there are men ploughing, planting and weeding; men guarding the pumps that push water into the irrigation canals; children pulling paddy seedlings. The men yell encouragement and rage at their bullocks. A boy sits on a bund singing, making up the words as he goes along: "I am a poor man, a very, very poor man." He stops and calls out to us cheerfully in English: "The sun rises in the East!" There are no women in these fields.

So far we have passed the statistically visible economy of Bangladesh — the busy local trade, the lorries from Tangail and Dhaka, the growing of crops and livestock; the irrigation technology. Not to mention government and donor interventions via the road system and the boy with an Education. This is the world that figures in the GDP and dominates development plans and the aid industry.

Now the road runs out of the sunlight and into an island of trees. This is a village, or part of a village. Here is where the women are. In this area of shade, are the village houses enclosing the village women, physically and economically invisible and confined to their domestic tasks. At least, that is the picture they fill in so many reports, usually highly judgmental, of the condition of women in Bangladesh. But, I would argue, that is the view of a (usually) male outsider coming from New York, from Dhaka, coming in from the main road. Because this is a book about women, I would like to describe the village from their viewpoint, (as far as I am able as an outsider), beginning in the *bari* and moving outwards.

Bangladeshi village women are not isolated in houses like a Western housewife; or locked into walled compounds like the third world middle-class. They live in a *bari*. This is a swept earth courtyard framed into a rough square by the houses of close relatives. The houses face inwards with blank back walls. The houses themselves and short, low walls of jute sticks or banana leaves define a *bari*; but they never entirely enclose it. The *bari* is above all *permeable*. Gaps and alleyways, shaded pergolas of beans and marrow vines, easily connect one *bari* to another and each *bari* to the outside. Outside there are intermediate areas containing haystacks and cowsheds, tube wells and vegetable plots, where women tend their livestock, gather food and draw water. From here paths lead through clumps of bamboo and bananas and groves of palms and fruit trees to the ponds, where poor women wash clothes and bathe themselves and their children. Beyond that is the true 'outside' — the starkly sunlit, open fields.

The paths and alleyways that link the *bari*s to each other are symbols of the social networks which link the people who live there. In the same *bari* are usually the houses of a woman's husband's brothers and their wives and families, and his parents, if they are still alive. At the level at which we were working — that of the village poor — women rarely shared a kitchen with their mother or sisters-in-law. Their nuclear families ate separately and managed their own budgets. But most of the women's work is done in the common courtyard, and the women are together much of the day.

Bari cluster together into a *para*, or neighborhood. In Ratnogram these are physically distinct, separated by ponds and stretches of open field. They are loosely based on *gusti* or lineage groups, so that neighboring *bari* are related in a widening circle of kin. This is the group within which the woman is located; enmeshed in networks of protection and social control, but also mutual help and economic transactions.

There are three *para* in Ratnogram. The smallest and most prosperous, Kahpara, is based on the *gusti* from which it is named and contains an elected

Newly cut wheat drying on the *bari* floor, the production floor for almost all agricultural processing. Note the cow dung drying in the left foreground and the sheltering circle of betel nut and fruit trees.

Photo Credit: Rudolphe de Koninck

Union member. The largest, Musjidpara, boasts the mosque and school, and the large cement and brick houses of both the largest landlord and his bitter rival. Beparipara is the poorest. Most of it is occupied by the Bepari caste of mustard oil makers, with some very poor non-Bepari living on its outskirts. Although the entire village is Muslim, pre-Islamic caste divisions remain important and the Bepari are one of the lower castes. They marry only with other Bepari and until very recently Bepari girls were married as children into the villages of their husbands. The reason for this is apparent as soon as you enter this *para.* Where the dominant mid-morning sound in Musjidpara is the rhythmic thump of the *dheki,* the foot operated, wooden mallet that pounds the husk off the paddy, in Beparipara it is the painful creak of the *ghani* — the stone mill with long wooden arms pushed by two or three women or girls, occasionally relieved by a cow, which crushes the mustard seed into oil. A new bride is automatically used as unpaid family labor on this *ghani.*

Overlaid on the kinship and *para* divisions within the village are *dol* or factions, headed by landlords with patronage to distribute — notably, opportunities to do daily labor, land to sharecrop or lease, and cash or rice to lend. These *borobari* (big houses) are important to poor women on their own account. In this part of Bangladesh, they offer the only kind of paid labor available to women — as servants or as helpers during the post-harvest processing. It is to the big houses that poor women sell the labor of their children, and contract to sell their milk or eggs. The landlord's wife is often a moneylender to village women as well. In Ratnogram one major landlord and his various offshoots formed five *borobari* (big houses — these ones *do* have high brick walls with locked doors) each with its own fan of client households. Another newcomer, a smaller landlord, forms a rival *dol.*

The kin networks, with their intertwining of social and economic relationships, extend, for the woman, beyond the confines of the village and back to her birthplace. Most brides come to live in their husband's village and become part of his family. But despite assertions in most of the literature on Bangladesh women that they are lost to their own families as a result, the women we studied retain strong links with their natal families. Their own families are both a refuge and an economic resource. This is made easier by the fact that most women come from nearby villages, often within walking distance — and women walk there and receive visits from their kin pretty often.

In addition, there are far more *ghor jamai* marriages — where the husband comes to live in the *bari* of his wife's family — than one would expect, given the hostility of Bengali males to this practice. There were seven *ghor jamai* marriages in our 62 member sample, and another couple who moved to the wife's village during the year, making up 13%. In addition, there were two women who had married men living in the same village and three divorcees who lived at home with their parents. Altogether 21% of our sample lived in their natal village. Women who live in their natal village generally move more freely within the village and can rely on many kinds of kin support.

The village of Bonopur, from where the other half of our sample was taken, is about 30km away from Ratnogram in the next Upazila, or district. It is only four kilometers from the large town of Gopalpur, which is the Upazila center, a place much larger than Ghatail with many shops, a large government hospital and the upazila-level police station and Government offices. Around three kilometers to the west of Bonopur is Shajanpur, a one-tea-shop place where the Grameen Bank branch office is located.

Unlike Ratnogram, where the *paras* have been built up, by hoe and basket, into raised islands above the paddy fields, Bonopur is spread out, linear fashion, along a natural plateau surrounded on three sides by a river bed. The river is dry in the winter and a swamp during the rainy season. In Bonopur the *gusti* overlap and the *para* merge into each other, marked only by the ponds. On the plateau are fields of vegetables from which this village gets a large part of its income, trading them as far as Dhaka. Although we chose this village because of its relative isolation — the road from Ghatail to Gopalpur and from there on to Modhupur is mud and almost impassable in the wet season, although a new road was under construction. But during the dry winter season, when this village bloomed with cauliflowers and cabbages, it was in much closer contact with distant markets than the more conventional paddy farmers of Ratnogram.

For the women in their *bari*, looking outwards, the concept which defines the space within which they live and work is the idea of 'inside' versus 'outside'. But the defining lines are neither fixed nor clear. Just as there are intermediate areas between the *bari* and the open fields, so the notion of 'inside' is flexible and can be pushed outwards. Although I never saw women working in the open fields that led to the main road, I quite often saw women in the fields between the *para* or next to their houses, staking their goats, collecting straw, helping their sons harvest paddy or cabbages or even pulling paddy seedlings. Whenever women were out in this ambiguous space they seemed to me to be expressing, in their brisk, purposeful body language, the message: "Don't mess with *me*. I'm doing my *family work.*"

How women negotiate more space and succeed or fail to push their boundaries outwards is the subject of part of this book. All I want to emphasise in this introduction is that I did not find that there was any fixed set of *purdah* rules that controlled women's activities. Rather there were ideas of 'proper behavior' around which were differences of opinion and room to maneuver, depending on a woman's age, relationships and power within her family. Moreover, the women defend their behavior as 'proper' regardless of how far 'out' their income work or their membership in Grameen Bank takes them.

They have no desire to confront or overturn the system in which they live, sanctified by Islam. Only one woman in our sample deliberately worked 'outside,' and she was a widow employed in the rural road repair program funded by CARE. All the others would calmly tell you, even while they were out in the field fetching their goats: "I only do inside work; outside work is the duty of my husband."

Although *purdah* proscribes being seen by strange men, that also is very flexible in practice. The family is widened when convenient by extending family terms of address and privileges to fictive uncles and brothers. Many families in the village have *dhormo* mothers and fathers (a religious relationship like a godmother or godfather) who are treated like family intimates. It is worth noting that, for the women members of the Grameen Bank, this admission to family status extends easily to the 10,000 largely male members of the Bank staff.

Certainly there were very few *burka* in the two villages. There were only two women in our sample who had elevated themselves into that black tent. One was a prosperous and aggressively status conscious Grameen Bank member. The other was the wife of a rather successful beggar in our control group. No doubt an appearance of piety is necessary in that profession. The lack of *purdah* clothing is in striking contrast to Malaysia, where Islamic dress, in the form of loose tunic and complete head covering, has enveloped the younger generation over the last decade.

Why You Should Read This Book
(and Not Just the Conclusion)

This book is about the impact of a decade of Grameen Bank membership on the lives of forty women who live in these two villages. Our research focussed on their household economies, but also on 'the politics of everyday life,' as they affected women's relationships within their families and within the Centers. You will not find the research results encapsulated in a series of elegant tables, since my concern is with the "noisier, messier understanding of social processes" (Kabeer 1994:133). We followed these 40 women, week by week, over the period of one year and compared them with a matched group of 22 women who were not members of the Grameen Bank. Nobody has systematically studied the impact of the Grameen Bank on its borrowers in this way before.

I think it is fair to say that Grameen Bank has been much written about but little researched. There are writings on its philosophy and operations by its practitioners, notably Professor Yunus himself (Yunus 1984, 1986, 1987, 1989, 1991); Huq and Sultan (1991); Shams (1992) and Gibbons (1990, 1994). There are the useful, but quite adulatory, accounts by Fuglesang and Chandler (1986,

1993) and most recently, a detailed look at the structure and management style of the Bank in the light of modern management theory by Susan Holcombe (1995). These accounts look at the Grameen Bank from the top end, a necessary perspective for an enquiry on what inspires it and how it works.

At the bottom end, the impact on the borrowers, important empirical work was done in the mid-eighties by scholars from the Bangladesh Institute of Development Studies. Mahabub Hossain (1988) surveyed five villages covered by the Grameen Bank and two control villages, and gathered systematic data on income, assets and employment. Atiur Rahman (1986a,b, 1989a,b,c) did several surveys on the impact of Grameen Bank membership on political participation consciousness and response to disaster, as well as on the nutritional impact of GB loans. Rushidan Rahman (1986) focussed specifically on the impact on women. These studies were done at a time when the Grameen Bank was very much smaller, younger and more equally balanced between male and female borrowers than it is now.

As one might expect, in the donor-driven research environment of Bangladesh, there are a number of surveys on whether Grameen Bank membership promotes family planning, the most recent and scholarly of which is Schuler and Hashemi (1994).

Hossain's work is fundamental to ours. His findings were:

- that investment in fixed assets and amount of working capital increased substantially amongst BG borrowers
- that the loans helped generate employment for poor women
- that GB members had higher incomes — and that the benefits spread to non-members in GB villages, who were better off than the landless in villages where there were no GB centers.

Hossain's field research, done in 1985, with a borrower sample of average membership of only 2.5 years, indicates that the potential impact on longer-term members could be dramatic. However, by 1992 when our research began, there was serious concern amongst the senior management of the Bank that the benefits to borrowers may have levelled off as local markets became saturated with the few activities funded by the loans.

Since 1985 there has also been a sea-change in the membership of the Bank. Hossain's field sample was only 55% female — and most of them were new members because of the shift towards women in the early eighties. The sub-sample selected for his in-depth household survey on economic impact was taken from the older centers and can be assumed to be mainly male. By 1992, when we went to Tangail, 94% of Grameen Bank's two million members were women.

Reflecting this background, the basic research questions we took to Tangail were:

1. Has GB type credit resulted in substantial decreases of poverty amongst the borrowers?

2. To what extent have women borrowers been empowered by access to this credit?

3. Is the impact, if any, sustainable over time?

To test these questions we needed a sample of long-term members, in their eighth to tenth year of borrowing. To reflect the composition of the Bank, all the sample should be women members.

But how large a sample did we need? Should we do a broad survey or a village study? Given that there had been almost no empirical work on the impact of GB lending for the past seven years and, as a result, a lack of information on which to base testable hypotheses, we decided on a village study, hedging our bets somewhat by selecting two quite different villages.

The sample we selected — of 40 Grameen Bank women in two centers and 22 non-members as a matched control group selected from the same two villages — was small enough so that David and I could get to know them individually and observe them continuously over the period of one year. Our goal was to trace their ups and downs through the seasons of lean and plenty, document their responses to crisis and disaster as these arose and observe how the loans and their proceeds were used within the family as this was happening. Through this almost anthropological method, we hoped to get an understanding of the *processes* by which women use their access to credit and negotiate their lives.

Our sample was carefully chosen (details on the selection of the sample and the methodology are contained in Appendix 1) but it is not statistically representative of either Grameen Bank members or the rural poor in Bangladesh. Tangail is only one of the eleven Zones in which the Grameen Bank is operating, each of them different. Moreover, women borrowers in their eighth to tenth loan cycles are still a minority in the Bank. Grameen Bank's rapid expansion after 1986 means that most of its women members have had an average of only four years borrowing and are probably younger than the average woman in our sample.

Our findings then are indicative of what *can* be achieved by women members over their first decade of membership, rather than the current situation of the average Grameen Bank member now.

However, for the kind of issues with which we were concerned our concentration on these 62 households was necessary. Many families were initially secretive about some of the economic data, particularly land matters and indebtedness. It also took time to uncover what members were actually doing with their loans and to get an accurate picture of the economic contribution of each woman, since some of it was deliberately hidden by the women themselves.

Much of the information we were seeking on processes and relationships is not quantifiable; it never appears in survey data based on standardized questionnaires. The balance of power in the household and the strategies women use to enlarge their space are particularly elusive to a one-shot interview, as we ourselves discovered in an initial questionnaire on 'decision-making.' My understanding of women's relationships grew slowly, based on piecemeal data gathered as things happened.

Some of our findings are preliminary, in the sense that they can be taken out and tested on a statistically representative sample, particularly our discoveries on the way women borrowers are investing in land. Some of the findings on women's centrality in their households can probably only be tested using a similarly anthropological approach.

On a personal note, there are people who relish the econometric elegance of surveys, and there are others, like myself, who revel in the noise and complexity of individual lives. The pared-down version of reality that arises from measuring hundreds of households would never have tempted me out of my durian orchard in the Jelebu hills of Malaysia and into the paddy fields of Tangail, and so this book would never have been written.

Our more general goal in conducting this research was to gather a body of empirical data against which could be tested some of the theoretical positions that have been taken on the Grameen Bank. These range from what Holcombe (1995:48) calls "casual criticism from the skeptical and cynical [in the development business]" to more informed questioning from scholars who nevertheless rely on secondary sources for their information on the Bank.

We should look at some of these theoretical stances and the questions they raise so that they can be dealt with in the chapters that follow.[2]

It took a long time for the academic world outside Bangladesh, or the development community, to notice the Grameen Bank at all, since it was an entirely indigenous creation and was mainly funded for its first seven years by Bangladeshi banks.[3] When they did, however, the reaction from the mainstream Women in Development (WID) practitioners and scholars was that it could not possibly be enough — credit alone could not substantially alter women's position in the absence of other inputs.

This group, broadly speaking, see poor women in Bangladesh as so disadvantaged by both poverty and gender that only a multipronged attack, through literacy and health education, the creation of market channels, skills training and conscientization *in addition to and prior to* credit for income creation could possibly have an impact on their situation (Chen 1986:232; BRAC 1980, 1983; Sobhan ed. 1991 Volume 1, Volume 7; Safilios-Rothschild 1991). The minimalist approach of the Grameen Bank, and its argument that poor women already have the skills and market information they need to escape from poverty, set it against the WID orthodoxy from the start.

In the donor community, a number of liberal feminists who have assumed powerful positions within both UN development agencies and USAID have been preoccupied with getting Asian women out of their domestic slavery and into paid employment, a route which has been of major importance in the liberation of Western women (World Bank 1990). Grameen Bank sins on that count as well. Far from busting women out of the *bari*, it gives loans for self employment so that women can earn income from things they already do at home. Yunus, in fact, has written that "wage-employment is not a happy road to poverty reduction" and exults that the woman borrower "does not have to leave her habitat or her children." (Yunus 1989:47-48)

More recently, the rapid expansion of the Bank and its continuing remarkable loan recovery rate have made it more difficult to ignore by mainstream economists, who are beginning to consider its macro-impact on poverty in Bangladesh. A recent study by the World Bank praises Grameen Bank on efficiency grounds, for hitting several birds with one stone:

> The Grameen Bank has deliberately targeted women, realising that their participation in social development is necessary for economic development because of their primary role in providing health, education and nutrition. Historically, women have been neglected by development projects, removing them from the growth and development process. (Khandker 1995:12)

However, amongst these economists and amongst almost all bankers who know anything about the Grameen Bank, serious doubts about its sustainability continue.

Far more critical of the Grameen Bank have been the structural feminists, who tend to see any efforts which do not aim at the overthrow of the capitalist and patriarchal structures which systematically subordinate women as, in Kabeer's words: "at best ameliorative, and, at worst, a co-opted form of feminism." (1994:67) They believe that women must organise to break the structures which oppress them; individual income gains cannot work alone. Since the Grameen Bank by policy does not confront the structures which exploit women, these critics assume that any income gains that women might make by using their loans will be extracted from them by male relatives or by the elites. There is ambivalence over whether the group and center structure of the Grameen Bank constitute the kind of solidarity group which could assert women's interests. Some (Berninghausen 1992:258) assume it does; others closer to the scene catagorize Grameen Bank groups as simply a delivery mechanism, not as structures which could empower the poor (Wood 1994:296).

Wood (Kramsjo 1992:33) characterizes studies of poverty alleviation and credit management as "pernicious, even when it includes participatory rhetoric, because it suggests solutions independent of the structures which produced the problems."

A less apocalyptic group of structural feminists who arose out of the SOW (Subordination of Women) group (Kabeer 1994:54) and who have done groundbreaking work on the politics of gender in a number of third world contexts, have raised some specific questions about the impact of Grameen Bank which must be answered in this study. First, is what I would call "the burden thesis," which argues that by adding income-generation to a woman's already multiple tasks, she is additionally burdened without necessarily benefitting *herself* — although her husband and children may be better off. Second, by extending credit to women, but closing one eye to male *use* of such loans, banks like the Grameen Bank are, in fact, forcing women to act as their debt collectors, again, without the women necessarily gaining anything for themselves (Goetz forthcoming).

All of these questions will be raised again and discussed in the light of our findings in the chapters that follow. Before outlining these findings, however, I would like to come down from these theoretical clouds to the slight but vibrant figure of Kia, because my relationship with her illustrates some of the problems we encountered in the data collection and the doubts that arose about its accuracy. Finally in this chapter I will describe the workings of the Grameen Bank centers in these two villages, as a necessary background to an account of the lives of its members.

"Tell Apa the Truth!"

I think most researchers working in a village sooner or later come across a "favorite" informant, someone, they convince themselves, who is more intelligent, more aware, someone who has the ability to step back a little from their own struggle for existence and comment on the bigger picture. All the virtues, in other words, that the researcher likes to imagine in herself.

I suspect that there is also something more personal in it. That person embodies some need or fantasy or prejudice of the outsider, just as the outsider does for the informant. Perhaps such relationships represent a marriage of the informant's desire to please the researcher (for her own reasons) with the researcher's desire to "discover" what she has gone there to find.

For me, initially, that person was Kia. Over the year she also came to symbolize many of the problems we encountered with the material we were collecting.

Her interest in me was, I think, tied up with her low caste status as a Bepari and her overwhelming determination to pull herself and her children as far as possible from anything that smelled of mustard oil. It was part of her strategy to befriend higher status people in the village and particularly to attach herself to those few outsiders from NGOs who came to work there. Despite my disappointing lack of a nose-stud or earrings, I came, at least, in a van, and so had some status to which she could hitch her ambitions.

For me, the attraction had much to do with her confidence and vivacity. If I was bored with meek women, there was absolutely nothing meek about Kia. When I was floundering in a fog of contradictions and evasions, she was refreshingly direct and never slow to advance a confident opinion. When I was hungry for information she prided herself on helping me — and often did.

Kia was 32 years old in 1992, with two sons aged 11 and 9. Her husband was a daily laborer on the farms of others. She lived on the edge of Beparipara, at the point where the non-Bepari houses began, and that was how she quite consciously saw herself — in transition; on the way out. She was well liked throughout the village, despite her caste status. In fact, one of the first dramas we encountered took place when Kia's loan proposal was denied by the bank worker, which provoked a strike in both the female and the male centers.

She had one of these finely-chiselled, mobile faces alive with expression — often laughter. She carried around with her such a field force of energy and zest that it took some time to notice how stick-thin and frail her body was.

Kia had a *ghor jamai* marriage — her husband lived in her parent's compound rather than she living in his village — and this certainly contributed to her confidence and dominance in her household, as well as the freedom with which she moved around the village. "I am the Lord!" she declared, explaining how decisions were made in her family, all five foot two of her chortling with amusement at the outrageousness of this idea.

I would often stop in her *bari,* squat down on the tiny wooden stool that keeps your backside about one and a half inches off the dirt, and ask the background to whatever had come up in the interviews that morning. If she knew, she would be delighted to tell me. If she didn't, she would oblige me by making something up.

Once when I was having trouble getting the facts of an old scandal that had deeply affected the life of Parul, one of the Grameen women in our sample, I asked Kia to help me persuade her to tell her side of this story. "Persuasion" didn't describe her method. She collared Parul, plunked us both under a tree and while I tried to gently extract the story, Kia stood over us, alternately fierce and cajoling, saying: "Don't just *sit*! Tell Apa the truth!"

Not having had the benefit of a post-modern education, or any other kind, Kia was sure she knew what the truth was — it was what had happened. I had more doubts, but having spent the last 15 years working as a journalist in Malaysia in the face of outright censorship, (being told at one point, for example, that poverty did not exist in Malaysia and so I was, forthwith, to stop writing about it) it still seemed a desirable goal to me. But even if you narrowed the problem down to just getting accurate information, was it possible for a

Kia busy with her fire, outside in the winter sunshine. Her house faces her parent's house across this *bari*, and the bamboo grove in the background separates her *bari* from that of her non-*Bepari* neighbours.   *Photo Credit: Helen Todd*

foreign outsider, working through interpreters, to get an accurate understanding of the lives of these women?

Did I even understand Kia? When the strike succeeded and Kia finally got her loan, she told the Bank and the research team that she would use it to replace her broken *ghani* — the stone mill that Bepari households use to crush mustard seed to produce oil. The mustard was being harvested; seed was cheap; other households were stocking seed, working their *ghani* well into the night and making the best profits of the year. "Where's the *ghani*? When will it arrive?" I asked Kia several times a week. "Any day now. Next week. Soon." she would reply.

After a month I knew that there had not been a working *ghani* in this *bari* for at least two years and that she had no intention of buying one. By then we were a familiar daily presence in the village and the Grameen members knew we were not reporting back to the branch office. So Kia was willing to tell us her plans.

"I am never going to push the *ghani* again for the rest of my life. I am not a cow. Neither my husband nor my sons are going to be involved in this Bepari business," she explained.

She had invested the loan in the lease of 20 decimals of paddy land. She would add to it, piece by piece, until she had transformed her husband from a daily laborer into a small farmer, like her non-Bepari neighbors.

She also had her eye on seven decimals of land for a houselot outside Beparipara, where she would build her own *bari* for herself and her husband, her two sons and their prospective wives and families. She was keen to build her own *bari* not just to get out of Beparipara. Although she owned the land on which her house stood in her own name, she feared that when her father died, a stepbrother (son of her father's second wife) would return and take over the *bari,* making the life of her family intolerable. (When writers lament the short-term perspective of the very poor, I think they have not talked to the women.)

Neither leasing nor buying land was allowed as a use of individual loan capital under the rules of the Bank. Borrowers should deal in land only out of their profits, or in collective activities, the Bank held. Officially, the Bank saw leasehold as a form of usury, one of the ways the more powerful in the village exploited and dispossessed the poor. That is why Kia — along with many other members — falsified her loan use to the Bank.

She had been trained as a *dai,* a traditional midwife, she told me, and painted me a vivid picture of racing off in the middle of the night to deliver babies, unpaid. "But I help them and they love me. They give me what they can afford. Most of the babies in this *para* have been delivered by me."

She also had a contract with a private hospital, who paid her a 500 Taka fee for any patient she referred to them. This brought her a lot of income, she said.

When we came back to the village the next winter we had eight months weekly data on every household. We knew what they earned and what they spent, what were their assets and debts, when they were ill, when without work and what their children were doing. Whenever the woman left her *para* we knew where she went and why.

Among the Grameen women Kia was one of the poorest. She delivered one baby in May and she attended two five day family planning courses in Ghatail, for which she was paid a daily allowance. But there was no other income recorded from work as a midwife and nothing was coming in from the hospital. The women in her *para* told me who delivered their babies and it was never Kia.

I remember the day I pushed her into admitting that in the last year she had delivered only one child and the only patients she had ever taken to the hospital were her husband and her cousin. Those remaining fragments of her fantasy of windfall income lay sadly on the beaten grey mud between us and neither of us could think of anything to say.

"She's completely unreliable," I told David that night. " I can't believe a word she tells me."

That was not the point, of course. I was disappointed and angry because I had wanted to believe Kia's fantasy almost as much as she did. It was not that the material I had gathered had proved to be false or unreliable. On the contrary. What had happened was that my false beliefs and preconceptions had, together with Kia's dreams, hit up against the hard rock of the weekly data, and collapsed. It was the beginning of a more accurate interpretation of the data and a more realistic understanding of her life.

This was to happen again and again during the last four months of interviewing. The weekly data sheets assembled in a mass of specific and often tedious detail the minutiae of village lives. They provided the touchstone against which all other material had to be tested and interpreted. It was also a springboard for further exploration. From it I could connect with the specific events and issues of immediate relevance to each woman — the purchase just made, the illness just overcome, the son just contracted out — and explore how these decisions were made and why one strategy for survival was chosen over another.

In addition, the continual presence of the research team in both villages over the period of a year positioned us firmly in the gossip networks (to which we contributed some items) and alerted us to many events which affected the women in the sample. All of the research team became involved with the lives of these women and our discussions often opened my eyes to the cultural context affecting their behavior. The smallness of the sample made it possible to cross-check much of the social information, as I did with Kia's babies.

By the spring I was asking myself why it had taken so long to accept that poor women have dreams and that a woman of Kia's energy and determination should have elevated hers to the level of semi-reality. By then I understood that the Walter Mitty side of Kia's character tended to obscure both her real tragedies and her real achievements.

Three years earlier, Kia had been making reasonably good progress towards her goal of respectable landedness. She operated a *ghani* and used her first three Grameen Bank loans as working capital to buy the mustard seed. She didn't want her husband to trade from village to village in mustard oil, although that was what he had done in his father's house, because when he did he used to "sell his oil and then hang around with rich people, spending money." So she asked the husband of her non-Bepari neighbor to take him with him doing daily labor "to break his shyness for that kind of work." So her husband did daily labor and went once a week to the *haat* to buy mustard seed and sell the oil Kia made to a retailer in the bazaar.

We ate from his daily labor; I repaid the Bank from selling the mustard cake and we saved all the profits from the mustard oil, although profits are often not good in this business. First, I bought this houselot from my father for 3,000 Taka and took a housing loan to build a Grameen Bank house. Then, when I had saved another 6,000 Taka I leased in a *bigha* (one-third of an acre) of paddy land. Saving was easier after that because we had our own paddy to eat. I needed 10,000 Taka to buy the new houselot. My father agreed to buy back this lot and I had 3,000 saved in my hand. I was already talking to the landlord when my husband and I both fell into disaster.

Kia was cooking *murri* (puffed rice) in red hot sand. Her sister's child got in her way when she was lifting the pot and she tipped the sand all over her leg. She was on crutches for a year and the *ghani* stopped — permanently. Shortly afterwards, her husband was diagnosed as having tuberculosis.

"My leg cost 3,000 Taka and we spent 10,000 Taka for his TB. I gave back the leasehold, used all my savings and my general loan and group fund loan. We were both cured, praise to God, but we were back again to zero."

After this she used her connections with the family planning workers who come to the village and with the private mission hospital in Modhupur where her husband had been treated to be included in a government family planning scheme for village *dai*. (She talked her way into it. She is not known in the village as a *dai*.) At the beginning of the year of data collection, she used her general loan to take a land lease, as we have seen. At the end she got a seasonal loan for 4,000 Taka and immediately put it into another 15 decimal leasehold. When her eldest son completed Standard Six, the last year of primary school, she worked through her husband's family to get him apprenticed to a furniture shop in Gopalpur. Her younger son, who refused to go to school, went to work for a woman landlord whom Kia had been cultivating for some time.

Just a week before I left the village I saw tragedy almost engulf her again. Her younger son, busy in the predawn, winter darkness with his "master's" shallow tube-well, got his shawl caught in the flywheel of the pump. This slammed his head against the open motor and tightened the shawl around his neck until it began cutting through the flesh. Only the quick reaction of the "master" saved his life. When the news came to Kia all she was told was that the boy, unconscious and bleeding, had been taken to hospital. She was beside herself with grief and terror.

Only a week later I watched as she talked to the founder and Managing Director of Grameen Bank, Professor Muhammad Yunus. Her vibrant face and her son's shaved head and scars stood vividly out of the crowd.

Earlier we had briefed Professor Yunus on our research, including our finding that many members were putting their loan capital into leasehold land just as fast as they could. We had urged that the borrowers should be allowed to do what they were doing anyway; that they saw leasehold as an investment in food security and the most sustainable way to raise household income. We argued that they were right and that loans should be made available specifically for the leasing in of land. Dr Yunus listened but did not commit himself.

"Let's go to the village," he said.

When we stopped in Kia's *bari* she and the boy related the drama of the accident and showed the tattered pink shawl he still wore as a kind of talisman.

Then Professor Yunus questioned Kia about the new special loan. "Do you want one?"

"Yes, sir!"

"What will you use it for?"

I saw Kia hesitate for a moment. Then she looked the Managing Director in the eye.

"I won't lie to you," she said. "I am going to lease in some land."

In the last few weeks of our eight months in Tangail I found myself rushing obsessively to tie up all the loose ends, answer all the unanswered questions, plumb the remaining mysteries. My desperation must have been apparent; I was impatient with our research assistants and pushed for more time with the village women at what was one of the busiest months of the year, when the *amon* paddy and the wheat were piling into their *bari* for processing.

Mohiron, a widow in her 60s who lived in Bonopur, was one of the "loose ends" I was pursuing; I had called at her house everyday for a week and always she was somewhere else. One day as I approached her *bari* I caught a glimpse of her bent and scurrying back, her faded blue sari pulled well forward over her head, hugging the very edge of the road as if that would make her invisible.

So I never did find out why Mohiron sold half of her houseplot to a complete stranger, a man who had money but no work and who sat in the *bari* most days eyeing Mohiron's daughter-in-law doing her kitchen chores until she retreated into her hut. I will never know why Mohiron was so afraid of him that she kept her money with the landlord's wife and wouldn't talk to me if he was there.

Nor did I ever penetrate the mystery of Zainon. She was a widow, not a

Grameen member, and worked as a maidservant for the landlord whose house overlooked her own. Some years before a man had been expelled from his family at a village *shalish* (court) for having an affair with her. Zainon quarrelled constantly and bitterly with her son who ate and often slept at his workplace and who gave her none of his earnings. Her 27 year old daughter did no work and was not married, an outlandish and scandalous state of affairs in the eyes of the village. When we analyzed the income data from her household we found that, judging by the amount of rice earned or purchased, all three of them should have died of hunger months before. As our questions became more informed and penetrating, Zainon was less and less often at home when the day for the weekly interview came around. Only her daughter would be visible, hanging about the landlord's front yard. She was an unusually dark, but very pretty girl, with dazzling white teeth. She sat on a log, nicely dressed, sleek with well being, smiling her perfect smile, as impenetrable as her mother's locked door.

Of course, the transgressions, the underlife of the village, are the most resistant to enquiry by outsiders and it may never have been possible to persuade people to open out their secret fears and shames to our scrutiny. We were not there long enough nor did we ever lose our distance as outsiders.

It was equally unrealistic to expect any kind of closure. The women I had known for a year were not going to tidy their lives into a package of neat conclusions just because I was about to cease observing them. We left several in the midst of various crises, without knowing what would be the outcomes.

There are limits to our findings imposed by cultural taboos, the time at our disposal and our own status as outsiders working through interpreters. But on the issues we chose to observe and on which we collected systematic and detailed data there is reasonable certainty about the conclusions. For all of our 62 member sample (we dropped Zainon and another member of the control group whose sons objected to our knowledge of their debts) we have an exhaustive week by week picture of their economic lives, through each season, the scarcity and glut of harvest and employment, their borrowings and lendings and the use of the Grameen capital. Amongst the poor in the context of village life, so much else depends on this economic base and on the success or failure of their economic strategies for survival. Through this detailed data we could map the woman's contribution to the cash income and to the wider economic life of the household and explore how decisions within the household were negotiated. We could see how she used her earnings, if she had them, and what benefits derived from them for herself and her children. Finally, I could make a judgment — only a judgment, but one based on a year of observation and anchored to economic realities — on the woman's confidence and self-esteem and how she related to the members of her own *bari* and to the village world outside it.

The Grameen Bank Approach to Rural Poverty

When the Grameen Bank field workers first appeared in the Ghatail area in 1980, the "Bank", then just a Project with fewer than 3,000 borrowers, was four years old (Grameen Bank Annual Report 1989:71). It was based on principles which made it then — and still make it — unique amongst development efforts aimed at redressing poverty. Professor Muhammad Yunus, who began giving small loans to poor people in Jobra, a village next to Chittagong University, as an experiment in 1976, was motivated by a belief that poor people already have the skills that can lift them out of poverty. What they lack is the capital to use these survival skills for their own benefit.

The poor are capable in many activities, Professor Yunus argues. In his own words:

"What do you do? " "I do odd jobs here and there." This is the life story of many a landless person. He has lost the foundation of his household. He has no land. No homestead. No barn. No cowshed. He is left with only his two hands. With these he does tidbits of odd jobs. He does something whenever he has the opportunity. He has to get his meals. ...

The person who does tidbits of odd jobs, is looking for opportunities all the time. He is like a hunter. He strikes at the opportune moment.

[However, because of his poverty] he is unable to utilize all his skills to their fullest extent because he does not have the essential capital base. ... He can only use his skills subject to the wishes and needs of the capitalist.

Only if the poor person acquires control over the capital needed for the independent application of his skills can he move in the direction of fuller utilization of his productive capacity. He can then begin a process of ensuring the continual increment of his assets and income.

With financial resources at his disposal, an individual is free to build his own fate with his own labor. Nothing can match the spirit of a free human being. (Gibbons 1992:27, 28, 32, 44)

In his Jobra experiment, Yunus found the conventional commercial banks hostile to the credit needs of the poor. But he discovered that the poor are credit-worthy, under certain conditions:

- when loan repayments are frequent and small
- when the bank business is conducted openly, in the village, using simple procedures
- when borrowers form peer groups who give support and exert pressure for repayment

He also formulated his own version of Gresham's Law: "in the world of development, if one mixes the poor and the non-poor within the format of a single programme, the non-poor will always drive out the poor." (1984:57)

During the Jobra experiment the basic organizational structure of the Grameen Bank evolved as an expression of these principles. The field staff of the Project were trained to seek out the poorest households in their areas and motivate them to form groups of five "like-minded" people. These groups were trained by the bank staff to sign their names and memorize the rules and principles of the Project. A senior staff member tested the groups and visited their homes to ensure that they were indeed poor. The definition used was ownership of less than half an acre of cultivable land or assets worth less than the value of one acre.

Groups joined together into centers, which held weekly meetings in the village, ideally in their own center hut. Here all the business — loan proposals, group and center approval of them, repayment and savings — was conducted. Groups and centers elected their own leaders. Group chairpersons and center chiefs were supposed to be changed each year.

The Grameen Bank Project came to the Tangail District in 1979 under the sponsorship of the Bangladesh Bank. In the eyes of the commercial bankers who were instructed to provide the loan capital, the Project was still being tested. Could a one-man experiment in a few villages be institutionalized into a district-wide credit programme, far from the University, and still retain its high recovery rates? During the Tangail period the Project continued to evolve and refine its rules and practices. An important change was a shift in focus to women, so that male centers have become a tiny minority in the Grameen Bank. This shift was partly in response to a serious repayment crisis which hit the Bank in Tangail in the mid-eighties, which led to a number of organizational changes.[4] In 1983 the Grameen Project became the Grameen Bank under its own charter and in 1986, the Bangladesh government sold most of its shares to the borrowers, so that they became the majority owners of the Grameen Bank.

Two Village Centers

This is the general history against which we can set the particular development of the two centers in Ratnogram and Bonopur. Although they cannot be seen as representative of the 60,000 centers in the Grameen Bank, they are the structures through which the Bank impacts on the lives of our sample.

The Grameen Bank branch at Ghatail began operations in January, 1980, while the Shajanpur Branch started work in the area that contains the village of Bonopur in March of the same year. At first, however, both branches concentrated on recruiting men and forming male centers, a focus which was general throughout the Tangail district at that time. However, later in that year,

Bank workers began talking to women in these villages and motivating them to form their own groups.

The Bank worker who came to Ratnogram was married into a family in the next village, which made her work easier, in the sense of placing her within already trusted women's networks of information. Although she visited the houses of poor women, motivating them to join, it was her mother-in-law they went to talk to about their doubts.

Five Bepari women formed the first group, led by a woman who subsequently left the Bank. Its members included women who had least to lose — a childless divorcee, a desperately poor widow with four young daughters, an embattled second wife. The second group was initiated by a woman from Musjidpara. Although very poor, her family belongs to a strong *gusti* in the village and is allied to the dominant landlord. Both of these women's husbands were already members of the male center formed earlier. Over the next four years the center expanded until it reached its current size — six groups of five members each. One group comes from Kahpara; one from Beparipara; three formed themselves mainly from Musjidpara and there is one mixed Bepari-Musjidpara group.

Perhaps because this is a small village, quite a few of the women who joined the center were married to men who were already members of the male center, a diffusion of responsibility and a doubling of debt which would lead to problems later. The biggest landlord and *matbar* (leader) in Ratnogram was quite supportive of the formation of these Grameen Bank centers in the village; the woman in Musjidpara who initiated the second group, was later center chief for many years and arranged for the center hut to be built on her family land, is one of his clients. None of the poor families associated with the rival *dol* became members of the center. Its landlord leader made insulting remarks about the "favors" Grameen women members must be giving to the male staff of the Bank in return for their loans. But whether his opposition stopped his client families from joining or whether they were excluded by the other members, I did not find out.

I think that this must be fairly typical of the response of the local elite to the arrival of Grameen Bank in their villages. There are many stories of landlords and *mullahs* opposing the creation of new Grameen centers. Most village studies, written from a Marxist perspective, dwell at length on the oppressive and exploitative landlord class. But I think that it is likely that some landlords were supportive and some not, according to their own factional rivalries, rather than all landlords seeing Grameen Bank as a threat to their class interests. The center in Bonopur is a case in point. The first group was formed by the niece of a *matbar* who later became Union Chairman. Although she was poor, she had the support of the main faction in the village. There is one end of the village, however, with many poor families but no Grameen members because of the very strong opposition, expressed in terms of Islam, from the major family there.

In the mid-eighties, when the leadership of the Bank believed that the route to higher productivity and substantially better incomes was through collective activities, financed by collective loans, the male center in Bonopur took a collective loan to buy a shallow tube well for irrigation. When the center members fell out amongst themselves over its management, they sold the machine, pocketed the proceeds and failed to repay the Bank. The male center fell apart, and very soon members of the women's center also began to drop out and stop repayment. The story of how a small group of women worked with the Branch staff to put the center together again is told in Chapter Eight.

In these centers, already nine and ten years old, group formation and group training took place long ago. The groups are of five women, who come from landless families (less than half an acre of land). They selected each other, and were of similar economic status but not close relatives. Since it did happen long ago and the rules of the bank have evolved and become more rigorous over time, there are a few members in each center who were not qualified to join, and a few neices and aunts in the same groups. The great majority, however, were very poor before joining Grameen Bank. A study of the No 1 Forms, which record personal information on the assets and occupations of the member's families at the time of their group training, reveals that only two households reported having any agricultural land at that time. Six out of ten male household heads were daily laborers on other peoples' land. We discovered that some of this information was fictional, of course, but almost all these families owned much less than half an acre of land (the amount used to define the "functionally landless") ten years earlier. In the intervening decade some have advanced faster than others, and there are very wide differences in their status now.

Although their group training took place nearly a decade ago, members are still expected to know the basic rules of the Bank and the 16 Decisions which make up its social program. During the year the branch manager questioned a widow in our sample before he disbursed her loan and found that she did not know some of the rules. He stopped payment of her loan until she relearned them.

The center meeting is held every Sunday morning in Ratnogram and every Tuesday in Bonopur in neat bamboo and thatch center huts built by the members. In Bonopur the meeting starts on time, with a salute but no exercises. The meeting in Ratnogram is supposed to start at 9 a.m., but it is the second center meeting in the Bank worker's day (the first starts at 7 a.m.) and he is usually late. So the women start to walk towards the center hut from their various *para* when someone spies the bank worker wobbling on his bike over the potholes in the distance and passes the word around.

Attendance at these weekly meetings by active members is excellent. As one member told me: "I feel uneasy and lonely if I ever miss a meeting." Recorded attendance, however, is only 83% in Bonopur and 84% in Ratnogram. That is because there are around five members in each center who have effectively dropped out, some many years ago. They never attend meetings and are no longer borrowing. They are kept on the books because they still owe money to the Bank. According to the area manager, these members could be replaced by new members even if their arrears are not settled. But in practice there were several empty places in the groups, although there is a strong demand in both villages from poor women who want to join.

Almost all active members take a general loan each year. This is repayable over 50 weeks in equal installments. When it has been repaid, the Bank worker calculates the interest (20%, which amortized over the 50 weeks is an effective rate of around 10.15%), which must be paid before the next loan can be proposed. The members decide themselves, without any coaching from the bank worker, how they want to use their loans and they take individual responsibility for repayment. But the loan proposal is made at the center meeting and must have the support of the group and the center chief if it is to be approved. The bank worker can also block the loan or reduce it if he is doubtful about the activity or the member's capacity to repay. The agreement of the center is a matter of much serious discussion amongst the members. If anyone fails to repay, her fellow group members may not be able to get further loans and the whole center will be under pressure to pay hard cash. Both centers have had to bail out defaulters in the past and they don't want to be stuck with them again.

The members all know who is doing what with their loans. But this is usually different from the loan use that is written on the proposal form that goes to the branch office. For example, Rohimah, an elderly widow in Bonopur, has been taking loans for seven years for "grocery shop." It is true that she hawked *biri* (locally rolled cigarettes) and *paan* (betel) around the village on a tray during the first two years of membership; but she has long ago given that up. According to the Bank records, 35 of our 40 member sample took loans in 1991/92 for either "paddy husking" alone or "paddy husking/ cow fattening." As far as we could tell, only four women did any paddy husking for sale during the year and that only for limited periods. Two young women who lived in the same *bari* had taken their last few loans for "cow fattening." Although I was in and out of their *bari* for seven months of the year, I never saw hide nor hair of any cows. Our analysis shows that only 17% of the loans taken in Bonopur during the year of data collection were used at least in part for the official purpose, and 28% of those in Ratnogram, as shown in Table 1.1.

The difference between the "official" use of the loan and the real use has become so much part of the culture of these two centers, that when a new member was admitted to the Bonopur center during the year that we were there, she gave "paddy husking" as the use of her first loan. She did buy paddy, sold it two weeks later (at a loss) and promptly put the money into a land lease.

There are two reasons why the center chief and Bank worker write these historical or fictitious uses of the general loans on the proposal form. The loans have to be approved by first the branch manager and then the area manager.

TABLE 1.1 Loan Use: Approved and Actual

Activity	Number of Loans		Amount of Loans (Taka)	
	Approved	Actual	Approved	Actual
Paddy husking	20 (50%)	0	73,500 (38%)	0
PH/Cow	8 (20%)	0	46,000 (24%)	0
Cow	7 (17%)	4 (10%)	42,500 (22%)	19,300 (10%)
Ghani	4 (10%)	2 (5%)	23,000 (12%)	5,760 (3%)
Grocery	1 (2%)	0	5,000 (3%)	0
Ghani/Sweets	1 (2%)	0	5,500 (3%)	0
Land Transaction		20 (49%)		70,320 (36%)
Loan Repayment		16 (39%)		24,720 (13%)
Paddy Stocking		12 (29%)		27,134 (14%)
Lending		7 (17%)		6,849 (4%)
Rickshaw		3 (7%)		6,137 (3%)
Dowry/Wedding		2 (5%)		5,075 (3%)
House materials		1 (2%)		4,680 (2%)
Others				8,192 (4%)
Not Known				16,833 (9%)
Total	41 (100%)		195,500 (100%)	

Taka: 40 = US$1.

Bank workers know that if the loan use is the same as the year before, and that loan had been successfully repaid, no questions would be raised about the new loan. Second, quite a few members were using their loans for activities which they thought the Bank would disapprove, like leasing in land or funding a husband or a son's business. So although their group members knew, and approved, the real loan use, it was not written on the form.

There is no particular reason why these two centers should be unique in this fictionalizing of loan use. As a result, the things women did with their loans in their first few years of membership, like paddy husking and livestock fattening, are still appearing in the records of the Bank as *the* major activities financed by its loans. Since these are typically activities of low productivity and minimal return to capital, the Bank has been criticized by economists for lending to sectors which will keep women poor. (Hossain 1984 found a negative rate of return to paddy husking, a finding the women have also made for themselves.) While the Bank's statistics on loan use and the economist's criticisms of them drone on like a stuck record, the women themselves have graduated into areas where they do get higher returns.

Loans are disbursed at the branch office four days a week. This is a big social event. The borrower whose loan has been approved walks to the branch with her center chief and her group chairperson (the group leader who is elected each year), sometimes accompanied by a few other members who feel like an outing. It takes about half an hour to walk from Ratnogram to the branch office in Ghatail and about 20 minutes from Bonopur to the Shajanpur branch, by shortcuts across the fields. While they wait with others from all the villages in the branch area, they exchange stories and swop news. In Ghatail, the branch and area offices occupy a four-story building, by far the tallest and most handsome building in town. The two-story, brick branch office in Shajanpur also dominates this one tea shop, one (empty) health center town. The borrowers are aware that they own these buildings, just as they own the Bank, and they come up and down the stairs, excited and a bit shy, but emboldened by each other's company, and into our room to look at our thick red quilt and the photographs of our children.

Seven days after this loan disbursement, the group chairperson, the center chief and the Bank worker are supposed to check that the loan has been used for its stated purpose and that it is successfully generating income. Since the stated purpose is usually incorrect, it follows that this check is also a formality. It is not that the bank worker is ignorant of the loan use, in most cases. For instance, five members took loans for "*ghani*" in Ratnogram. The *ghani* is a very large stone mill which is set inside the *bari* under its own hut. Anyone walking through Beparipara could see that three of these women had no *ghani* in their compound.

It makes some sense to waive the loan utilization check in long-established centers like the ones we studied. Most of these borrowers have already established, beyond doubt, their credit worthiness, by repaying eight or nine loans in succession, and they are highly motivated to keep this credit opportunity open by continuing to repay. Within the center, members know each other's strengths and weaknesses intimately. There is a great deal of mutual pressure and (less often) mutual help, to keep repayment regular.

But it does mean that the Grameen Bank, as an institution, does not know what its loans are being used for. It also means that the Bank may be slow to learn of misuse which either threatens repayment or women member's control over their capital. Amongst the members, those who *were* affected by the lack of a rigorous loan utilization check were those few women who were in real trouble — usually because of a serious illness in the family — who could not use their loans to generate income and so were falling deeper and deeper into debt. There were also some women, mostly elderly widows, who were not using the loan themselves but passing it to sons or other relatives in circumstances which allowed them no control over the proceeds. In a few rare cases the woman was being exploited by a male relative outside her household, so that she got no return from her loan except the repayment. But this information was not available to the officers of the Bank.

Apart from the general loan, which comes around every year, members are eligible for several other kinds of loans. The most popular is called an irrigation loan, introduced in the Tangail Zone in 1989 to help members operating land to pay for the inputs needed for the irrigated *boro* [dry season] rice crop. Thirty five of the 40 members in our sample took this loan. Not all of them operated paddy land. Some used it as a mid-term capital boost and some to help them get through the lean season of March and April.

Each week each member deposits one Taka into her group savings fund, a safety-net fund from which they can borrow for any purpose, with the agreement of the rest of the group. In addition, 5% of every general loan and seasonal/irrigation loan is deposited in the group fund of the borrower. This is "our money" members feel and they make full use of it. Almost all members have a group fund loan outstanding. During the year, one member borrowed from her group fund to take her seriously ill child to hospital; another ran out of money to complete her new house and so got her group's agreement to take out enough to buy the final bamboo wall. Several used it to buy paddy to get through the lean pre-harvest months of September-October. Several others, however, faced a crisis but were unable to take money from their group fund savings when they needed it. The flip side of the members' conviction that this is "our money" is that it is not regularly repaid. In two or three groups the fund was no longer functioning because one member had a long-outstanding group fund loan unpaid. In one group this had been the case for three years.

All GB members also contribute five Taka on every 1,000 Taka received as loan into an emergency fund, which is designed as a kind of insurance cover for death, default, disaster and accidents. There was only one payment to any of our 40 members from the emergency fund during the year. The husband of one of our GB members, who was himself a member of the male center in Ratnogram, died suddenly. There was a ceremony in which the branch manager handed a letter of condolence and a 5,000 Taka payment from the emergency fund to the widow. Immediately after the ceremony, the bank worker took back the 4,984 Taka that the husband still owed to the Bank, leaving the widow with the letter and 16 Taka.[5]

Fifteen women, mostly in Ratnogram, had taken housing loans and built a solid and roomy Grameen Bank house. This meant that 15 women had legal title to their homes and the land on which it stood, since this is a pre-condition to approval of this loan. Another six had taken tube-well loans, so that they had clean water conveniently within their own *bari*.

At the end of the year, the Tangail Zone introduced a new loan which was immediately very popular. Called a seasonal loan, it replaced the irrigation loan and was aimed to finance cultivation by any member of the household. Unlike the irrigation loan, which was never larger than 1,500 Taka in the year of our study, the seasonal loan was almost as large as the general loan. The term of the seasonal loan was also one year, but repayment was initially more flexible within that period. Later payment was standardized at 2% per week, as with the general loan. The seasonal loan effectively doubled the capital available annually to those members who got it. By the time we left 13 members in Ratnogram had got seasonal loans of between 3,000 and 7,000 Taka, but disbursement had not yet begun in Bonopur.

According to the zonal manager, these loans were to be given on a selective basis to the stronger members, whose families operated land and who could carry the nearly doubled burden of repayment. In practice the Bank worker in Ratnogram steered a course between this concept and very strong pressure from the center to disburse these loans to nearly all members.

Notes

1. A bicycle with a two wheeled wooden dray on the back, usually loaded with sacks of paddy or other produce, and sometimes a whole family going to town.

2. I am indebted to Naila Kabeer here (1994) for her guidance through the thickets of Women in Development theory.

3. Readers who dispute this often forgotten fact should consult Grameen Bank's Annual Reports, Hossain 1988 and Khandker 1995.

4. An account of this period and the institutionalising process is contained in Gibbons (forthcoming).

5. The contribution to the emergency fund used to be 2.5% of the interest on each

loan. The Bidmala or Constitution and By-Laws of the Grameen Bank allow a wide range of uses for the emergency fund, including to repay loans of members who face disasters such as the death of a cow or the destruction of a rickshaw purchased with a GB loan. In practice, however, the emergency fund has been used only for payment of grants to the relatives of members who die. These payments are made from the interest accruing on the money in the emergency fund, leaving the fund itself intact. In 1994, a decision was taken to utilise some of this growing fund to finance a pilot health scheme in six branches in Tangail.

2

What Credit Can Do:
Women's Contribution

The poor Bangladeshi village women who people the pages of the academic literature and the real women who live in Ratnogram and Bonopur seem to belong to two different species. The woman in the books is so oppressed that she has lost all sense of her own value; she is therefore easily exploited and deprived. She is powerless to control her own life and can take almost no part in the decisions which shape it, whether it be the economic fate of the family or how many children she should have. *Purdah* makes her "invisible," Islamic constraints make it impossible for her to move an inch in any direction. Worst of all, she is so meekly subservient to the patriarchal ethos which devalues her that she perpetuates it by actively discriminating against her own daughters and terrorizing her daughters in law.

In a discussion of the position of women in South Asia, Judith Bruce (1989:982) summarizes the received view of women in Bangladesh:

> In Bangladesh, in particular, women's access to income earning opportunities is severely limited; their legal inheritance rights are generally forfeited; their chances of becoming widows (because of age differentials between spouses at marriage) are a near certainty; divorce and abandonment are realistic possibilities; and control of women by patriarchal structures is extreme.

Westergaard (1983:9) writing from a village near Comila, highlights the "lack of decision making power and control on the part of the women" over the economic life of a rural family, because it is men who control the means of production.

> In Bangladesh women are entitled to ownership and control of land, but in actual fact most land is owned and controlled by men. ... Men are also in control of the major inputs in the production process, including draught power, seeds

fertilizers, etc. ...When it comes to control over the distribution of output, it is most often the men who decide how much of the harvest is to be kept for consumption and how much is to be sold.

After a mental preparation like this, the Grameen women of Ratnogram and Bonopur come as a bit of a shock. We are talking to Jamilah, a Grameen Bank member in Bonopur, the "young," 35 year old, second wife of 60 year old Mir Ali, trying to disentangle the complex structure of their landholdings. This is her father's village, she tells us. When her husband was cheated out of his inheritance in his own village she left him and came home. He followed, with a bevy of adolescent children from his dead first wife. Jamilah joined Grameen in secret against his wishes, and used her first two loans to negotiate a seven decimal houselot from her father. Two loans and two cows later she did another deal with her father, exchanging the cows for a doubling of her houselot. Since then Jamilah has bought the paddy field next to her house from her father, 10.5 decimals in her own name, and is buying another 22 decimal field from her sister. In addition, she has leased in no less than six separate fields totalling 67 decimals. Mir Ali supports the family, *as he is expected to do*, with his work as a mason. When he fails to bring home enough wages to meet the family's food needs there is a row, and he suffers the rough edge of Jamilah's tongue. The land and the leases accumulated with Jamilah's capital are managed by her and she rolls the income derived from them into the accumulation of more land.

Jamilah explains the division of labor involved. Her husband hears about land available for lease in his travels around the area. She decides if she can afford to take the land and sends him off to negotiate with the owner. Most of these lots are sharecropped out and at harvest it is Mir Ali's job to check that they are getting their full 50% share and bring it back to the *bari*. Jamilah is in charge of its disposal from then on. As she describes this situation, Jamilah is at pains to make the power relationship clear to us. She pauses as a happy thought occurs to her and she allows a rare smile to cross her sour face. "Listen. He is like my daily laborer. He does not spend one *poisha* without my consent."

According to the academic literature, it is women's lack of access to markets because they are not allowed under the rules of *purdah* to go out of the *bari*, which makes it almost impossible for them to earn substantial income, let alone manage the family finances. Their seclusion makes them both too ignorant and too dependent on others to do business on their own account.

Purdah means that a woman is heavily reliant on the family menfolk for information and ideas (although much information is imparted by other women) as well as for the means to operate in "male space." She...would not normally be consulted by her husband on any matter which is not domestic in nature. (Abecassis 1990:56.)

Abercassis qualifies this statement with reference to some poor women and some older women, but sees these as exceptions. For similar views see Jansen (1987) and Blanchet (1984).

Banu, a Grameen Bank member in Ratnogram, has two daughters working in a garment factory in Chittagong, one widowed and one still unmarried. Her eldest son lives with his two sisters who support him as he finishes his secondary schooling in that city. In addition, they send remittances home which Banu invests in leasehold land. She arranges these leases herself through her uncles-in-law in the same *para* and so far has accumulated 90 decimals. She regards them as partly in trust for her widowed daughter against the day when she will give up the factory work and come home, so she stocks half the harvest, sells when the price is high and uses the proceeds of this, as well as her Grameen loans, to lease in more land. Her eldest son operates these fields, with help from her vegetable-vendor husband at peak seasons, together with the two *bigha* which her husband inherited in his own name. But there was no doubt in our minds after a year's observation about who controls and manages the finances of this family. Banu is the managing director of the family firm. Nor, it seems, is there any doubt in the minds of the daughters.

After the *amon* harvest, Banu's husband took the long trip from Ghatail to Chittagong to see his three children. They feted him for a fortnight. Then the eldest daughter gave him 1,500 Taka to take back to her mother for investment, which he duly delivered to Banu on his return. For their father the two girls bought a *lunggi* and gave him the train and bus fare home. That was all.

When David went to interview the husband about the family's farming operations, Banu kept chipping in.

"What do you want to talk to him for?" she asked. "He doesn't know anything about this business."

In his book on the role of Islam in rural Bangladesh, David Abecassis (1990:55,57) writes:

The reality of a poor women's life is that she is regarded in every way as an inferior form of human life. She is all-too-often treated with little or no respect, viewed by her husband and parents-in-law more or less as a chattel, too foolish and ignorant to have any valid opinion on affairs outside the *bari* and of too little value to be accorded the same level of concern, love or care which wo.ild be accorded to a male.

Among rural poor women, there is a very widespread feeling of inferiority, induced by their subject status, which they start to internalize from their earliest years. Their labor and their contribution to society are undervalued. They are cut off from the mainstream of society and from the most important processes of power and decision making, not just by *purdah* but by the attitudes which lie behind it.

Banu (right), the manager of her family's finances, proudly showing off one of her newly leased paddy fields. Alia (left), the ex-Center Chief, and also the manager of her family, grazing her sheep on the bunds between the open fields.

Photo Credit: Nurjahan Chaklader

"My contribution is twelve-sixteenths!" states one of the Grameen members confidently. (This method of expressing proportions is common in the village and I presume it dates back to the time when 16 *anna* made a *rupee*.) All day I have been getting similar responses to a question on how much they reckoned they contributed to the overall income of the household. Astonished, I rephrase the question and explain it more carefully. But still the women reply: "My contribution is very great!" "I do plenty! (*khub beshi, onek beshi*)" Salma, a member of the control group, sitting in her *bari* milking her goats while her husband is out at the new road, excavating earth for a daily wage, claims that her share is "sixteen-sixteenths."

I had thought I would get some measure of self esteem by seeing how each woman estimated her contribution, compared to her actual contribution as measured in our weekly data. I expected varying degrees of underestimation. It had never occurred to me that they would *overestimate* their contribution. As for Salma, I knew she worked hard, but I also knew that her cash income was quite small. She cared for her goats and a calf and sold the odd chicken and pumpkin. She worked as a domestic servant in the harvest season. But in our calculations of household income her contribution was only 31%.

"How can that be?" I ask, rather crossly. "What do you earn that is more than the money your husband brings home from his daily labor?"

"My husband is gone all day. He doesn't know what is needed here. Everything is my responsibility. It is true that my husband earns a daily wage, but he puts that into my hand. And why shouldn't he? I am the manager here; the main person."

So it was not direct cash earnings Salma was talking about but her management of the household and its budget. But whatever the accuracy of their estimates of their economic contribution, none of these women seemed to be lacking in self-esteem. I looked in vain for "widespread feelings of inferiority."

In their dated but still influential study of Jhagrapur, Arens and Van Beurden write:

> Women are in general confined to their homesteads, but sometimes they do come out perhaps to fetch water or to visit relatives. When a woman goes outside her homestead she has to go veiled. ... When she goes outside her village she must go either in a bullock cart or palanquin. (1977:62)

What follows is a randomly-taken winter day in the life of Meena, a married woman in her thirties from Bonopur, who joined Grameen Bank during the year of data collection. Her husband leaves before dawn for his digging job on the roadside. Not long after, Meena is on the road herself, hurrying on foot to her natal village about half a mile away to get back the 500 Taka plus interest she lent to her cousin three months ago. She fails. By late morning she is in

Shajanpur, the small town more than a mile in the opposite direction, to accompany a member of her group getting a loan from the Grameen Bank branch. On the way she stakes her goats in a field to feed. She husks padi at home most of the afternoon and sews dried kapok back into the pillow cases. Then she walks back over the fields to fetch her goats. She stakes them in a nearby field while she cooks, then she goes out and fetches them home for the night. Her husband returns after dark and they eat together with their two children. He is tired so she makes the bed for him. Then *again* she goes out, this time accompanied by her aunt, to try to get the money back from her cousin in the next village.

Meena, whose goats, moneylending business and Grameen Bank membership take her constantly outside her *bari*, tells me in all honesty: "I try to do as much work as I can do, but I only do inside work. I don't do outside work."

Why does the literature on poor rural women in Bangladesh prepare one so little for many of the women we actually met in Ratnogram and Bonopur? Here were women operating land, managing the finances of their families; women who valued themselves and their work and who were remarkably mobile.

It is not that the statistical outlines of women's condition are wrong. Women's life expectancy *is* slightly lower than men's, mainly because of very high maternal mortality rates. They seldom take the land which they inherit. Women are usually widowed in their fifties. Girls are less likely to stay in school (Rahman 1991:122-129). It is almost impossible for women to operate in a "male space" like the weekly *haat*. *Purdah* does restrict their movements.

But the "litany of grim statistics" (Arthur and McNicoll 1978 quoted in White 1992:17), with which so many accounts of the condition of women in Bangladesh begins, simply does not explain a Jamilah or a Banu or a Meena.[1] And these women cannot be discounted because they are in some ways exceptional. Outstanding women are not uncommon in our sample. The dogged, largely theoretical focus on the oppression and confinement of Bengali women obscures what they actually manage to do in their day to day lives. What is supposed to follow logically from the "facts" about the situation of poor rural women just did not seem to follow in these two villages. It is not true that they could not earn income, that they had no access to markets, that they could not buy and sell on their own behalf, that they could not exercise control over land or other assets or that they were unable to manage the family finances. As for *purdah*, Meena's approach to it shows that it is less a rigid set of rules than a mindset open to interpretation.

The problem was, we were not doing a village study, but a study in two villages of the lives of 62 women in order to evaluate the longer-term impact of the Grameen Bank. I was very diffident, therefore, about disagreeing with what appeared to be the consensus amongst scholars, even in relation to the small sample of women we were studying. The last thing I wanted was to take on the "Women In Development" establishment about the "status of women" in Bangladesh in general.

So I was very relieved in the course of the year to come across a village study which does confront the received view and which tries to explain the colonial and aid politics behind the singleminded focus on misery.[2]

In a discussion of women's economic activities in a village in Rajshahi, Sarah White writes:

> ...it is simply not true that Bangladeshi women do not go out, but rather notions of "inside" and "outside" are open to complex manipulation. ...While women do not commonly appear in the market place, this does not mean that they do not participate in markets; their activities often underlie transactions in the *haat*, and there are extensive female networks for the exchange of goods within villages. (1992:78-79)

This important book brings into sharp focus the transactional world where women are able to operate, both its extent and its limitations. Its approach gave me a theoretical context in which I could better understand what individual women in our sample were doing. It also gave me a sharper eye for the maneuvering, and sometimes subterfuge, they used as they extended their range and ambitions.

If you believe in the received view of the huddled masses of rural woman, locked in their *bari*, despising themselves, then the documented success of the Grameen Bank in reaching them and raising their incomes is truly astonishing. It is unbelievable. I think this at least partly explains two predominant responses to the Bank. The first and most general are those, of many schools, who *don't* believe it. When Grameen Bank became too large and successful to be ignored, many tried to explain it away in terms of some unique circumstance which could not be repeated, like the charisma of its founder. Or they argued that its dependence on subsidy made it unsustainable in the long term. Or they argued that benefits would level off as the village markets became saturated with the few activities open to women [3] or as the system — in the shape of either landlords or patriarchs — moved to extract what little income poor women had been able to make.[4]

The other response is the "miracle" school, demonstrated in the books by Jayanta Kuma Ray (1987) and Chandler and Fuglesang (1986,1993) which show Grameen women and Bank officials confronting a hostile environment, but succeeding heroically against all odds. This approach has relied on one-shot life histories and extensive interviews with Bank staff and tends to be uncritical of the Bank.[5]

As my accounts of Jamilah, Banu, Salma and Meena show, all the negatives which are supposed to follow from the constraints on rural women in Bangladesh do not seem to follow in our two villages. We found that women have a number of ways of earning income, they buy and sell, they borrow and lend, sometimes at usurious rates of interest, they can get access to land and control the produce of it. Grameen women, because they have regular access to capital, are generally much more active in all these areas than non-Grameen women. There is also no doubt that the presence of a Grameen Bank center in a village stimulates the local economy in ways that benefit the non-member poor (Hossain 1988). Non-Grameen women in villages where Grameen Bank women have been operating for a decade have certainly been influenced by their example to be more economically active and assertive (Schuler and Hashemi, 1994). So this spillover affect has influenced our control group, who live in the same villages as our Grameen Bank sample.

What I am arguing is that Grameen women are not different in kind; they are simply different in opportunity. Many of the women in the control group — like Salma pictured above — do not look much like the browbeaten stereotype either.

If you look at the Grameen women in the context of a village world of transactions, many of them handled by women, which I believe is the real one, their environment is not hostile to women's enterprise. They have a springboard. It may be narrow; it may be characterized by low productivity, but, with capital, they can harness their other resources and get on. Nor do I think they see themselves as confronting or overturning social norms. It could be better described as a kind of sidling around the constraints, while strenuously insisting that everything is being done according to custom.

If you look at the Grameen Bank in this context, then its success is neither unbelievable, nor "heroic" in the sense of achieving the impossible. It is explicable. The Bank has succeeded at its most fundamental level because its village clients have been able to make enough money from their loans to repay the Bank. The women clients have done this, not by jumping out of *purdah* or by confronting the society in which they are embedded, but by using or manipulating elements in their culture which allow their enterprise. If they had not been able to do this, the Bank would have failed. This seems so self-evident that it would be embarrassing to state it, if it were not for the amount of hype that has been written by admirers of the Bank.

Sarah White, who describes an "enterprise culture" which includes women in the village she studied, writes:

> During my time in Kumirpur I observed that women were extensively involved
> in market transactions. There was, however, no development agency promoting
> small business, nor bank which was providing loans to the poor. ...In channeling
> new resources to women, development programmes may extend women's options.
> It is a mistake, however, to see these as breaking down a monolithic local culture,
> or to underestimate the flexibility that already exists. (1992:71)

Our data on Grameen women show that the provision of credit by the Bank, and the use that most of them have made of this facility, has done a great deal more than extend their options. Over the decade in which they have been members of the Bank, and because of the regular and reliable injections of capital they have received each year, more than half of these women in both villages have been able to pull their families right out of poverty.

There has been considerable argument amongst Bangladeshi academics about where to put the poverty line — whether at a per capita income which would support a daily intake of 1800 calories or one which would support 2112 calories. The majority defend the lower poverty line of 1800 as more realistic. If we follow this lower line, adjusted for inflation, an annual per capita income of 4,787 Taka becomes the cutoff point for the year of data collection.

(A poverty line based on calory intake is, of course, a very poverty-stricken measurement of real lives. I use it here as an entry point, and will look at other needs, like housing and health, as well as the human need for respect and agency, in the chapters which follow.)

The households of 23 women members of Grameen Bank, in our sample of 40 households, had incomes above this poverty line. In other words 57.5% of the GB group were no longer poor. Only four of the control group households were no longer poor, or 18%.

Some 17 of the Grameen Bank families were still poor (42.5%), compared to 18 families (81.8%) in the control group. But within the poverty group the depth of poverty differed greatly.

FIGURE 2.1 Household Poverty Status: Grameen Bank Sample (N=40)

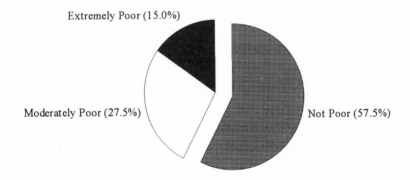

Extremely Poor (15.0%)

Moderately Poor (27.5%)

Not Poor (57.5%)

FIGURE 2.2 Household Poverty Status: Control Group Sample (N=22)

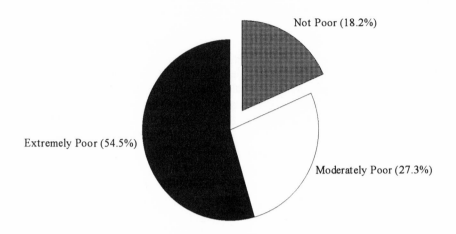

Not Poor (18.2%)

Extremely Poor (54.5%)

Moderately Poor (27.3%)

Only six Grameen families were still amongst the hard-core poor, compared to 12, or more than half of the families in the control group. Eleven families in the Grameen sample numbered amongst the moderately poor, compared to six such families in the control group.

If we use the higher poverty line of 2112 calories per day it alters the numbers, but not the sharp contrast between the Grameen Bank households and those of the control. At this poverty line, which is 5617 Taka per capita per annum, 18 GB households are out of poverty, or 45%, compared to three households in the control group, or 14%. Some 22 GB households are still poor (55%), while 19 control group households are still poor (86%).

Two Enterprising Women

To show what this means in the lives of the families involved I would like to focus on two of the women in our sample in order to try to pinpoint the differences that have arisen because one has had access to Grameen credit and the other has not.

Begum, who is a Grameen Bank member, and Shireen, who is not, are both 31 years old. They both have husbands who work as daily laborers and widowed mothers-in-law living in the same compound. Begum has one son of 13, Shireen two sons of ten and eight and a four year old daughter. Both are hard working women; both express a strong desire to build a better life for their children.

That is where the similarities end. Begum's family is no longer poor; their annual net earnings are Taka 28,302, more than three times the earnings of Shireen's family, at Taka 7,077. Begum lives in a solid house, financed by a Grameen Bank loan and owned by herself. It is twenty feet long with a rain-proof tin roof supported by flood-proof cement pillars. There is even a desk covered with her son's schoolbooks. Shireen's house is so small that the sleeping mat takes up more than half of it. The walls are a haphazard jigsaw of dilapidated bamboo matting and rice straw. If you stand up too fast in Shireen's house you are in danger of putting yet another hole in the thatch.

Life was not so good to Begum fifteen years ago, when she came to this village as a bride. Then she lived in a jute stick hut much like Shireen's, except that most of the time she lived in it alone. Like many landless young men her husband was bonded on a labor contract to a nearby landlord. These labor contracts are heavily weighted in the landlord's favor. They work in such a way that they offer food, minimal clothing and some security to the laborer, but almost certain misery to his wife and family.

Although the landlord's property was just across the fields, the "master" wanted him on 24 hour call, so Shakeeb was allowed to come home only once a week. He usually came empty handed. He was adequately fed at his workplace, which had the benefit to his employer of keeping him fit for work, but he rarely had any cash. His "pay" was Taka 3,000 per year, paid in kind twice a year in the form of paddy at the time of harvest. This paddy he brought home. Begum stored it and attempted the impossible task of stretching it out over six months.

When she needed cash she would husk a few kilos from her food store and sell it. Occasionally Shakeeb would bring back some extra padi for Begum or Taka 100. But to eke out the rice over the year Begum and first one son, then a second, lived mainly on *roti* — an unleavened pancake — and flour soup, a very unpleasant and unfilling slop which is how the village poor stretch out their flour supply when they are truly desperate. When her second son was one year old, he caught pneumonia in their leaky hut and died of it.

It was her sister in law, who lives in the same *bari*, who persuaded her to join Grameen ten years ago, but she was too malnourished and depressed to be very interested. "She was so weak I had to drag her along to the training sessions," her sister-in-law exclaimed.

It is hard to imagine now that this large, dark, strong-boned woman, constantly busy, could ever have been too listless to walk.

Begum's work, and the capital she brings into the family through her Grameen loans, contributes fully 63% of the income of her household. Shireen's household, despite her constant attention to her calf and chickens, is still numbered amongst the very poor, with a per capita income of only Taka 2022 a year. To this income Shireen contributes only 12%.

What do these figures actually mean in the fabric of their daily lives? Begum is a quiet, serious woman compared to the more exuberant sisters-in-law in her *bari,* but she has an air of calm confidence. She knows her value. "My share is very much," she says, when asked about her contribution to the household income. "My husband works in the morning, then he comes home and eats and in the afternoon he rests. I am always working. He earns much Taka, but if you valued my work in Taka it would be a great deal, more than his," she says, putting in her cool fashion the WID position for counting women's labor into both domestic and national accounts.

We record a day in Begum's life and get a measure of the *sharedness* of the life she leads now with her once-absent husband. It is the *amon* harvest season and both wake before dawn. They pray and Shakeeb goes off to his leased field to cut paddy. Begum makes dung cakes[6] from the droppings of their own cows and slaps them on to the path to dry. She fetches water, feeds the cows and lets out the chickens. Then she puts three maunds of paddy to boil, sweeps out the compound, washes the fireplace and hurries to cook rice, spinach and eggplant paste for breakfast. At 10 a.m. Shakeeb comes back from the field and they eat together with their son and Shakeeb's mother.

The rest of the day Begum spends spreading out the boiled paddy to dry, turning it, keeping the chickens out of it and drying straw for fuel. By 4 p.m. the dried paddy is swept back into baskets and stored, the straw neatly stacked in the kitchen hut and the compound cleared for the next round. Begum escapes to the pond for her bath. Again she fetches water, feeds the cows and puts the chickens away for the night. At 4.30 Shakeeb lopes in with a huge pile of paddy on his head. Together they thresh and winnow it, working until well after dark. Seeing how busy they are, Begum's mother-in-law lights the lamps and cooks rice and a fish and radish curry, made from fish the son caught after school. The moon has risen by the time the paddy is put into baskets and they all sit together to eat dinner.

On the other side of the village, in Kahpara, Shireen looks harried as she rushes in from cutting grass for the calf to cook *roti* for her children. She is petite and fair skinned, with a kind of starry-eyed prettiness. You can understand why Forman, her husband, married her in the teeth of his mother's outrage more than a decade ago.

But nowadays Forman never bothers to buy oil for her hair. It is dry and dull; her mouth falls in discontented lines. A ragged petticoat drags out from under her *sari.* Nobody in the research team likes the weekly interview with Shireen. She is often bad tempered, probably because she is often hungry, and she resents the time we take with our questioning.

"In all things I am under my husband," she says. "He decides what we should do." In April, one of the cruellest months in the Bengali year, when the sun beats fiercely on the cracked earth and there is almost no work for people like Forman, he decided to take their ten year old son out of school and contract him to the house of a landlord for 500 Taka a year. Earlier, in February he leased out their only piece of agricultural land — 11 decimals — for 1,400 taka.

Begum has consistently used her loans to get access to paddy land so that she can turn her husband from a labourer to a farmer. Behind her is her large tin-roofed and cement pillared Grameen Bank house.　　　*Photo Credit: Nurjahan Chaklader*

He used half of it to go to Dhaka looking for work. When he failed to get it, they used the rest for food. "Where will we get the Taka to redeem the land? Shireen asks bitterly. "We don't even have Taka for bamboo to mend the house for the rainy season."

Shireen's sights are set on mending her house against the next rainy season, stocking enough padi for the next month. She seems to be always running to stand still. At her most ambitious, she longs to bring her son home and put him back in school. Begum has the option of a much longer-term view and more ambitious plans. She has, in partnership with her husband, taken her life into her own hands and is shaping it in the way she wants.

Taka 1,400 (the amount Forman got in exchange for his land and then was forced to use up in consumption just to feed his family) is exactly the amount of capital Begum used, from her 7th Grameen loan, to buy a cow which she sold this year for 2,500 Taka. With that she bought a second bullock to make a pair to pull a plough.

From the very beginning — when Shakeeb was still working out his labor contract — this couple has systematically used the GB loans to acquire land. The first two years they leased in 10 decimals and then 15 decimals — which they sharecropped out because Shakeeb could not work it while he was contracted to his landlord. Meanwhile, with the balance of the loan amount they bought paddy, which Begum boiled, husked and resold, using the profit to make her repayments. After Begum took her third loan, she bought a cow and Shakeeb left the labor contract and came home. Now he worked the leasehold land himself, using the cow for ploughing (borrowing another cow to make a pair from another GB family) and doing daily labor to meet their cash needs.

Begum worried at first about the leasehold land and kept very quiet about it, because it was against the GB rules. But they both wanted to salt this unaccustomed capital away into investment — into the "pure value" of land. Shakeeb says:

> If we had put all the loans into paddy, that would make us lazy, it would take away our impulse to work. We agreed to put as much as possible into land. Of course, it was hard to get through the months until the harvest. Often we didn't have enough to eat because we used our cash to make the repayment. It was very difficult in those early years but we had that land and we added to it.

For the past four years, Begum has done less paddy husking and invested in cows. She sold a cow to buy a plough and used her group loans to buy fertilizer. In the process she has helped turn Shakeeb into a leaseholder and a sharecropper, since both the cows and capital for inputs make him an attractive prospect to landlords wishing to sharecrop out their land.

Their joint ambition is to release Shakeeb from daily labor altogether and to turn him into a full-time farmer. During the year of data collection he was half way there. He farmed 59 decimals of sharecrop and 45 decimals of leasehold, which took almost half his time. There was always ample paddy in stock for the family's food needs, as well as a surplus for Begum to husk and sell. It is hard to overestimate the satisfaction and security that a full store of paddy gives to someone like Begum, who remembers the hunger of herself and her children.

When Shakeeb was not farming, he worked at the nearby brickfields, or at pond digging or road construction. The brickfields is very hard work cutting clay and carrying bricks, but it is well paid and much sought after by the village men. During the *irri* (in Tangail the irrigated *boro* crop is called *irri*, in honor of the Green Revolution) planting season, Begum's acquisition of the pair of bullocks made it possible for Shakeeb to hire himself out to plough the paddy fields. During the same season that Forman was earning Taka 175 per week as a general laborer, the best money he earned all year, Shakeeb was pulling in between Taka 400 and Taka 700 a week, because Begum's capital had made the bullocks possible. Despite Begum's comments about his afternoon rest, Shakeeb was always working. Forman was often unable to find work as a daily laborer.

When Begum finished paying off her eighth loan in November and became eligible for the next loan, her husband begged her to give him a break. "Let's stop for a while. I can't cope with so much work," he told her. He spent the winter bringing in the *amon* harvest and working in the brickfields, while Begum dried and boiled and husked almost daily. In January, in time for the *irri* planting, Begum took her ninth loan of 7,500 Taka and immediately leased in another 36 decimals for Taka 10,000. At this rate it would probably take them another two or three years to fulfill their ambition — for Shakeeb to give up daily labor altogether and work full time as a farmer.

The last time I talk to them together, Shakeeb is sitting on a stool in the house and Begum stands behind his shoulder, almost touching him, a little closer than village propriety allows. But she is perfectly at ease, leaning back against the platform on which stand her baskets of paddy, stretching her strong body as she raises one arm to comb her hair. Shakeeb explains:

There were so many things that I *could* do, that I *wanted* to do, but I had no Taka. Then Begum could take these loans. Each time we decided how we should use the loan and slowly our confidence grew; our love grew! I depended on Begum and together we have made much progress.

Nahar, translating, teases Begum, who laughs, the keys at the end of her *sari* jingling. "He never loved me before. Only when I bring Taka he loves me!" Shakeeb joins the laughing. Then he looks at me directly and says with great seriousness: "I love her anyway. Of all the Grameen Bank women in this village, she is the best. They will buy all kinds of things; call their relatives for feasting. Begum never. Everything she keeps for investment. That is why we have done so well."

The contrast with Shireen could hardly be more stark, with painful consequences for her family. Forman leased out the only agricultural land they owned early in the year and then spent the capital in a vain attempt to get work. This made the family effectively landless and dependent on Forman's daily earnings to buy rice. During March and April Forman was able to get work only three or four days a week, bringing home only Taka 60 to 80, when their minimal need for rice alone was Taka 100 per week. In October he was getting only one day's work a week and Shireen was buying paddy on credit at high prices and eating only once a day.

Forman managed to get land to sharecrop during the year — but with neither bullocks nor capital he is not an attractive prospect for landlords, so the 23 decimals was boggy land and much of the *amon* crop rotted. When the crop was harvested Forman's share was worth Taka 500 — against which they had already borrowed Taka 640 worth of padi in the hungry months that preceded the harvest.

When we look at Shireen we are not seeing a woman who is idle or who has no entrepreneurial skills. They owned a calf, which Shireen tended with care. By the end of the year it was a cow worth double its bought value. She also made an arrangement with a neighbor to sharefatten a sheep. The sheep produced two lambs during the year, one of which is now owned by Shireen under this arrangement. This small increase in their assets is wholly Shireen's doing.

Begum's only son is doing well in school, in Class V. He sits at the desk in her large house doing his homework. When he is not studying, he helps his father in the fields, catches fish and enjoys the loving attention of his mother.

Shireen's eldest son was at the beck and call of a landlord's household for six months of the year , during which time he rarely saw his mother. Then, as seems to happen fairly often, the landlord's children picked a fight with him and beat him shortly before the balance of the contract money was due to be paid by his "master." He ran home, angry and penniless, and spent the harvest period working in the fields with his father for Taka 10 per day.

Begum's mother-in-law lives in a partition of their house and eats with her son's family, in what appears to be a relationship of love and respect. Shakeeb rarely eats first, which is the tradition in village families. "He never sits and eats alone. He always says: 'You sit with me'," Begum explains.

Shireen and her mother-in-law also live in the same *bari*, but in an atmosphere of mutual hatred. There is a very strong cultural imperative in Bangladesh which makes the care of a widow the responsibility of her sons. In this *bari,* poverty has broken this social contract. Forman's mother, Bachiron, who is a member of our control group, is bent almost double and leans on a stout stick. She begs for a living. When she is too sick to walk from *para* to *para* asking for rice, she starves. Her daughters sometimes send her food, but she receives nothing, not even an occasional meal, from her son's household. For this situation. of course, she blames her daughter-in-law, Shireen, loudly and often, to whoever will listen.

Forman eats whenever possible at his workplace. He brings home less cash that way, but he gets enough to eat. When he is at home it is because he is jobless and he is often in a bad mood. He eats first with his sons. Shireen and her daughter get the leftovers.

Shireen's daughter is visibly wasted. When we measure her we find that she is only 72% of the international standard of weight for her height. Shireen herself looks severely underweight and anaemic and the child from her last pregnancy was stillborn.

One day I am talking to Shireen in the doorway of her tiny shack, when she begins a kind of crazed rush of sweeping and tidying. Then she throws a few handfuls of rice into a pot and, without a word, literally runs away from us to the fireplace to begin cooking. "What is wrong with her?" I ask a neighbor.

"If her husband comes back and the rice is not cooked he will beat her," she explained. Just then, Bachiron, her mother-in-law, comes stumbling up to talk to us and squats down in the doorway of her son's hut. We are deep in conversation when Shireen comes running back from her fire and starts hauling something out of the cowshed behind my head, almost knocking me from my stool. It turns out to be her door. Then she manhandles the door into place in the doorway, pushing her bent and half-blind mother-in-law out of the way in the process, so that Bachiron almost falls into my lap. All the time Shireen is muttering to herself like a mad woman: "He will be home; the rice is not cooked; the house is just standing open..." before rushing back to her fire.

The neighbors are so ashamed of this small incident, which contradicts all the norms of good behavior in the village, that a schoolgirl follows me out to the road, trying to think of something to say that will absolve it. Finally, she bursts out:

"When I get married, I don't care *what* my mother-in-law is like, I will always treat her with kindness!"

1993 was a good year in the Tangail district. There were no floods or cyclones. The rains were a bit late, but the *amon* crop was good. For Begum and Shakeeb this meant a paddy surplus which they sold and the confidence to invest in a larger leasehold for 1993. For Forman it meant enough work at the turn of the year to pay off the household's borrowings and to persuade his eldest son to return to school for 1993; back into Class Three. At the beginning of the data collection, Shireen had told us that they were usually short of food. At the end of the year she said: "Only sometimes." There was other good news too. During the year Shireen became a member of a saving and loans society called ASA. If she saves four Taka a week for a year, she becomes eligible for a Taka 1,000 loan. She was already making plans for another calf.

Despite these small improvements, however, the difference between the poverty and vulnerability of Shireen's household and the security of Begum's is stark. Very poor women and men have little control over their lives; the non-poor have much more. Shireen experiences frequent distress, little or no power over the decisions which most affect her life and a breakdown of social relations within her *bari*. Poverty meant her ten year old son stopped school in Grade Three and left home to work for abusive strangers. It means her daughter is so underweight that she may not survive the next bout of diarrhoea or a rainy season influenza. Worse, until she joined ASA at least, she had no weapons to change her situation. Although she is determined and can work hard, there is little that she can do but struggle on from day to day.

There are of course personal differences between these two families, Shireen is Forman's second wife; he ditched his first to marry her. Forman's mother (at least on hindsight) loved her first daughter-in-law and disliked the interloper, which underlies the hostility pervading this *bari* today. Forman is proud and quick tempered, which doesn't make him popular with employers. It is notable that even when he does similar work to Shakeeb, his daily rate is always lower. "I have no need to join Grameen. I will save my own capital and depend on no man," he declared when we first met him. We only later discovered that he had tried to join the male center and been rejected.

But who can say if Forman's prickly personality or Begum's serene calm are a result or a cause of poverty? There are personality and family differences which help explain the way the Grameen women use their loans and whether they are active or passive partners in the income earning process. In the control group there are women who are subservient. I cannot use the cliche "meekly subservient" because they were usually bitterly and angrily subservient like Shireen. There are a few who tell their husbands in no uncertain terms what should be done. During the year each one of these 62 women emerged as a distinct personality. But there are no systematic personality differences which can explain the graphic contrasts we found between the Grameen members as a whole and the women in the control group.

More Than Half

The economic contribution that these Grameen Bank women make to the overall income of their families after a decade of membership, as shown in Table 2.1, is quite remarkable. It is substantially more than the contribution of women in the control group. It is also well above the levels discovered by Rushidan (1986) in her study of women GB borrowers in Tangail and Rangpur during 1985, most of whom had been members for less than three years. In Ratnogram and Bonopur, the average Grameen woman was producing more than half the total household earnings — a contribution which is so large and so difficult to minimize or ignore, that it underlies our other findings concerning their empowerment.

In our Grameen sample, the women contributed, on average, 54% of the net earnings of their households. This compares with the 25% contributed by the women in the control group. Rushidan's study found that GB women in their early loan cycles were contributing 38% of total household income on average.

In this analysis I excluded from both groups those female-headed households where the woman lives alone or with children under ten years old, as these women have no choice but to earn all the income. There are amongst these "female-headed households," two beggars (including Shireen's mother-in-law, Bachiron) whose lives are so desperate that to talk about their "economic contribution" is to make a mockery of them.

This average contribution for the Grameen Bank members is somewhat skewed downwards by a few older women who have "honorably retired" and are now inactive — something none of the women in the control group can afford to do. But if we look at the number of GB women who contribute half or more of the net income, there are 24 such women, or 65% of the GB sample. Rushidan's study, which included women who were the sole support of their households, found only 22% of her sample who contributed half or more of the family income. In our control group there are only three women who contribute half the income or more, and two of them are female-headed households, one with a son of ten years old and the other with a 13 year old daughter.

In our calculations of income we counted income in kind as well as in cash. This covers a large part of the harvest income, since some of the harvested paddy is stored for consumption and some is sold. But it also covers most of the service work that women do. Maidservants working in the houses of richer villagers, for example, are rarely paid in cash. They receive their meals and a *sari* and sometimes a post-harvest payment in paddy, depending on the role they play in the processing of the harvest. The income of beggars also comes in a handful of rice and a few beans or radishes. We imputed a market value to these payments in kind, including meals, and counted it into the income.

Since in Bangladesh the woman's role in processing agricultural crops is very important we were careful to include the value of it in the calculations of household income. (For example, we imputed the value-added of the paddy processing women do at 15% of the total value, which is a conservative estimate.) But we did not put a value on some of the other subsistence or quasi-productive activities of women in the two villages, like gathering fuel or edible leaves, or growing vegetables for family consumption. In this sense we have underestimated the woman's contribution to full household income.

Hossain Zillur Rahman (Rahman 1991:215-217) calculates the value of all expenditure saving activities as 20% of the total household income of landless families. The major expenditure saving activities — gathering sticks, leaves and dung for fuel, and growing or gathering vegetables and fruit — are done by women. Only gathering house-building materials and fishing are mainly male activities.

Table 2.1 Female Contribution To Net Household Income (Excluding Women Living Alone or With Children Under Ten Years)

	GB (N=37)	Control (N=19)
Average Contribution	54.4%	25.4%
Numbers Contributing Half or More	24	3
% of Sample	65.0%	16.0%

FIGURE 2.3 Female Contribution to Household Income: Grameen Bank (N=37)

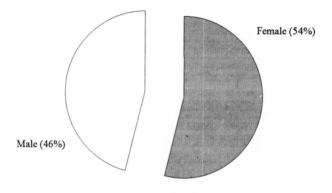

FIGURE 2.4 Female Contribution to Household Income: Control Sample (N=19)

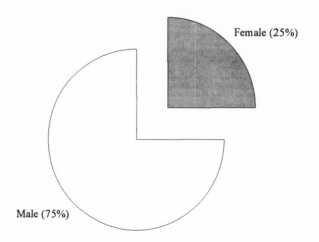

The women's share of the total income is calculated according to her contribution in capital and labor, regardless of who actually sells the product and receives the cash for it. In these decisions we have also followed village custom as we understood it. For example, all the income that is made from poultry and small livestock within the *bari* is counted as the woman's income, because that is how it is regarded in the village. Moreover, the majority of sales of poultry, vegetables grown in the houselot, bananas, milk and eggs take place within the *para* and are transacted between the women themselves.

Direct income from the women's own economic activities, like sewing quilts, husking paddy, making puffed rice or pushing the *ghani*, are, of course, regarded as her own.

Income from joint activities of wife and husband or mother and adult married son are divided according to the capital and labor contribution of each. The Bepari partnerships, where the wife managed the production of the mustard oil and the husband walked from village to village selling it, the income share of the wife in the sale of that oil was counted as 50%. When the mother makes sweets and the son peddles them the income is also divided 50:50.

Remittances from working children are counted as the woman's income if they are sent into her hand. This happens far more often than one would expect with only a reading knowledge of the Bangladeshi village, as with the example of Banu.

Women who used their loans to fund trading enterprises by their husbands or sons, received a proportion of the net profits of the business depending on how much capital they put up. Those who bought rickshaws or rickshaw vans for a relative to operate, got the rental value as their share of the income.

A large part of the income in both villages comes from agricultural produce. Women's role in these activities is quite strictly prescribed by custom. Women have no role in field cultivation although a few women are nibbling away at the fringes of these restrictions, as I shall discuss in Chapter 4. They do however play a major role in processing.

"Man's work is to cut the paddy and bring it home. All the rest is the duty of the woman," stated the husband of one of the Grameen members. In December-January of 1992/93 the men were literally "bringing the paddy home," walking back along the bunds with such a pile of cut rice stalks on their heads that only a tied up *lunggi* and a pair of stringy legs could be seen beneath it. When this walking haystack gets to the *bari*, the man is still responsible for threshing the grains from the straw, although in practice his wife often helps.

From then onwards, all the work is hers. She boils, dries, stores and husks the paddy. She can also be in charge of the occasional sales from her store to meet a sudden expenditure or to supply a needy neighbor. Major sales to the *haat* are handled by the men.

In our calculations of the harvest income we followed local practice in giving 50% of the value of the harvest to the owner of the land. In most cases the land owned by the family was inherited and so the legal owner was the husband. Even where the land had been bought it was difficult to determine from several years before how much capital for the purchase had come from which partner, so we followed the legal ownership — even where it was likely that the woman's capital had helped fund its acquisition.

Most of the land operated by our sample was, however, leasehold. In this case we gave the half share due to the "owner" to whichever partner supplied the capital to secure the lease. This was often the woman, using her Grameen loans. We computed 25% of the value of the harvest as the share of the male who did the cultivation. 15% went to the woman who did the processing and a final 10% to whoever supplied the capital for inputs like seedlings and fertilizer. Therefore, in those leaseholds acquired through the woman's GB loans, her "share" of the harvest usually came to 75%.

All borrowings, less repayment and interest, are counted into net income. When the borrowing is done by the woman, as with all the Grameen Bank loans, this is counted as the woman's share. Since many women in the GB sample borrowed much larger amounts of capital during 1992 than a year earlier, mainly because of the new seasonal loans, this boosted their contribution significantly.

Other researchers working in South Asia and computing women's contribution to total household income according to all of their productive activities rather than just waged labor have also found that they contribute substantially to household income. Mukerjee (1985) has estimated that Indian women contribute 36 per cent of India's net domestic product, not counting their services as housewives. This is larger than our finding in the control group that women contributed 25 per cent of the income of their households.

We expected that the Grameen women would be more substantial contributors to the total income of their households than the women in the control group. (It is surprising how seldom this question is asked, considering that women are 94% of the two million membership of the Grameen Bank. But it is implicit in Hossain (1988) that a substantial part of the increase in household income noted in the GB female group compared to his control was coming from the activities of the woman member.)

However, we knew that women's traditional *bari* activities in Bangladesh produce only low rates of return compared to the trading or agricultural activities of men. This can be seen with both the Grameen and non-Grameen women when the income from the *bari* is examined. It comes in small dribbles, now and then; a few eggs this week, next week a marrow, bananas or mangoes in season, then an emergency sale of a chicken to meet a loan repayment or medicine for a sick child. These *bari* sales are often vital to the woman, they can make the difference between fish curry or just a paste of wild leaves, but they are not big figures; nothing that would make an economist sit up.

Similarly, the activities for which we are told that most of the Grameen women use their loans — paddy husking and milch cows — produce very low returns. The net profit made by the six women who did any paddy husking during the year totalled a little over 2,000 Taka. One women made a loss. The returns for selling milk were better, but few cows were in milk for longer than a few months.

However, most of the women are not, in fact, husking paddy, except for their own consumption. Milch cows are a secondary activity. Our figures show that the bulk of the Grameen women's contribution to the household income is coming from various kinds of agriculture and land dealings. As can be seen in Figure 2.5, the largest contribution comes from net borrowings, followed by her share of the paddy and commercial vegetable harvests, followed by sale of livestock and other produce from her *bari,* and the proceeds of land transactions.

The large proportion of GB women's income coming from net borrowings requires explanation. In the last month of data collection 15 women took large seasonal loans, in addition to their other borrowings from the Bank. Since the repayments stretch over the next year, this gave them a sizable net position. Seven women took housing loans during the year of amounts between 12,000 and 20,000 Taka. Since repayment of housing loans are spread over 15 years, this also boosted the net borrowing position of these women.

FIGURE 2.5 Where GB Women's Income Comes From

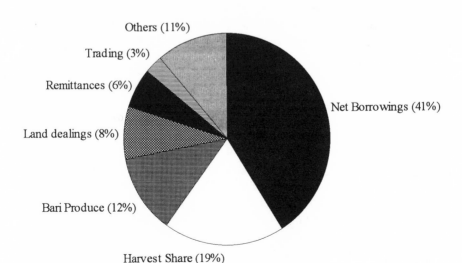

Others (11%)

Trading (3%)

Remittances (6%)

Land dealings (8%)

Bari Produce (12%)

Net Borrowings (41%)

Harvest Share (19%)

Apart from borrowings, by far the largest slice of total women's earnings (19%) came from their share of the harvest of the land operated by the household. The women's share of this is substantial because many have used their loans to lease-in land. Therefore their income share includes the proportion due to their "ownership" as well as their processing and capital inputs. Another 8% comes from dealings in land, mainly redeeming leaseholds taken with earlier loans and leasing out of land owned by the woman. It is clear then that a major part of women's earnings revolve around cultivation and dealings in land, an area which is traditionally dominated by men.

Some 12% of total female earnings are still coming from traditional activities in the *bari* — the sale of poultry and goats, vegetables and fruit, milk and husked rice. Another 2% comes from the sale of cows and calves.

In contrast to their participation in cultivation and land transactions, few women made much income from non-agricultural trading. Although some women contributed capital to their husband's broken glass or aluminium pot businesses, only the two Bepari women making mustard oil played a major role in a trading business.

More important to these GB women were remittances, from sons (and in one case daughters), working away from home, and reflects the hold they are able to maintain over the earnings of unmarried children.

All the kinds of earnings which are typical of very poor women in the village — domestic labor paid in kind, sewing, gleaning, begging, even paddy husking — are insignificant (less than 1%) in the earnings of the Grameen women. Of the sources of survival income of this kind, only gifts and relief are still of some importance, although they comprise only 2.5% of total earnings. Most of this is coming from the Government's Vulnerable Group Development (VGD) fortnightly wheat distribution, which is going to widows in Bonopur.

If we go back to Begum and Shireen and look in detail at their economic contribution we find the following breakdown. Begum contributes 63% of the income of her family in the following ways. Her annual income from paddy husking and selling produce from her *bari* is less than 1,000 Taka, 2% of household income, compared to Shakeeb's wages from daily labor which come to Taka 5,564 over the year. But during the year Begum brought in Taka 9,700 in loan capital, taking at various times a special loan, a group fund loan and her general loan. Her net borrowing, less repayment, was 2,343 Taka. She gets 75% of the harvest income because she provided the capital to lease in the land (50%), the capital for agricultural inputs (10%) and the processing of the crop (15%). She also gets half the ploughing income, as the owner of the bullocks. Finally she sold assets bought with previous Grameen loans — a cow and a calf — and she returned a plot of leasehold land. All that boosts her income share to 63%.

Shireen earns more than Begum from her *bari*, because she has a banana patch and grows some vegetables. She gets the 15% processing share from the sharecrop Forman cultivates. But there is so little to process from this poor harvest that her share comes to only 222 Taka. They cultivate no other land. The bulk of the family's meagre earnings comes from Forman's daily labor, in which she plays no part. Not even the traditional, domestic service part, since when he works she seldom cooks for him. He prefers to eat the more substantial meals provided at the landlord's house.

It is their landlessness and Shireen's lack of access to capital (it is Forman who borrows from the moneylender when they are desperate) that reduces her contribution to 12 per cent. This is lower than most of the control group.

What is surprising about these findings is not just the sheer weight of the GB woman's contribution. It is also the fact that most of the GB loans are going into agriculture. For almost a decade, debate on the economic impact of Grameen Bank lending has been rooted in the conviction that most loans were going into non-farm activities. This conviction is based on studies done by various researchers at BIDS from 1981 to 1985, at a time when GB membership was less than 100,000 and the majority of the members were still men. It is our finding in these two villages that the non-farm sector is no longer of much importance for investment. The implications of this on both the household and the village economy are far-reaching, but that is David's turf, and will be fully explored in his forthcoming book.

What is important here is the heavy involvement of Grameen women in a sphere which is regarded as traditionally male. Recent critics of Grameen Bank, and of rural credit programs for women in general, have argued that women are likely to lose control over their loans when they are invested in activities "culturally ascribed as masculine." (Goetz *draft*:10.) When a woman loses control over the use of her loan, she is forced to shoulder the burden of repayment without any payoff in terms of her own welfare or empowerment.

We have already met a number of women in this chapter who would make any observer pause before jumping to conclusions about control. The husband may be highly visible out there ploughing the field and bellowing at his bullocks, but that says little about his wife's interest in the field, or how much of her capital, labor and management goes into the production from it. Most of the earnings shown in Figure 2.5 do not come from the sole activities of the woman loanee. We have already seen that activities "culturally ascribed as female" are limited and give low returns. Most GB women in our sample have graduated into more profitable uses for their loans. But these investments depend on joint activities of husband and wife, or mother and son. Does this mean that they have also lost control of joint enterprises funded by their capital? This is one of the questions which the next two chapters will try to answer by looking more closely at what the women do and how they relate to others in their households while they are doing it.

Notes

1. The World Bank 1990 *Bangladesh: Strategy Paper on Women in Development* actually begins with a league table of statistics on such items as maternal mortality, female education, etc. On more than half these items Bangladesh scores the worst in Asia. This failure on all fronts then provides the backdrop for World Bank prescriptions of what should be done.

2. White points out that the interests of the "donor raj," as Kramsjo and Wood (1992) call it, dominate discussions of gender in Bangladesh. At its worst, this results in judgmental and racist comparisons of women's 'status' with other societies and helps feed such policies as the experiments with birth control techniques that are banned in the West. At best, it produces confusions like that displayed in an NGO newsletter which showed a woman squatting on the roadside breaking bricks in the sun, and heralded this as liberation because she was "out at work."

3. I have telescoped here quite a number of criticisms and comments on the Bank by economists. Von Pischke (1991:304) sees Grameen Bank as unique and non-replicable both because of the charisma of Professor Yunus and the particular "market niche" it has carved out in rural Bangladesh. Yaron (1992:110-118) another World Bank economist argues that it is expensive and "heavily dependent on subsidies", a view which still prevails in the World Bank despite Khandker's more positive 1995 analysis. That Grameen Bank borrowers will saturate local markets is argued by S.R.Osmani in *The Bangladesh Development Studies* 1989 and subsequently debated in that journal. All of these objections are faithfully repeated in the Bangladesh Task Forces report on poverty alleviation (Sobhan 1991:32).

4. Kramsjo and Wood (1992).

5. This is not the view of Professor Muhummad Yunus, nor the senior officers in the Grameen Bank. The underlying philosphy of the Grameen Bank is that many poor women are already involved in various enterprises which can be capitalised by small loans, so that women can take the profit for themselves rather than have it extracted by moneylenders and wholesalers. Every staff member knows that the first loan went to a woman making cane stools, which freed her from the clutches of the wholesaler who had previously supplied her with the cane at a high, disguised rate of interest.

6. Cow dung made into pizza shaped rounds and dried for fuel.

3

Wives and Partners

Habibah is a formidible personality. She is an angular, hard-faced woman in her late forties, with a husband not much older and an unmarried son of 21. Her only daughter was married out of the village years ago. Habibah's ambition is simple — she wants to be rich. Habibah has been the center chief in Bonopur for eight years. Recently, in deference to the rules of the Bank, which require the center chief to be changed each year, Baby was elected. But that change was purely cosmetic. Habibah still rules the center with the same combination of rewards, forceful leadership and scalding remarks as she rules her family.

I never met anyone in Bangladesh to match her mouth. Once she leaned forward to me and whispered, about an officer of the Bank: "He is a crook (*tout*) and he taught us to be crooks..." Then she cackled, obviously pleased to have had such a useful education. We will meet her again in the chapter on the organisation of Grameen groups and centers, because she is the pivot of the center in Bonopur.

Habibah must have been a strong woman even before joining Grameen Bank. This is her village. She was the eldest daughter in a family of three girls and no sons, so she inherited a third of her father's landholdings and persuaded her husband to settle in her village. In the past decade she has devoted herself to recreating the very large *bari* where she grew up by buying out the shares of her two sisters, who are married outside the village, and to acquiring the land adjacent to her house. She inherited 54 decimals of agricultural land and a 12 decimal houselot. By the time we met her she had got back the entire 35 decimal original houselot as well as a ten decimal garden next to it. This is a productive jungle of date and betel nut palms, bananas, lemon trees, bean vines, carrots and tomatoes. In addition, she has bought both sisters' shares of her father's half acre of vegetable land and was completing the purchase of his paddy land — a final 22 decimals which she had been leasing from her sister.[1]

Altogether, Habibah, her husband and adult son, have bought more than an acre of agricultural land over the last few years, reassembling her father's landholdings and adding to them. With leasehold and sharecrop, they cultivate almost two acres. It is Habibah who uses her family networks to buy and lease land and who negotiates land to sharecrop. She even decides what to plant and when to plant and can be seen out in the field near her house on market days with her two men harvesting her vegetables.

"While we are harvesting I am thinking: 'What will we plant next that will give the fastest and best return?' Then in the evening we discuss it; but I make the final decision."

Twice a week Habibah sorts and washes the vegetables and her husband and son carry them to the *haat* to sell. She gets an accounting when they return and the proceeds go into her tin trunk. When purchases have to be made she doles out the money to the two men. I think it is fair to say that Habibah is the head of the family business and her husband and son are her hands and feet.

One day I was eating my lunch in Habibah's large two-roomed house when a row erupted outside. Habibah had discovered that some of her radishes had been stolen from the field and she was tearing a blue strip off her husband.

"Of course people will steal them if you are not watching over the field! Do you expect me to do everything?"

Habibah's dominance is reinforced by other resources. While her husband is illiterate, she has a Grade five education. She also does other business on her own account. During the year she used her general loan to buy large amounts of paddy at the lowest prices, stocked it and sold it when the price was high. And like many of the better-off women in the village, she lends money and paddy at high rates of interest. She used the returns from selling paddy stock and from moneylending, as well as from the sale of harvests of mustard seed and winter vegetables to pay for her sister's land.

However, by no means all of the land has been bought in her name. The large houselot is owned two thirds by her and one third by her son. For the agricultural land, about half is in her son's name, with legal ownership of the rest divided 1:3 between Habibah and her husband. To this extent she has conformed to custom, rewarded the two men for their contribution and maintained the harmony of the household. But she has also arranged it with a clear eye to her own interests. "It's O.K. to put their names," she explains. "I have kept ownership of one third of each main field. They can't do anything without my agreement."

A *ghor jamai* marriage puts Habibah in a strong position in operating the village networks. But she keeps these networks well oiled with favors. She frequently lends small sums without interest to Grameen members who are short of cash for repayment, although she never helps those she considers "bad" members. (Her definition of "bad" members seems to be those who are often in difficulty.) Similarly, she lends paddy to certain relatives and neighbors without interest. Others pay between 50% and 140%. After each harvest she sends paddy

Habibah, unchallenged leader of the Bonopur center, her *bari* crowded with children and some of her poor women hangers-on.   *Photo Credit: Nurjahan Chaklader*

to her in-laws in Gopalpur. Just as she has taken over the father's land, so she had taken on the responsibilities of a son. During the year, her 70 year old mother joined her household permanently.

The *dheki* is usually pounding away in her bari, but I have never seen Habibah working it. There is always a small retinue of ragged-looking women around her. Although she denies employing them it is likely that they do her husking and other chores in exchange for payment in paddy.

There were other signs of Habibah's rising social status. Her house sprouted iron bars across its windows during the year. Before the *Eid* festival she sent her men's best *punjabi* suits out to the *dhobi* (laundry) to be ironed! Hers was the only family in Bonopur to sacrifice a goat for *korbani,* the Muslim festival of sacrifice. At *Muharam,* the Muslim New Year, when each family in the village makes a contribution to the mosque, she was assessed by the village elders to pay 130 Taka, as against 30 Taka for most of the other Grameen families.

Habibah's largesse, as well as her unchallenged control of the Center, make her a powerful figure in the village. I listened one day while she talked with the wife of the elected village member in the District Council — a local landlord. When this lady expressed an opinion to me about a doctor who treated some of the people in the village, Habibah cut in: "We Grameen Bank people don't agree with that." And proceeded to tell the landlord's wife what "Grameen Bank" thought about the doctor. The lady looked a bit non-plussed, but accepted it, which surprised me — until I learned that Habibah had recently lent money to her husband (without interest) to help him mend his shallow tube well.

But the most potent signal to me of Habibah's steady and sustainable rise in the world came in the form of a four year old charmer called Amir. Amir is Habibah's grandson, the eldest son of her only daughter, who came permanently into her care during the year. He is the shape of the future and he is plump and fair, unlike any poor child in Bonopur. He is encouraged to talk and make demands and they are immediately met, by the retinue of women who are always in Habibah's *bari.* He is already a little *borolok* (a landlord). Habibah has undertaken his education and fully intends to see him through college. She is already teaching him his alphabet. Meanwhile she shows him the business. Amir demonstrates proudly to me how he can pull carrots and wash them and pack them for the market.

This is not an attractive picture of Habibah; she is not a likable woman. But I respected her, as did most people in the village. She was a skilful and successful manager. Her judgments of other Grameen members were harsh but shrewd and she had played a key role in pulling the Grameen center together when it had almost collapsed five years earlier. Neither the richer villagers nor the Bank officials could browbeat her when she stood for the interests of the members. Most of all there is about her an honesty and directness which is rooted in her powerful self-confidence.

David was talking to her one day when a beggar came by. She told one of the women to give him a handful of paddy from the store. Then she commented (as the haves usually do about the have-nots): "Actually, he can work, but begging is his profession."

"Would you give to him if I was not here?" David teased her.

"I am expected to give," she replied with dignity. Then she favored David with one of her crooked, sardonic smiles. "Usually I would scold him first and then give. Because you are here he missed the lecture."

How much has membership of Grameen Bank contributed to the empowerment of Habibah? It seems likely that she was already dominant in her household before the Bank began operating here, otherwise how would she have persuaded her husband to move to her *bari* when he had inherited land in his own village? Even without Grameen, she would have been a capable manager, using her kin networks, the labor of her two men and the absence of other mouths to feed to build up the assets of the family.

But access to capital from Grameen has dramatically increased her ability to use these strengths. Without it she would not have been able to complete the buy-back of her father's landholdings, retain the loyalty and obedience of her husband and son through the accumulation of land they partly own and strengthen her networks with gifts and loans. Amir would not be headed for a college education.

Habibah's management has brought prosperity to her family. They are one of the better off families in our sample, with an annual household net income of 30,436 Taka. To this income, her capital and industry, and ownership of much of the land, contributes 68%. During the year she was able to raise 21,000 Taka to complete the buy over of her sister's inheritance. She was the only woman in our sample to operate a personal bank account.

Just as Habibah has strengthened her management of her own household, so she has become a figure to be reckoned with in the village. In the absence of Grameen there would have been little opportunity for Habibah to exercise her considerable powers of leadership.

Women in Charge

In our sample of 62, there are nine woman who were in our judgment in full control of the financial management of their households. Eight are GB women and one is in the control group. Four of them are widows, who have been forced to take control of young families. (There are other widows or divorcees who were clearly not in control of their lives and I have not included them in this group of "managing directors." Two of these widows are beggars, pathetically dependent on the largesse of others. Two live alone and manage their own budgets, but are still under the authority of male relatives in the same *bari*.) Among the women with husbands, there are four who are similar in power to Habibah. They run their families, making almost all the decisions, including those about the cultivation of land, a sphere which is traditionally male in Bangladesh. All of them are Grameen women. Their average age is 41, rather early to become matriarchs by age and tradition alone.

They have other things in common. Three are in *ghor jamai* marriages. They are Habibah herself, Jamilah, who was introduced in the Chapter 2 calling her husband her daily laborer, and Kia, the intrepid *dai,* who taught me so much in Ratnogram.

In an environment of scarcity where almost all opportunity is mediated through ties within *gusti* or between a landlord and his faction, these husbands are initially dependent on their wives' *gusti* even to get daily labor, let alone access to land to cultivate. In such marriages, also, the wife is often able to persuade her father to gift or sell her land for a *bari* or for cultivation, and such land is often registered in her name. This is what both Jamilah and Kia were able to do.

A woman in her childhood setting knows all the levers she can use to her advantage and she can move much more freely without attracting the kind of comment she would get in her husband's village.

There are two Grameen women, however, who have negotiated this position of power within the *bari* of their husband's kin. We have already met Banu, who has two daughters sending her money from Chittagong, which she uses to deal in land on her own account. When David finally managed to get her husband on his own and asked him about the management of their finances, the husband said that he managed his own vegetable business. But apart from that, he explained, everything else, including directing the son in cultivating their land, he had willingly turned over to his capable wife.

The other "managing director" has the full backing of her in-laws in her assumption of control. When we first arrived in the village of Ratnogram, Alia, the ex-center chief, was handling three streams of income from two working sons and her son-in-law. Earlier, she bought one son a rickshaw-van, but he was offered a good contract operating a shallow tube well for irrigation. He discussed this chance with his mother and she encouraged him to take it. Rather than sell the rickshaw, she invited her son-in-law to live with her and drive it. Alia was delighted to have her daughter and grandson back in the house and her son-in-law put all his daily earnings into her hand. Her husband, who is thirty years older than Alia, can no longer work and spends most of his time sitting in the sun.

When we arrive back it is winter and the arrangement with the son-in-law long ago collapsed in acrimony. He has left, taking Alia's daughter and grandson with him, to her great distress. The rickshaw has been sold. Her old husband is sitting as usual under a tree near the path, gazing at the stubble in the fields. Alia looks tired, but quietly triumphant, and her *bari* is covered with drying *amon* paddy. We sit shelling peanuts for the sweets she wants to make, while she tells us how yesterday she helped her younger son harvest their paddy, tying up the bundles in the field and stacking them on his head. Then they worked together in the *bari* until midnight, threshing and winnowing the paddy by the light of the full moon.

The talk turns to her husband and her management of the household. He can supervise the ploughing, but he is too old to work in the fields any more, she says.

"My husband was never very smart," she admits sadly. "He's a thick one."

Then she tells us of the thousands he has lost to thieves and pickpockets in his cow business. In the last disaster before "retirement" he bought a bullock for 5,000 Taka in a *haat* on the other side of the Jamuna River. The boat he hired sank, with cow, on the way back across the river. He also lost the 2,000 Taka he had hidden in his *lunggi* while saving himself.

"Loose brain," chimes in a very old lady squatting in a corner. This turns out to be his mother. "Lazy! It's only my daughter-in-law who keeps this family going."

It was not the last time I noticed a mother-in-law throw her support behind a Grameen wife (the one with the cash) when her son had proved himself lazy or incompetent. The survival of the family as a whole could often depend on it.

Partnerships

In 19 of the 40 Grameen households in the two villages, or nearly half of our sample, wife and husband worked and made decisions in partnership. When these partnerships seemed more or less equal we described the wife as a "partner", meaning that she not only held the money but was actively involved in the decisions taken about its use. When the wife seemed to be the dominant voice in this joint decision making, we described her as a "banker", since she had the edge in directing the use of the household earnings. In the control group there were four partnerships: two of which were the more dominant bankers.

In all such households, major decisions were intensively discussed and the outcome was usually some kind of consensus. There was no question of the husband making arbitrary decisions on his own without consultation, except occasionally in relation to his own business. Matters concerning the house, the *bari*, major purchases, the land operated and the children were settled together. But such relationships amongst the control group were unusual. The fact that they existed, however, supports my point that Grameen women and non-Grameen women are not different in kind, despite the Grameen women's decade of access to credit and participation in Group and Center. All the women in the villages had some resources they could call on and many skills, and a few had used these to carve themselves a position of some influence within their families. But the non-Grameen women were starved of one resource — regular access to credit — and the lack of this had made a telling difference.

Sometimes it is not easy to tell if a woman is a partner or a banker — equal or dominant. These are quiet negotiations in the privacy of a marriage. Except for Jamilah, whose fights with her husband were famous, these women took care to preserve the appearance of family harmony. In a society where men had so much socially sanctioned authority over women, even dominant women took care to observe the norms of "womanly" behavior. In this way a woman protected what was a most vital resource — her good relationship with her husband.

So usually we made a judgment about the power each woman wielded within the family based on outcomes. When we knew, for example, that the husband was opposed or doubtful about any course of action, we watched to see if the woman would win his agreement to do what she wanted to do. If she did then we would catagorise her as a four, or the dominant voice in decision making, even if she appeared quite submissive.

When Nahar and I walked into Zarinah's *bari* in the early afternoon she was bathing in her petticoat in a secluded corner, water streaming over her hair and breasts. We sat in the cool of her roomy, new house until she had finished. Then we chatted while she stored her scented soap in a tin, oiled her hair and rubbed "snow" onto her face and arms. When she had achieved a proper matt finish she was ready for serious talk. Zarinah, at 28, moves and speaks with self possession and grace; she is very concerned with proper behavior. When she smiles, which is not often, she is suddenly beautiful.

The day before, I had seen her in the field with her goats and I am interested in the concept of "inside" and "outside" and how far women can push out their boundaries. I ask her if she attracts any comment by going into the fields. Her normal low-key calm deserts her and she replies with passion:

"Why would they criticise? Will the ones who talk feed me? This is *my bari work*!" Then she calms down a little. "If you go in the proper way people won't say anything. If I go gently there is nothing to criticise."

This is a sore point with Zarinah. Years earlier her trips to the center meetings on the other side of the river and to the Bank's branch office did attract criticism. Her husband was teased about his young wife and her group members "walking along the open road like a herd of water buffaloes." At the time there were also problems in the center and he insisted she withdraw. It was a year before she and the bank worker persuaded him to let her return. Her relationship with her husband is central and she is careful with it, just as she is careful to preserve her beauty. Her concern with proper behavior is a way of saving him from shame, while she gets on with what she wants to do.

On another occasion we are discussing her contribution to the household. Just as I am warming up, her husband walks in. So I ask him. "She does a lot," he replies. "She does all the inside work. And for that I have given her 4.5

decimals of this house land. In future I will give her much more." There is something a bit smug about the way he says this, as if it is a tribute to his kindness alone. He doesn't mention that it is a requirement of the Grameen Bank that the wife own the land on which she builds a house financed by a Grameen Bank housing loan. "If you want the proportion, I think we each contribute about half," he concludes.

Zarinah nods. When he has gone, she does not contradict the fifty-fifty assessment. But she adds: "I do the inside work, but I do the outside work too. My husband goes out early to do his peddling business and comes home late, so it is all my work."

In fact, Zarinah contributes 55% of the income of this household, so her husband's estimate is not far off. This family dramatically improved their economic position during the year. They bought three new paddy fields, a total of 35 decimals; they leased in 53 decimals of paddy land; they built a new house. It cost them 35,000 Taka for the land, 8,000 for the leasehold and 15,000 for the house. In the decisions involved in these ambitious purchases, both husband and wife were involved in exhaustive discussions. But it was Zarinah who was the risk taker, and her husband who was persuaded.

The housebuilding and the purchase of two of the paddy fields all took place in the space of a month — a huge burden for this couple, whose average monthly income is less than 6,000 Taka. Initially, they planned only to build the house. Zarinah applied to the Grameen Bank for a 15,000 Taka housing loan. Her husband was worried about taking so much, but Zarinah persuaded him that she could handle the repayments, by selling some of her numerous chickens or ducks if necessary, something she often did when they were a bit short. She clinched it by reminding him that she had already bought the tin sheets for the roof, even before the loan came through.

The house was almost finished when a landlord approached Zahir with the offer of two fields for sale adjacent to Zahir's own inherited fields. Zahir brought the news back to Zarinah. It was a tempting opportunity; it would be bitter to miss it. But he was worried and reluctant to take on any further burdens. "Can we do it?" he asked her.

> I was very strong. I told him we had already sold 9,000 Taka worth of paddy stock from the last harvest and the IRRI crop was almost ready to be cut. I could sell three goats and my calf. Then Zahir said we could lease out both the new fields and raise 12,000 Taka, as well as return a lease for another 6,000. Yes, we could do it!

Zarinah also had to take a group loan of 1,000 Taka and with a bit more scratching here and there they finally paid the entire purchase price of 30,000. The pinch was so tight the next month that she had to sell a bronze plate her mother had given her to cover her loan repayments. But Zarinah's determination to manage somehow, and her willingness to take a risk, paid off for the whole family. They ended the year with assets worth 133,423 Taka and the highest average per capita income of all the sample at 23,069 Taka, an outcome which surely further strengthened Zarinah's influence in the family.

As a young woman living in her husband's village, Zarinah is vulnerable to criticism if she oversteps any of the many social boundaries that circumscribe women's behavior. In self-defence, she is very prim and proper. She never opposes or contradicts her husband and puts a lot of effort into maintaining her looks and keeping him sweet. I can hear feminists screaming already. But what looks like submission, can also be seen as a strategy for getting what she wants. Zarinah is, in fact, bolder and more ambitious than her husband. She has a class five education; her husband is illiterate. She has two sons and has been delaying for years trying for the daughter her husband wants. She is determined to get a better life for her family as fast as it can be done. And judging by the outcomes during the year, it is Zarinah's ambition that is pushing events and Zahir who is working — and worrying — alongside her. That is why, despite the claims of both of them that theirs is an equal partnership, I have classified Zarinah as a "banker."

The capital from Grameen Bank is playing a crucial part in this process. Zarinah's irrigation loan paid for the inputs for the *amon* crop, which they stocked and sold to purchase five decimals of land from Zahir's brother. (This was crisis sale within the family. The brother was arrested by the police and needed money to bribe his way out of jail.) Part of Zarinah's irrigation loan she invested in boosting her flock of ducks and chickens, many of which she later sold to help with this land purchase. Zarinah's general loan and part of her housing loan paid for the lease of 53 decimals mid-year, which tripled their IRRI harvest, which helped to buy the landlord's two fields. They also raised 6,000 Taka for the land purchase by giving back part of this lease. Earlier general loans had bought the cows and goats whose offspring were sold to help fund the land purchase. Zarinah's housing loan built the house. Finally, her group fund loan bridged the last gap between the cash they had and the price the landlord wanted.

The price of that purchase, of course, was that both the new fields had to be leased out, and they gave back a leasehold field, so that in the next year they would cultivate less land and harvest less paddy. But the new seasonal loan, together with her next general loan, would enable Zarinah to get back most of this within a year. Once that had been achieved, they would be operating 157 decimals and harvesting plenty of excess paddy to stock and sell. Then Zarinah's new loans and the profits from paddy would probably fund another round of acquisitions.

One incident concerning Zarinah sticks in my mind as a kind of symbol of the seriousness and passion she put into their acquisition of land. One day the research assistant arrived at her house and found this self-possessed, quiet woman in angry tears. "The Government has taken away my land," she cried. "I paid 15,000 Taka to lease in that land; I would get the harvest in two months and now they have taken 35 decimals to dig a canal!"

Her seven year old son, also crying, burst out with great drama: "Why are they cutting our paddy? How will we eat rice?"

"She was overwhelmed with sorrow for her lost land," noted the research assistant in his diary. There was actually no great reason for such an outburst. They lost the value of a half grown crop and the inputs they had used. She and Zahir were, of course, paid back the full sum of the lease. And for several years this family has never had to worry about eating — they produce enough rice to always have paddy in stock as well as excess to sell when the price reaches its highest point. But small setbacks in Zarinah's road to landedness are occasions of great distress.

Managing to Succeed

Partnerships are by far the most dominant pattern amongst the Grameen women in both villages. They are only a minority amongst the control group. Some readers might share with me a certain prejudice in favor of partnerships. On the other hand, there are many men in the village, not to mention men in the Grameen Bank in their personal lives, who would think it a most unnatural arrangement. But if these ideological mindsets are put aside for the moment, and we look at each of the 62 households in terms of their level of economic success, an interesting relationship emerges. 19 of the 27 households which have risen out of the poverty group (70%) are partnerships or are run by a dominant woman.

One would expect a relationship between the economic contribution of active female loanees and the success of their households. Two or three incomes are better than the one traditionally earned by the male household head. Several incomes make a family less vulnerable to disaster in any one line of business. Rushidan's 1985 study makes a similar, though weaker finding in that the families of her female loanees earned a slightly higher average income than the families of male loanees.

What is more surprising is a relationship between the female *management* of the household and its success, particularly in an environment where women are supposed to suffer such strong disadvantages in running anything at all.

It is possible to speculate that women who have been poor are highly skilled at managing scarce resources. In the village, women are expected to get some kind of meal ready — even when their husbands have brought nothing home. So they become expert at stretching the food supply so there is something for the days when there is no work for their husbands. When they get some income they are highly motivated to squirrel it away into assets for their own and their children's security. Several women in the control group who did not even have enough to eat, amazed me during the year by producing "secret savings" and investing them in assets. Many of the Grameen women have extended these scrimping and squirreling skills, during their ten years of experience of taking loans and using them in various enterprises, into managing an impressive build up of assets.

Both these relationships — several streams of income and capable female management — can be seen in Zarinah's household. There are three major streams of income fueling the success of this family. Zahir operates a successful broken glass business, collecting scrap glass, metal and plastic from surrounding villages and selling them to a wholesaler in Gopalpur. He runs this business without help from Zarinah's Grameen loans, and it contributes 11% of the family income. Zarinah gets a healthy return from her livestock — milk, eggs, chickens, ducks, goats and calf fattening. Some of her Grameen capital is used to add to her stock, but the major items, the cows and goats, were bought with previous general loans, and continue to give her new kids and calves each year. What Zarinah makes from her *bari* activities contributes 9% of the family income. But the largest source of regular income for this couple is the harvest from their land, which brought in 26% of their 1992 income. Just over a third of this Zahir inherited from his father, but the rest has largely been financed by Zarinah's capital, which also supplies inputs of seedlings, labor and fertiliser.

Because of the land purchase, Zarinah sold livestock and they leased out land to raise funds. These one-off sales raised 37% of their income during 1991. The balance was Zarinah's net borrowings, which are large because she took a housing loan as well as her general loan during that year.

Zarinah's constant work tending her livestock, as well as her contribution of capital to the acquisition and operation of land and of her labor to process the harvest from it, have substantially boosted the income of her family. But we have also seen that her role in decision making has been to push the family's fortunes forward much faster than if Zahir had been in sole charge. I would speculate that Zarinah is the risk taker because she knows from past experience of poverty that she can manage even when they run down their cash resources to almost nothing. This gives her the confidence to take on burdens that Zahir would probably not have risked if he had taken the decisions on his own.

In household terms, this hardworking young couple has the third highest income in our sample. In per capita terms, because they have only two children and no other dependents, they are the highest income earners. But the family size is also Zarinah's decision. Zahir wants a daughter. Zarinah says maybe later, and is openly taking the pill.

Slightly Less Than Equal

The tightest partnership in Ratnogram is a Bepari couple, Norjahan and Nurul, who are engaged in the traditional Bepari business of mustard oil. In some ways they are more interdependent than Zarinah and Zahir, since they each form half of one business — Norjahan makes the oil and Nurul sells it. But in their case the power relationship is tilted in favor of the husband — we classified Norjahan as a "treasurer," not a "banker."

Interviewing them is like a conversation with Tweedledum and Tweedledee. Nurul became a good informant about the business side of life in the village, so I was often in their house. (I grew fond of their eldest daughter, Aini, who already, at 13, was running little enterprises, so that I would occasionally buy from her one egg or a raffia coaster and watch her squirrel away the money in her clothes.) It was impossible to ask Nurul anything about trading or farming without Norjahan also answering. And if I asked Norjahan about the *ghani* work, Nurul would chip in. Both would stonewall any question which implied that Norjahan's interests might be different in any way from Nurul's.

The success of this strikingly close economic partnership is based mainly on the oil business. But there is also income from two *bigha* of wheat and paddy land and the steady but modest takings of poultry, goats and vegetables from their very large *bari*. These various sources gave them a net income of 42,000 Taka a year.

But, on balance, Norjahan is less important to this partnership than Zarinah is in hers; and the Grameen capital is less crucial to their success — nowadays, at least. Both facts must contribute to the third; that Nurul has the edge in this partnership. No-one would describe Norjahan as either submissive or passive; she takes a most active role in all discussions. Her behavior is much more aggressive than Zarinah's. But when it is all talked through I think it is Nurul who has the casting vote. He also seems to be the brains behind the financial management of the oil business.

Mustard oil is made in a rather crude looking mill called a *ghani*. The grinding part of this mill is made of stone, but it is turned by three wooden arms on a pivot. These arms are weighted heavily with stones and pushed around and around endlessly by three women. Three hours of pushing produces around 1.25 kilos of oil, depending on the capacity of the *ghani*. The women who do the pushing get 2.5 Taka each per three hour shift. The painful, heavy creak of this *ghani* and the grey, zonked-out faces of the women and girls who push it are the image of Beparipara which sticks in my mind.

Norjahan manages the *ghani*, filling the central hollow with cleaned seed, arranging the stones and organising the shifts of women to push it. Sometimes she puts the cow on it between shifts. But, as she explains to us, without irony, pushing the *ghani* too long is bad for the cow, and women are faster. The resulting oil seed cake she sells in the village as animal feed. The oil she measures, mixes with soy oil and bottles.

All the marketing is handled by Nurul. Selling the oil is a skilful business. Since they have capital, Nurul no longer sells to a wholesaler. He makes much more profit selling oil at the *haat* and from village to village by exchange — of mustard oil for paddy, or wheat or mustard seed. He must know the current prices of all commodities and be prepared to sell what he exchanges at the next *haat.* Price fluctuates with season and the profit margins are tiny, so all sellers mix the expensive mustard oil with cheaper oils, like soy, in order to make a living. They compete with machine-milled mustard oil, which is cheaper. The only reason they survive is the customers' belief that *ghani* oil tastes better and is more pure than the heavily mixed oil from the town mills. So Nurul trades on his "Bepariness" as well as his market knowledge and treads a thin line between adulterating his oil to make a better margin and adulterating his reputation.

Nurul more than doubled his turnover during the year and he also branched out into trading coconut oil and kerosene as well, a business to which Norjahan makes no contribution. During the slack season, when mustard seed is scarce and the demand for mustard oil low, the *ghani* stops for four months, and Nurul sells only machine-milled oil. As a result, Norjahan's contribution to their total net income was 48% — rather less than Zarinah's.

Norjahan took three loans during the year of data collection. Her general loan of 8,000 Taka was spent entirely on rebuilding their already large house. Her group fund loan of 2,000 Taka increased the capital Nurul had available to buy kerosene and coconut oil. Her seasonal loan of 5,000, taken just before the *ghani* restarted operations in February, was mainly spent on stocking mustard seed. However, the doubling of Nurul's turnover, and his new ventures into kerosene and coconut oil, took place before either of these loans and were largely funded out of his profits.

By their own account, the capital from Grameen has been important but not crucial to their success — and was more important in the past than it is now.

When Norjahan came to this village as a bride, at the age of ten, she pushed her father-in-law's *ghani* and lived in his house. She started before dawn and worked until well after dark, she remembers. By the time Grameen Bank arrived in the village, the couple had formed a separate household and had their own *ghani,* which Norjahan pushed. But Nurul bought the seed on credit and sold the oil to the same wholesaler at a heavy, disguised interest. Norjahan's early loans gave them the capital to escape from the wholesaler's clutches.

Within a few years they had built a bigger house and gradually tripled the size of their houselot to a third of an acre by buying out the interests of Nurul's sisters, mother and unmarried brothers who built themselves a new *bari* half a

Norjahan and Nurul, now the most successful mustard oil traders in Beparipara. In this formal picture that they demanded, Norjahan is resplendent in her silk *sari* and Nurul in the glasses he put on for the picture. They sit in front of their new tin-shed house and both hold protectively the favourite son.
Photo Credit: Nurjahan Chaklader

mile away across the fields. They also bought out the sister's inherited paddy land, at low prices, so that they now have 60 decimals. This land supplies them with rice, wheat and potatoes throughout the year. Norjahan used one loan to buy a bullock which both ploughs and helps push the *ghani*. But in the year of data collection, Grameen capital (net borrowing minus repayment and interest) represented only 17% of the household income — in Zarinah's household it represented 23% and their land purchase would have been impossible without it. This difference somewhat reduces Norjahan's contribution to the household. This combines with other factors to reduce her influence within the family. Nurul is a very astute businessman and a strong character. He is also ten years older than Norjahan and numerate, where she is illiterate.

But there is more to it than that. Despite her contribution and her active participation in all decisions, Norjahan is, in reality, less essential to the oil business than her husband. He would make less profit, but he could manage without her. She could not manage without him. He could buy his oil from the mill in Ghatail and stay in business. Without him to buy the seed for the *ghani* and sell the oil she makes, Norjahan would find it difficult to make a living, let alone sustain their current income. In the next *bari*, a member of her Grameen group in the same kind of partnership, was making good income at the beginning of the year. When her husband fell ill with typhoid and was unable to trade the oil she made, their mustard oil income abruptly collapsed. It is this dependence on their husbands to trade their oil which makes Bepari women vulnerable and undermines their status, just as does their custom of sending illiterate child brides into the homes of husbands very much older than they are.

But there is another reason why both Norjahan and her husband are keen to down play the role of Grameen in their lives at present. They are the biggest mustard oil traders in the village and are now one of the more prosperous families in Beparipara. But they are extremely sensitive to the odor which attaches to this business and to the Bepari caste. I got some hint of this edginess in my very first meeting with them. It was our first week in the village when I knew nothing about anything. But there was something different about this *para*, so I stupidly asked: "Are you Muslims?"

"Some people say we are not Muslims because we are Bepari. But we are just as good Muslims as anyone else," Nurul replied, very dry, looking me straight in the eye.

This couple strive intensely towards a higher social status and a position of respect. Their route is quite different from Kia's, who wishes to dissociate her family altogether from the traditional Bepari activity of making and selling mustard oil. Nurul and Norjahan are parlaying their growing wealth into status. Hence the new house, which sported some middle class touches like barred windows and a large, locked tin trunk, and whose completion was celebrated with a lunch for 30 *mullahs* (religious teachers or leaders). At *Eid* they sacrificed a goat, the only Grameen family in Beparipara to do so. Weekly they save a small sum in a savings society for the future education of their only son. But in their most ambitious status bid yet — the marriage of their eldest daughter, Aini — they have run headlong up against the culture of the Bank. When Aini turned 14 she was taken out of school in order to be married. It is rumored that they have found a salaried boy for her — a coup which will cost them 20,000 Taka in dowry. (Norjahan would admit to only 6,000 Taka and said: "They are Bepari like us. We don't want to marry her to a family who will look down on us.")

Since Grameen Bank proscribes both child marriage and dowry in its 16 Decisions, Norjahan was getting flak from some of her center members as well as (I'm sorry to say) from some members of the research team.

At the end of the year both husband and wife became disciples of a religious leader in the next village, and attended a night of prayers and lectures there once a week. It is possible that this group formed an alternative source of social support and approval to the Grameen center and legitimised the things they were doing anyway, like marrying Aini before puberty.

Apart from their determination to marry Aini, there are other aspects of their family life which remain traditional compared to other Grameen partnerships in the village. Norjahan had three daughters before she achieved a boy. This boy, now six years old, is blatantly favored over his sisters. One day I was eating in their house and I gave Norjahan two pieces of bread from my lunchbag to give to the children. She divided one piece into three for the three girls. The other piece went to her son. He has more clothes, a savings account for his future schooling and pocket money on demand. "It's all going to be his anyway," explains Nurul a bit defensively, as he dolls out yet another Taka to the boy from the tin which hangs down from the ceiling.

When I look at Norjahan, now in her mid-thirties, I see a very thin woman with a body like a stunted child. Although married at ten, she tells me she did not menstruate until she was twenty. When the babies came she often carried and breast-fed them while pushing the *ghani*. This happens even now, very soon after childbirth, in Beparipara.

But Norjahan seldom spends long on the *ghani* nowadays. She hires other women, while she manages the oil making, tends the cow and poultry, the vegetables and fruit trees on her large *bari*, waters the adjacent wheat field, boils and dries the paddy and does the hundred other things that keep women in middle peasant families busy all day. The winter months, when the demand for mustard oil is at its peak, and the *amon* harvest must also be processed, is the busiest time. "I don't have time to eat!" she exclaims proudly.

Far from regretting the more than 20 years she has slaved on the *ghani*, Norjahan attributes to *it* (rather than to Grameen) their present success. "All our prosperity comes from that hard work. From that we built up our capital. Some we invested in land and some went back into the oil business, and so day by day we grow."

But it is clear that none of her daughters are ever going to push the *ghani* from dawn to dusk. Aini, who already has a flock of chickens of her own, will become a busy housewife — or *bari*wife is a better word for duties and opportunities which extend well beyond the house, with a husband who will not be poor. The other two are in school. The boy will probably go at least to high-school and perhaps to college.

Pushing the *ghani* is now the role of Rezia, an 11 year old poor relation, whose mother is dead and whose father is half-mad. Every day I saw her ragged pants and dusty legs going round and round in the half dark of the *ghani* shed as I passed. One day the *ghani* stopped for repairs, but there was still no rest for Rezia. She was put on to the washing. From the top of their steps, Norjahan and her three bright-faced daughters threw out their things, chattering and laughing. The frozen misery of Rezia's face never changed as she gradually disappeared behind the pile of dirty clothes.

Entrepreneurs Without Capital

It could be argued that women like Zarinah and Norjahan did not become economically active and entrepreneurial because they had access to capital through Grameen Bank. On the contrary, they joined Grameen Bank *because* they were active and entrepreneurial. Therefore we would expect to find Grameen women to be more active economically and more influential within the family circle than women in the control group.

There is some limited truth to this argument. Obviously, a woman like Habibah and a couple like Norjahan and Nurul, who were already engaged in activities that required capital — and were borrowing it from wholesalers or moneylenders — jumped at the chance to join Grameen Bank when it came into their villages. However, there is something unreal about the assumption behind this argument — that women can somehow be classified as "entrepreneurial" or "passive." Here in Ratnogram and Bonopur, at the bottom of the social heap, there are not many "inactive" women, in either the control group or the Grameen group. Poor women must hustle to survive. Whatever they can do to bring a few Taka into the household they do and most women are doing several things at once. Some are more astute than others, but the real differences relate to the resources at their disposal.

When we look at a woman like Shireen, who appeared in Chapter 2 tending her calf and share-sheep and scratching each day for enough food to feed her family, we see a woman who is hard working and grabs at whatever chance she gets. But she has neither land nor capital. Her own family is too poor to help and, as an unwelcome second wife, she has few allies in her husband's *gusti*. As a result, she can do little to boost the fortunes of her family and is completely dependent on her husband for her survival; a fact which is reflected in her subordination.

There are women in the control group who do make an important contribution to the family income. There are two who are dominant and two who are equal partners. But when we look closely at these women, we find that they have used some other resource to negotiate this position of power.

The most dominant and entrepreneurial woman in the control group is Kadeera, who was not in the village when the Grameen center was formed ten years ago. She was living with her husband in her father's house in another village. Moreover, she belongs to the wrong *dol*. The four households that make up her *bari* are all poor relatives and clients of the Khan's — a landlord who is at war with the dominant faction in the village.

Kadeera is tall, with very large feet and an ungainly shuffling walk as if she has a hip deformity. She must have been an unusual bride. She arrived in her father-in-law's household here 12 years ago, bringing with her a dowry of 2,500 Taka, and the revolutionary idea that this money belonged to her. Kadeera soon discovered that she was married to a man who disliked daily labor. "He would work one day and rest for four," she remembers. When her father-in-law "broke" her dowry and began to use it to buy food, she demanded the money back. She got back only 1,000 Taka and returned to her father's house.

There she had the full support of her own kin. She used what was left of the dowry to stock paddy, selling in the lean season and rolling her capital until it had grown to 6,000 Taka. Meanwhile her husband joined her in her father's house where they stayed for eight years, producing two children, a son and a daughter. His dislike for work did not change. "He seldom worked, but was never shy to eat," Kadeera says.

Then her father died. Her mother gave Kadeera a cow (the means to an independent income?) and told the young couple to take the 6,000 Taka nest-egg and make their lives in Ratnogram. In Ratnogram they built a house next to her father-in-law and put part of Kadeera's capital into a leasehold field and bought a calf. With the cow to help with ploughing Kadir persuaded the Khans to give him two fields to sharecrop. But even in a separate household, Kadir's character did not change, Kadeera recalls. In addition, both the children were dogged by illness. In the year previous to the data collection, their daughter became seriously ill with a liver disease. What was left of Kadeera's capital went on medicine; they gave back the leasehold and spent that capital as well; but the girl died.

The daughter's long illness and the shock of her death seems to have transformed Kadir. He is now as hard-working as any man in the village. He hires himself out with their two cows to plough during the season; otherwise he takes whatever daily work he can get. He sharecrops two fields, as well as seven decimals owned by his mother. But the death wiped out Kadeera's capital and sent them back to zero.

Kadeera's dominance in this household has come partly through default — until very recently all the push for improvement was coming from her. She also made full use of her kin networks in her father's village, and still does. She is one of the most outspoken and self-confident of the women in the control group. When I asked *her* about her contribution to the household, she replied directly that she provided 12/16ths of the income, and proceeded to give me a list of her activities, starting with 'Planning and Advice.' In cash terms, it was an overestimate. Her contribution was 47%. But because of her contribution this was one of only three families in the control group who were no longer poor.

Kadeera simply shuffles right through any social conventions which stand in her way, including the respect and care she is expected to show to her in-laws in the same *bari*. I saw her often in the fields collecting straw for fuel and grass for the cows. She helped Kadir plant wheat and harvest it. She did the watering. "If I do the outside work, then he is free to earn money from daily labor," she explained matter-of-factly.

Kadeera visited her mother's house no less than eight times during the year, often for a week at a time, usually collecting gifts of money or food. But the father-in-law who "broke" her dowry all those years ago, never got a Taka from Kadeera's scarce resources. Old Samoj lay on a mat in the wintry sun all day right outside Kadeera's door, unable to walk and with nothing to eat. He simply waited for his old wife to come back from doing odd jobs at the Khan house. She brought home her "wages" — a meal that she shared with him. At *Eid,* the *bari* was deserted. Although Kadir gave 20 Taka to the mosque for the *Eid* prayers, he gave not one *poisha* to his father. Both the sons spent *Eid* in their wives' villages, leaving the old couple to the infrequent charity of the Khans. A month later old Samoj was dead.

It is clear that Kadeera could use far more capital than she has been able to gather through her own resources. Her story of the nest-egg she built up and then lost in her effort to cure her daughter is depressingly familiar amongst the control group. Women with the same determination can roll a windfall inheritance or build up some small savings from share-fattening livestock. They can invest in an asset like a cow which will produce an income. A young couple working hard together, with some help from their kin, can do the same even faster. But amongst the Bangladeshi poor, disasters like illness or crop failure are frequent, and it takes only one to wipe out these painfully-gathered assets. Grameen members face the same disasters. But they have access to special loan funds to pick themselves up afterwards, and they have the general loan and seasonal loans each year to recover their capital. They are less likely to have to liquidate their assets and start again from nothing.

Kadeera was making her third attempt to build a nest egg in the year we were there. Before her daughter died she had joined ASA, a savings and loan society which held weekly meetings in the next village. We got a detailed look at how she used these loans and what difference they made. ASA loans are small. The first was 1,800 Taka. Kadeera spent 800 Taka to repay money they had been forced to borrow for food in the lean season and to buy the fertiliser needed for the sharecrop. The balance of 1,000 she lent to a middle farmer. After four months he repaid her 1,500, partly in cash and partly in paddy. The paddy fed them through the next lean period, while the cash went into fertiliser for the next crop, food for the cows and loan repayments. Her next loan was larger at 2,800 Taka, but its use followed the same pattern. More than 800 of it went into the inputs required by the sharecrop and 600 to repay debts. The remainder she lent out again on the same terms.

Returns from sharecropping are very thin, since the sharecropper supplies the inputs and the landlord takes half the harvest. This means that half the benefits of the capital Kadeera put into the sharecropped fields were, in fact, going to the landlord. But if they skimped on the inputs, Kadir was likely to lose the sharecrop to someone with more capital. Moreover, when they were short of food — which they usually were while Kadir worked the sharecropped fields rather than working for a daily wage, Kadeera borrowed at very high rates of interest from the wife of the same landlord. These debts were settled from the next ASA loan. After these payments, what was left of the ASA capital was simply not enough for this couple to make the jump from sharecrop to leasehold, so that they could enjoy the benefits of the entire harvest for themselves. This was a jump that many Grameen members in the same village, with their more frequent access to larger loans, had been able to make many years earlier.

Kadeera was astonished and scornful when I told her she was not poor. But because they only have one surviving child, Kadeera and Kadir in per capita terms were out of the poverty group in 1992, with an income of 6,958 Taka per capita per annum. They were doing better than any other control group family and better than quite a few GB families. With Kadir's new attitude to his responsibilities, and Kadeera's skills at least partly capitalised by ASA, they are likely to further improve their position. But they will be slower than the successful GB families. Kadeera has access to far less capital than she has the competence and entrepreneurial capacity to use.

The advantage Grameen women have over the control group, in terms of access to capital, increased dramatically during the year. In 1992, the Bank introduced a seasonal loan, which replaced the irrigation loan and could be applied for during the *amon* and IRRI planting seasons. However, it was much larger than the irrigation loan. Members in good standing could take as a seasonal loan up to the amount that they were borrowing in their general loan. In our centers that meant that they could borrow between 5,000 and 8,000 Taka, thereby almost doubling the amount of loan capital they had access to in one year.

As of February, 1993, the center in Bonopur was not yet disbursing seasonal loans. But in Ratnogram, 15 members had already taken a seasonal loan in addition to their general loan, and the others were clamoring for their turn. In Ratnogram, this additional capital was going mainly into the acquisition of leasehold land and could be expected to greatly accelerate increases in income and assets for those households who could carry the additional repayment. Within another year it would probably have considerably widened the gap which already existed between the incomes of Grameen households and the incomes of other poor families in the village, even those like Kadeera's who were doing reasonably well.

Buttering the Networks

The women I have introduced in this chapter are resourceful — in the sense of having resources which they put to use to improve the economic status of their families. Credit from the Grameen Bank adds a powerful new economic weapon to their arsenals. But it does more than that. It enables them to use their *other* resources with more effect. The most important of these for all the women in our sample — important in their scope for economic action as well as their sense of worth — is their network of social relationships.

We saw Habibah, for example, using her existing advantage of living in her natal village, surrounded by her own kin, to lease, sharecrop and purchase the land of her sisters and other relatives. She uses the same networks to pursue her paddy stocking and moneylending businesses. She creates clients in the center and even amongst the village elite by giving interest-free loans and maintains a retinue of followers by giving employment. The fuel for these activities is her Grameen Bank capital. The prosperity that her use of her loans has brought her enables her to partake fully in the ceremonial life of her kin group as well as of the wider village, which adds to her influence and status. She takes gifts to weddings and entertains her sister's families to long winter *pitta* visits.[2] Her house is a regular stop for beggars; she contributes to the mosque and slaughters a goat to distribute to the poor at *Korbani.*

Habibah is exceptional; but all the women in our sample depended on the circle of their husband's kin in the village and on their own families in their natal villages for various kinds of transactions and support. Grameen Bank women used these kin networks specifically to advance their Grameen Bank projects, for borrowing and lending and for physical help when they were busy. In turn, they used their capital and growing prosperity to oil these networks, through gifts and small loans, through having Taka to buy livestock and lease land from others in their *gusti,* and through offering the kind of ceremonial feasts and contributions that signal their full membership of the social and religious life of the village. For the most successful Grameen families, this process has advanced to the point where they have become patrons rather than clients.

I did a fairly rough and ready analysis of the strength of these social networks by looking the activities of each woman across five areas: the amount of support and interaction with her in-laws and with her own natal family; the extent to which she was able to lend money or materials or offer employment to others; her participation in any organization or group outside of her kin group; her leadership role within such groups and her performance of social obligations over the year, like circumcision feasts, hosting visitors with suitable food, gifts and religious offerings. I used the weekly data sheets, which record all transactions and expenditures, borrowings and lendings, visits and journeys, as well as my own observations of interactions in the *bari* and *para* to assign a score out of ten for each area.

Out of a possible score of 50, Grameen Bank members averaged 18 points over this spectrum, compared with an average of 8.5 for the control group. They were closest in the area of kin support, with the GB women averaging a score of 6.2 over 10, compared to the control group average of 4.8. The Grameen Bank group gave twice as much employment and loans as the control group. In terms of performing social obligations, the average of both groups is low — this is still a feature of only the most prosperous GB families. Nevertheless, the Grameen Bank women were twice as likely to give feasts and make contributions as the control group.

I included participation in organizations and social groups because this creates a network of support and interaction independent of kin groups. Although there were a few members of ASA and other *somity* (society) amongst the control group, and one trainee in a government veterinary programme, the GB women, because of their membership of the center and some in other organizations as well, were far more participant, scoring an average of 6 out of 10 in this category compared to only 1.4 among the control group. None of the control group women played any leadership role in any organization. Some 16 of the GB women played some leadership role, whether formally, as group chairperson or as center chief, or informally, as with Habibah's unchallenged leadership of the Bonopur center.

I will return to the GB women's participation in their groups and Centers, and what it means to them, in Chapter Eight. All I want to stress here is that credit is important for more than income generation. GB women have used it to strengthen and extend their social networks, because they are now in a position to do favours, rather than being always supplicants.

By stressing resources, however, I do not wish to imply that these women are simply individuals, with personal strengths and weaknesses, within each household. The individuals are important — the Grameen Bank system puts the responsibility for choosing loan use and repayment squarely on the individual woman. But in her *bari* she acts within structures which are heavily weighted on the side of her husband and her male in-laws. All these women, except those in *ghor jamai* marriages, came to these two villages in their teens, sometimes before puberty, as strangers, without allies, constantly watched and criticised, at the bottom of the family pecking order. At that point in their lives, almost all the material resources, houses, land and animals, were the property of the male lineage. The young bride was an assetless dependent.

Social structures in Bangladesh are weighted against women because they are patrilocal — women move into their husband's *bari* and village on marriage and are usually much younger than their husbands. They are patrilinial — property is in practice inherited by men. And they are patriarchal, in their assumption that women stay in domestic space, they are economic dependents and need constant male protection. But we need to be cautious here. All the *patri* words are terms of abuse in the feminist literature. But the women I got to know in these two villages do not view their society as hostile to them. It is a given, within which they see opportunities and levers they can manipulate. The very fact that many of them have reached a position within their *bari* so different from the one they occupied as young brides indicates that their way of looking has validity. It is from this perspective then, what they can do rather than what constrains them, that I want to look at the position of our 62 women within their families in the next chapter.

Notes

1. Individuals are not qualified to enter Grameen Bank unless their landholding is less than half an acre (50 decimals) of agricultural land. Habibah inherited 54 decimals and her husband inherited 65 decimals in his own village. But Habibah sold 15 decimals of the land she inherited to raise the money to buy her sister's share of the houselot. Meanwhile her husband gave 29 decimals of his land to his daughter and sold the rest. That would have brought their joint holdings down to 39 decimals. Depending on the timing that this was done and other land purchased, Habibah may have been qualified to join the Bank.

2. The cold months after the *amon* harvest are traditionally visiting time, and special cakes, or *pitta,* are made for them.

4

Taka Talks:
Centrality in the Household

In the last chapter we met some energetic and capable Grameen Bank women, women who have won a central position in their families. The strongest amongst them have taken over the management of their households, but the majority work in a more or less equal partnerships with their husbands. In describing them I sidestepped the issue raised by feminist critics about who controls loan use. ("Who Takes the Credit?" is the catchy title of the Goetz study.) I also delayed answering the question posed in the Preface: if women are generating income through the use of their loans, but men are selling most of their produce, who is *getting* the income that she generates?

The calculations made in Chapter 2 on the percentage contribution each woman makes to the total household income are done in a typical economics vacuum. We could sit behind our computers and calculate how much Taka the woman's work and capital earned. We could say, for example, that Norjahan got half the income from the sale of mustard oil so long as she was producing it on the *ghani*. But did that mean that Nurul separated his profits from his working capital each night and gave half the profit to Norjahan? That was what her work actually earned. But did she GET it?

The first thing I discovered when I raised this issue with the women in Ratnogram and Bonopur, was that it was, to them, a very odd and irrelevant question. First of all, the typical village husband returned from a day's trading would give *all* his cash to his wife — not because it was regarded as hers, but because, as the one who stayed at home, it was her customary duty to safeguard the money. More fundamentally, neither husband nor wife thought in such individualistic terms.

Village women have only one career option — marriage and family. Banu's daughters, one unmarried and one widowed, who work in a garment factory in Chittagong, are the only women in our sample who have a living outside the family structure. Until Bangladesh becomes much more industrialised such women will be a rarity. The life of a village woman is subsumed within that of her family — a notion which extends well beyond the nuclear group which eats from one rice pot, in widening circles out from her *bari* and back to her natal village. She seems to have no conception of a life outside of it. She defends her work as family work, no matter how much it earns or how far out of the *bari* it takes her. Her plans and ambitions are centered on the advancement of the family and the future of her children.

Most women in the village are themselves the family bank — they hold the family cash for safekeeping, including their husband's earnings. In poor families, all the income earned has to go immediately to the survival of the family. Now that many of the Grameen families have some surplus it is being put into building up family assets. Quite a few women keep "secret savings," but this is a small hoard against emergencies or security against a feckless husband; it is not destined for any individual expenditure but for the survival of the family in a crisis.

It follows from the lack of choice women have in any life outside of marriage and family that the concept of autonomy, in the sense of an independent, individual existence, supported by a separate income, has little meaning for them. For instance, a large part of their contribution to the household income comes from their share of the proceeds of the harvest. But in practice, of course, the paddy that comes in from the field is not divided into husband and wife shares, the way we divide them in our analysis. There is no paddy basket labelled "His" and another basket labelled "Hers." The paddy is a joint family resource, just as its production is a joint family effort. What is of importance is whether the woman's contribution in producing that resource is recognised and valued by herself and others in the family and what entitlements she has, as a result, over the use that is made of it.

However, autonomy, in the other sense of holding assets, of earning an income, of being an important economic actor in the household's survival, is certainly relevant. It is also clear in the case studies, that women do have separate interests within the family. When Habibah keeps part ownership of all the main fields, she is consciously protecting her own interests against those of her husband and son. We have seen that she keeps a personal bank account with the GB branch office. Several women in their forties in our Grameen Bank sample are already planning their fall-back position in the event of widowhood. Their plans are based on control over the product of land they own or lease (when they become a single-woman household, *not now)* and their ownership of the family house and the houselot. There are in our case studies intrafamily conflicts in which women either get what they want or are overruled, according to the strength they bring to the negotiating process.

But the idea of separate control over separate earnings within the current family unit is not very useful in understanding these intra-family negotiations, particularly since so many of the activities funded by the loans are joint activities of husband and wife. What is more useful is the concept of the "centrality" of the woman in the management and decision making of the family. This concept places the woman within her web of relationships, which is how she sees herself, and has the convenience, for the researcher, of looking at family politics from the outcome end, where they are easier to observe. Sarah White comments that this notion of centrality "focuses analysis on relationships, rather than assuming an essential individualism, [and] seems a more appropriate term than autonomy as a way of conceiving interpersonal power in the Bangladesh context." (White 1992:140)

I think the best way to illustrate this is to begin with a negative case — a woman who is not central but marginal, a woman who makes a significant contribution to the family earnings but has so little power that she cannot even sleep or eat where she wants to.

No Place of Her Own

Parveen, a woman in her sixties and a Grameen Bank member, was helping her daughter-in-law husk paddy this morning. The pounding end of the heavy wooden beam of the *dheki* missed the pounding hole and landed on Parveen's hand as she was sorting the husked grain from the chaff. It looks like some bones are broken and she is in great pain. I give her some analgesics, but it is not until the next day that her son finds time to take her to Gopalpur to have her hand set.

There has been a big improvement in the fortunes of this family and the evidence is all around us — two brand-new houses on a big, new *bari,* facing the rich, black earth of a ploughed vegetable field. In a corner of the *bari* is the raised mud foundation of a third house. It has four corner posts, but no roof or walls. "This is going to be the kitchen," the daughter-in-law tells me, proudly showing me around her new *bari.*

"This is going to be my house," Parveen tells me when I visit her the next day, pointing to the same place.

In the old *bari,* Parveen lived and ate with her eldest son and his family in the house where she had spent her life since she married into this village at the age of 12. Her estranged husband lived with the youngest son. Recently, her husband died. Then her sons sold the old lot and bought this 15 decimal *bari* and vegetable field and built houses for themselves. They have decided that from now on Parveen will sleep and eat for one month with one son and one month with the other. Parveen's protests have been ignored.

> I am an old lady. I want to sleep in my own house and eat with my eldest son. I want to sleep in one place and eat in one place and not be shifted from one to another. But now they say they cannot afford to finish my house. I haven't been able to sleep since we moved here. It is too cold.

Parveen points to a mat on the floor. It is winter and the packed mud floor is so cold it chills my bare feet. Then she beats her good hand on the wooden bed on which we are sitting. "This is my *choki* (platform bed), and I gave it to them."

This household had the fourth highest household income in our sample and Parveen's loans from GB have contributed to this prosperity. They have helped to buy 43 decimals of land and a 24 decimal lease. She also helped to buy the new *bari*. None of this property is in her name. Her general loan of 4,500 Taka was used for the *bari* purchase and the sale of her cow, goats and poultry raised another 4,000 Taka. Her contribution to the overall household income during the year, from the sale of milk, her livestock, net borrowings and her part in the processing of their paddy harvest, came to 28%. Her contribution to the purchase price of the new *bari* was 38%. But Parveen has always handed over her loans to be divided between her two sons and she has no influence over the use of them. Even the milk money she makes from her cow is not under her control. When she visited her daughter in the middle of the year, her son collected the milk proceeds and used them to buy a small piece of land needed as a seedling nursery.

But although Parveen is unhappy about the way she is treated within the family, she does not see her interests as separate from it, nor does she use her loans as bargaining chips. When I suggested to her that she might delay applying for her irrigation loan until her sons completed building her house, she looked at me quite puzzled.

"But we need that money for the *shaak* (spinach) seeds and the fertiliser," she said.

Even if it occurred to her, Parveen does not earn enough from her own livestock (now all sold for the new *bari* in any case) to support herself. So even if she were willing to take a tougher line in negotiating with her sons, her fallback position is not very good. None of the assets that her loans have helped to acquire are in her name or under her management, including a place to live. She is dependent on her sons. Although she makes a contribution to the family income, it is not large enough in this fairly prosperous *bari* to be crucial to the survival of the family. And since she has never used the loans herself or even directed the use of them, they have not empowered her. She is simply regarded as the agent by which they come into the household.

On the other hand, both her sons are successful vegetable traders and their households are much better off than was Parveen's household when her three boys were children. As a result, the material conditions of Parveen's life are much better than they used to be. So as well as conflict, there are shared gains and mutual interests which hold this family together. There are other widows in our sample who are much more "autonomous" than Parveen. They are forced to fend for themselves, because, in the words of one of our research team, they have been "chucked by their sons." Their level of living, in terms of food and clothing, are much worse than Parveen's and their lives are full of insecurity.

Parveen, one of the most marginal Grameen Bank women in our sample, just after the joint family moved into a new *bari* in which she had no place of her own.
Photo Credit: Helen Todd

If we look at the function of Grameen Bank loans in Parveen's life, they have not altered her dependence or the customary trade-off dependent women make between current needs and future security. All they have done is strengthen her claim on her son's support and protection because they want this access to credit.

There is only one other woman amongst the 40 Grameen members in our sample who is as marginal as Parveen. She also "pipelines" her loans to her husband and son, who make a good income driving rickshaws. Unlike Parveen, she has no livestock. They cultivate little land, so she has no role in processing. Her capital contribution is less important than Parveen's because her husband is also a Grameen Bank member and is taking larger loans. Her economic contribution to her household is only 5%, which makes her completely dependent on the kindness of her husband and sons. Her influence is minimal. For instance, she tried to persuade her eldest son, who was employed in another village on a labour contract, to come home and get married. He gave her some money and renewed the contract.

However, the research team always joked about her being the "happiest" — as well as the most idle — woman in our sample. She wanders freely around Musjidpara with a great wad of *paan* in her mouth, smiling her goofy smile, and looking for anyone willing to stop and listen while she unloads her store of trivia. Her husband and unmarried sons regard her as a bit loose-brained, but they treat her with a kind of amused tenderness.

Pipelines for Credit

As is clear in these two cases, the most marginal women are those who do not use their loans themselves; who "pipeline" them to male relatives. This practice gives them stronger claims on the support and "kindness" of these relatives, but it does not give them any independence.

Ten of the Grameen Bank women in our sample were passing on all or most of their loans to others under circumstances that gave them little control over the use of this capital. This is 25% of our sample, a proportion which is higher than that found by Rushidan at 12% (1986) and Goetz at 10%.[1] I think the difference is largely attributable to the more intimate knowledge we had of these families. Since GB women are supposed to use the loans themselves most would not admit either the real use or the real user in a first interview.

This same intimacy with our sample makes it impossible to take a simplistic, judgmental position on "pipelining." The reasons, and the results, are very diverse. One young divorcee, for example, was passing her loans to her mother who was running the household. Some elderly women in their sixties were passing their loans to their sons in an implicit contract to secure their support. Also the situation is far from static. Two women whose loans had been appropriated for years by male relatives were in the process of wresting back control in the year we were there — after eight years of borrowing. I will return to this issue when examining the reasons why six of the Grameen Bank families in our sample are still amongst the hard-core poor. However, that pipelining is a poor option for most of the women concerned is acknowledged by nearly everyone in the GB centers; not only because it is against the rules of the Bank. As I pointed out in the last chapter, there is a strong relationship between the woman playing an active role in both productive work and the management of the household budget, and the success of that household. It is notable that those households where women had little control over the use of their loans and, as a result, played a minor economic role, were amongst the least successful in our sample. In seven of the 17 GB families who were still in the poverty group, the woman member had little role in the use of her loan. Parveen is the exception.

Centrality

I have discussed the two most marginal of the GB women, not because they are typical, but because they throw into relief the centrality of most of the Grameen women in our sample. As described in Chapter 3, 27 of the 40 Grameen Bank members, or 68%, are either partners or are dominant in the economic management of their households. Over the ten years they have been borrowing from Grameen Bank these women have negotiated a central position in the family and considerable influence over all the major decisions made.

There are five women in the control group (23%) who have the same kind of centrality; two of them head their households. But the majority of the non-Grameen women have little influence and are quite marginal in the decision making process. In decisions which directly affected their interests they were often overridden or ignored. There was a 38 year old woman who was ill and unwillingly pregnant for the eighth time. There was another who was watching her eldest son die of malnutrition and could do nothing to help him. There was another who had been saving for a year in ASA to qualify for a loan. When the time came her husband forced her to withdraw.

What gave the Grameen women more say was, according to them, the capital they brought into the household and the results of that capital in terms of increased income, more assets and enhanced security against lean times and disasters. Clearly, Taka talks. For families who have previously suffered extreme poverty, the change in their lives has been dramatic. Before they were landless and depended on daily labour to survive. In the pre-harvest months of *Choitro* and *Kartik* they went hungry and into debt. Now they have land to cultivate and paddy in store. Their houses are roomy and do not leak in the rains. They eat rice three times a day instead of once. At *Eid,* everyone buys new clothes.

It is hard for husbands to minimise the contribution their wives have made to the well-being of the family when it affects such basic aspects of their everyday lives. In these small villages, the contrast which now exists between the very poor families whose women joined Grameen ten years ago and those who did not, is known to everyone. As we saw in Chapter 2, 65% of the Grameen women contribute more than half the household income. A contribution of this importance cannot be ignored.

The crucial quality of the Grameen credit which makes this contribution possible is its reliable arrival year after year. So long as the woman repays her loan she is guaranteed of another, usually larger loan, the next year. When it is time to buy fertiliser for the IRRI crop she can get a seasonal loan. When there is a crisis she can (usually) get a loan from her group fund. And the Grameen Bank has proved that it is not one of the NGOs that arrive with a flourish and then collapse and disappear — like many that villagers in Tangail have encountered.

The importance of the recurrent nature of the capital input by the Grameen women is illustrated by the life of a member of the control group. Four years ago when Shahera's father died her brothers sold his land and gave Shahera the 6,000 Taka which was her share of the inheritance. This she gave to her husband to lease in some land. This one-shot contribution of capital has not improved her very marginal position in the household. He already operates more than an acre and earns a good income from trading, so her contribution did not substantially alter their economic position. He has a steady source of capital in the shape of his father, who is a Grameen Bank member who divides his loans between his sons in exchange for their covering his repayment. There is no more money coming from Shahera so he is under no pressure to treat her well. And he doesn't. Shahera has so little control over the family finances that she cannot tell us what he earns. He beats her. Although they have an income just above the poverty line, Shahera cannot direct his earnings to the welfare of their children. The two youngest are amongst the most severely malnourished in the sample.

In the process of exploring the issues of centrality and control I developed a series of six categories to describe how the finances and economic decisions of each household were organised and how much control the woman exercised over them.

In the first category are women who play no role in the household finances, not even the role of holding the money safely. These women, including Parveen, who are quite marginal in the management of the household, score zero in FIGURE 4.1. Next are the "cashboxes" — women who play the traditional domestic role of holding the money and safeguarding it, but who have little or no control over the use of it and little say in family decisions. Those defined as "cashbox plus" are a little more central. They hold and safeguard the money and have some influence over its use and some say in family decisions, although this influence is still mainly confined to domestic matters.

"Partners" and "Bankers" are the partnerships described in Chapter 3, where husband and wife, or a woman and some other male relative make decisions together in mutual consultation and the woman plays a central role in the management of the family. Where the woman's voice is dominant in the partnership, like Zarinah's, she is a "banker," who holds the money and has a primary role in investment decisions, but a secondary role in implementing the day to day management of the larger assets, like land. Finally, the "managing directors," like Habibah in Bonopur. These women make the investment decisions and manage the income or product of them, directing their menfolk like their hands and feet. Few things are decided in their families without their consent.

Female headed households presented some difficulty. An elderly widow, abandoned by her sons and forced to beg for a living, is not answerable to anything but the demands of her stomach. But there is something obscene about describing her as a "Managing Director" of her hunger. In addition, there are divorcees and young widows who head households but live in the *bari* of a father or brother-in-law and fall, in various ways, under male authority. So I have placed these women according to my judgment of how much control they have over their lives.

Placing each woman into a category involved a judgment based on a year's observation of her economic activities and questioning of the process by which major decisions were arrived at as they arose. The results of this year long observation differed quite markedly from the results obtained from a questionnaire administered at the beginning of the data collection.

Questionable Questionnaires

I think it is worthwhile to describe this questionnaire, because it is, in fact, the way most surveys of decision making are conducted and it highlights the unreliable results which can be obtained from them. We drew a box divided into neat squares. For each category — cultivation, purchase/sale of assets, schooling, marriage — the member of the research team conducting the interview would ask the respondent if decisions concerning that subject were made by her husband alone, by herself alone or by both together. The resulting collection of ticks were supposed to stand for the decision-making process of the household.

Looking back at them a year later, the ticks bore only limited relation to the reality we had come to know. If they had any usefulness it was to demonstrate a cultural ideal — the way our respondent felt families *ought* to behave, rather than the way they actually did. But in terms of the ideal, there *was* an interesting difference between the control group and the Grameen women.

If we exclude women living alone, who have few choices, and just look at the nuclear families, 84% of the Grameen women said that decisions were made jointly. This was also an ideal amongst the control group women, although not nearly so strongly. Some 47% claimed to make family decisions together. Not one of the Grameen women told us that decisions were made by her husband alone. However, 37% of the control group said their husbands made major decisions on his own without their participation. Only five Grameen women admitted that they made decisions on major matters for the family without their husbands, and three of them had husbands who were clearly physically or mentally incapable. Even hatchet-faced Habibah, who ruled her husband and son with a tongue that could cut leather, when asked in the initial interview, replied sweetly that all decisions in her household were made by consensus.

If we take these results as a description of how the respondents thought their family ought to behave, or the desired image she wished to present to the researcher, rather than a description of reality, then nearly all the Grameen women clearly valued the jointly-made decision and the ideal of family consensus. Even where they dominated the decision making process, it was culturally too risky for them to admit it in a first interview.

In the control group also the ideal of joint husband-wife decision making was claimed by almost half these women, including those families where we later observed the husband making major decisions in the teeth of his wife's opposition and interests. But there were still more than one out of three women in the control group who accepted the traditional norm that household decisions are made unilaterally by the male head.

Our experience with this questionnaire has given me a deep suspicion of the value of one-shot interviews to gauge anything as complex and culture-laden as decision making within the family. Our more time-consuming and intensive method, although it restricted the size of the sample, enabled us to make judgments based on observing the process of decision making as it took place. Although we were still reliant on what the respondent chose to tell us, we got well below the level of myth. There is room for debate in some cases. For example all the research team agreed that Shireen was a cashbox, but was Begum an equal partner or a more powerful banker? Another researcher might assign some cases a degree up or down. But given the wealth of data collected and the number of meetings between interviewers and respondent, I am confident that these results are reasonably accurate.

FIGURE 4.1 shows large differences between GB women and women in the control group. Fully 68% (27 women) of the GB sample can be described as central in their households; they are either Partners, Bankers or Managing Directors. Among them, eight women have a more than equal influence and another eight are the dominant voice. The control group by contrast are quite marginal in the decision making process. The largest group — eight women or 36% — are cashboxes. They have the traditional responsibility of safeguarding the money of the household, but they have little influence over its use. Five women have some influence. Another five can be described as central in the decision making process, or 23%. Only one women is the dominant voice in her household and she is a widow whose eldest son is 10 years old.

FIGURE 4.1   Central or Marginal? Influence over Household Decision Making
(Grameen Bank sample N=40; Control N=22)

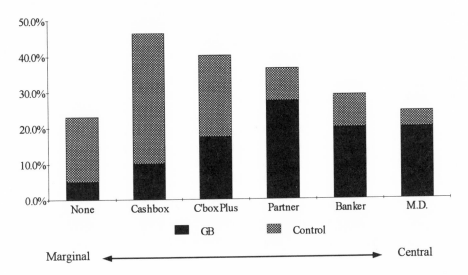

The power that GB women have in their households is closely related to their economic contribution — although there is by no means a perfect fit. Women's contribution correlates at a .66 level of significance with their centrality in decision making.

Some GB women have *more* influence in their households than one could predict from their economic contribution. This is because, even when the woman is not directly earning income from her own activities or from her capital contribution, she may be able to control the earnings of other members of her household, particularly her unmarried sons. I will describe this process later in this chapter. Other women are strengthened by the leadership role they play outside their families, within the Grameen Bank center.

These results are quite remarkable and they have to be qualified in two ways. First, these GB members have been borrowing for a decade and have had that time to build and consolidate their position in the family, just as their husbands have had time to adjust to and accept the increasing centrality of their wives. It should not be expected that GB members in their third or fourth loan cycles (which was the majority of GB woman members in 1992/93) should have yet reached a similar position — or that it could be reached without some conflict along the way.

In addition, nearly half of the GB women in our sample are in their forties or early fifties, at a time in a woman's life cycle when she is most likely to exercise the greatest influence over her household — although it is still a bit early for full-blown matriarchy. The control group were on average a little younger; 37.5 years as against the GB average of 39 years. This difference is too small to be of much significance. What might have affected these results more is that of those women in the control group over 40, most were widows and very poor, a combination which left them with little control over their lives.

The second qualification which it is necessary to make on these results, is that they reflect decisions which *were made* during the year. As several writers have pointed out (White 1992:23-24; Kabeer 1994:225) many issues simply do not come up for decision. Social and economic structures eliminate some choices. The paths to be followed are laid down, by poverty or by restrictions on women. Even with the support of her family, a woman cannot choose to take her cow to the cattle *haat* or open a tea shop on the road. She can't ask her husband to cook because she is busy boiling paddy. She is unlikely to have much say over *waris* land — the land which is inherited through her husband's kin group. She cannot choose a boy for her daughter without the consent of the elders of the *gusti,* nor can she represent the family in the village *shalish* or court. She can use her loans to educate her son, but if she cannot afford the bribe, she cannot get him a salaried job.

But even given these qualifications, these findings strongly support the assumption behind most "income-generating" programs for women — that increasing women's earnings will increase their decision making power and raise their status in the household.

Empowerment as a Process

This assumption has come under increasing attack from feminist writers, for reasons which must be taken into account. They reflect a concern that women are targeted, not to liberate or empower them, but to harness their labour for development. Their "income-generation" increases an already heavy work burden, adds to the household account and the GNP, without much payoff for the women themselves.

There are a number of third world studies which show this happening, particularly in relation to women moving into wage employment. They exchange the authority of father or husband for the authority of male supervisors; they are diligent, docile and underpaid; their incomes are appropriated by the family. (Ong 1987; Bruce 1989). Harriss (1992:353) asks if contributions by wage-earning women translate into greater control over the use of that cash in subsistence decisions about who gets what amounts and kinds of food. "Existing evidence suggests the answer is no," she writes, citing evidence from Tamil Nadu. She cites Jain's (1980:4) more general conclusion that "income does not guarantee improved female status within household or society."

Against these studies we have to put the findings above which show without doubt that women who have a decade of Grameen Bank loan use behind them exercise much more power in their families than do similar women without such access. They also show a high correlation between the woman's contribution and her centrality in decision making, meaning that it is the loans and the use to which she has put them that have made the difference.

Of course, Grameen Bank borrowers are not wage slaves. They are self-employed in their own *bari*. No bosses have been added that they did not have already. Borrowers choose their own loan use and work in their own setting; there is little conflict between their domestic duties and their income work.

But I would like to emphasise that there *are* a substantial minority of GB women who have not benefitted much from their loans in income terms. There are also a third of the GB sample who are marginal in the household decision making process. There is no *automatic* progression from access to credit to income generation to centrality. This is clearly illustrated by the case of Parveen, with whom I started this chapter. Empowerment is a process. And this process by which women move from the margins to the center of economic management is complex and long-term. It is often underground; it involves the politics of bedroom and *bari* and can be seen by the outsider only in terms of outcomes. As we see with Parveen, it can go badly wrong.

But looking at empowerment as a process changes the focus from the negatives in the environment which constrain women to what the women are able to do. Both the ideology and the structures of village society are undoubtedly hostile to the empowerment of women. But if you look instead at how they can manipulate family relationships and the levers they use to acquire more influence, the centrality of Grameen women becomes more explicable. What follows is quite impressionistic, but it describes some of the structures and beliefs I observed women using to achieve influence and even predominance within their families.

Cashboxes

It is traditional in these villages for the wife to hold the money that her husband earns. Since she is in the *bari* from day to day, a relatively secure place surrounded by trusted kin, money is safer in her keeping than in his. She hides it in a hole in the roof or locks it in a trunk and carries the key tied to the end of her *sari*. This custom does not mean that she has any control over the money, even less does it mean that she can refuse to hand it to her husband when he asks for it. But she is the cashbox; she has the power of information at least. She knows what he earns and how much is saved; he has to ask to get the use of it. In the face of a woman with the kind of self confidence that most of the Grameen Bank women exhibit, it must be fairly daunting for a man to take money from her cashbox for a purpose which is not in the family interest.

In many societies — in Egypt, for example, and in many parts of the West — a wife has no idea what her husband earns or how he spends his earnings (Bruce 1989). It was noteworthy in these two villages that, with a few exceptions, illiterate women were able to give us an exact account of what each member of the household earned on each day of the preceding week, as well as every item of expenditure, right down to the one Taka her profligate husband spent daily on *biri*.

Social Networks

If information gives power, then women's networks are crucial sources of the knowledge women need to assert control. As we saw in Chapter 3, Grameen Bank women use their social networks to advance their income-earning projects and in turn strengthen their networks by the way they use their loans. In turn, the alliances they make amongst their kin group as well as their membership of the center give them more clout within their own households.

I was sitting in Habibah's compound on a *haat* day when her husband and adult son returned from selling vegetables. She broke off to interrogate — that is the only word — both of them about what they sold, for how much, until she had every detail. It was clear she knew the current price for every vegetable they had sold. Then she gave her son the key to put the proceeds in her tin trunk.

Women are not cut off from information by their exclusion from the larger markets. Women who were dealing in mustard oil or paddy or the sale of milk and eggs knew the fluctuations of local price down to the last *poisha*. Although not being able to attend the *haat* was a serious constraint on women, and in the absence of a man a crippling constraint, it is hard for men to pull the wool over the eyes of women like Habibah when giving account of their transactions.

Sarah White writes from Kumirpur to overturn the common view of women isolated within their own households:

> There is a wide-reaching skein of relationships binding women to one another...few women can fulfil their household responsibilities without calling on the network: for labour, for loans, for help with child care or marketing. (1992:91)

Nor are these purely female networks, although the channels are often via the wives. Most of the land leases Banu holds are from her husband's kin group, most of whom are not poor. When you ask her who decided to spend the loan money on leasehold land, she says, as is customary: "We both decided." But this is how it actually happened when she took a lease in December, 1992.

From her sister-in-law in the next *bari* she heard that her husband's younger brother had his eye on a field he wanted to buy. To help pay for it he wanted to lease out another field he owned of 15 decimals. Ten days before this Banu had got a seasonal loan of 7,000 Taka which she planned to use to rebuild their house. But this field was too good to miss. When her husband came home from his vegetable trading, she told him: "This is a good chance. The house can wait a few months. Anyway I can apply for a housing loan. Your brother will certainly lease it to you rather than let it go outside the family." So her husband went to his brother the next day and arranged it.

It is interesting that it was Banu who heard of this chance rather than her husband. Like many traders in the village, he leaves early for the *haat* and comes back after dark. He travels around to all the *haats* in the area, six days a week, so he is rarely in the village during the day. It is Banu who is more likely to know the local "gossip," which rather tips on its head the notion that you have to go "out" to know what is going on. It is quite likely that the sister-in-law tipped off her husband that an opportunity existed for *him* in the shape of the cash that Banu had in hand.

Begum's husband's kin were more direct. In mid-year, a field that Begum and her husband had leased in two years earlier was taken back by the owner. He gave the money to Shakeeb, who handed it over to Begum for safekeeping. Then a relative from whom they were already sharecropping land approached Begum directly to lease one of his fields. She was keen and discussed it with Shakeeb when he returned from the brickfields. He agreed and arranged it with the relative.

Control over Sons

Several writers on Bangladesh have commented on the extraordinary hold that mothers seem to have over their sons. In our sample there were a number of women who puzzled me at first. They were confident, they exuded a kind of managerial air, but they had no actual income-earning activity. They took their loans for "paddy husking," but it was years since they had done any paddy husking for anything other than their own consumption.

"What do they *do*?" I asked the research assistant. "How can they be so strong when they are not *earning* anything?"

"They have grown up sons," she replied with a grin. "They are honorably retired."

What they were, it turned out, were executive directors of the family firm. Alia, the soft-spoken, graceful, former center chief of Ratnogram, is one such woman. Her husband, Hakim, who is thirty years older, is incapacitated and spends his days sitting in the sun. She has two sons. She set up the eldest with a rickshaw. They have not accumulated much land, but the second farms half an acre of sharecrop and 31 decimals that Alia has used her Grameen loans to lease in. When he is not in these fields he does daily labour for others. When the eldest got a more lucrative contract operating a shallow tube well he left home and Alia invited her son-in-law to live in her house with his wife and child and operate the rickshaw. This was the situation when we started work in the village. Alia was getting substantial remittances from the eldest. The son-in-law gave her all the proceeds from his daily plying of the rickshaw. (His takings were always in nice round numbers though, so I suspect he was using the odd taka in the tea shop.) Her second son handed over all his earnings from daily labour. In the slack season when work was scarce he bought peanuts, Alia made them into sweets, and he hawked them around the villages. Despite her husband's inability to work, she was handling three streams of income from the other three males in the household.

"I manage everything. When there is a decision to be made we all discuss it — like a meeting. But in the end I decide what is the best thing to do. When Enamul was offered the contract he wanted to take it, but he asked me first, and I agreed."

In Malaysia, which is also a rural, Muslim society, sons certainly do not hand over their earnings to their mothers, even when they are living at home. Unmarried daughters working in factories sometimes send remittances home, but regular remittances from sons are rare. In the West, parents may charge working children rent if they live at home, but it is most unusual for a son to hand his entire wage packet to his mother.

But in Bangladesh, it seems to be accepted that a "good" son should hand over all his earnings to his mother, at least until he is married and eating separately. Many of the women in our sample were in their forties and had unmarried sons at home. This custom is not unchallenged. One GB member with two sons received all their earnings at the beginning of the year, plus remittances from her husband who worked in town as a nightguard. But at the end of the year one of the sons revolted and refused to hand over his earnings, with his father taking his side. There was a major row and the son moved out of the main house and began to eat separately, although he was not yet married. Although his mother decamped to her natal village for two weeks as an expression of her displeasure, there was little else she could do to enforce his obedience.

But where it was accepted by the sons it was an excellent strategy for a Grameen woman to use the loan capital to get access to land for the husband to cultivate and then subsequent loans to set up one or two sons in business, and to manage all these income streams in such a way as to accumulate assets for the family.

Behind this strategy was the recognition that such control could not last. Sons would marry and eventually build a house and kitchen of their own in the *bari*. The wife would, over time, come to exercise more influence than the mother. Then, when the mother was old, her sons were supposed to support her. But everyone in Ratnogram and Bonopur could see painful examples of old women abandoned by their sons. It was necessary to have an insurance against widowhood.

Banu, who has four sons still in school and another understudying his father in the vegetable business, was already calculating her insurance against old age.

> My security is Grameen Bank. Even if my daughters-in-law turn out to be no good and disagree with me, I will still have land and Taka from Grameen Bank. I can always sharecrop out the land for my income and my food. I would abandon my husband and children before I would abandon Grameen Bank.

Entitlements to Assets

We also found embedded in the local culture another weapon that women were using to extend their control. The income earned from the small activities of women inside their own *bari* — the raising of poultry, the growing of vegetables, the sewing of quilts — these are socially accepted as the woman's own income, which she keeps separate and disposes of as she wishes. It is regarded as shameful for the husband to appropriate this income, partly because it is so paltry. It is clearly acknowledged at village level that women "own" these minor assets and have the disposal of them. What I think the Grameen women have been able to do over the years is to extend this recognition to cover some of the more substantial assets that they have been able to accumulate with their loans. This was certainly the case with larger livestock, like cows and bullocks, which have traditionally been the property of the male. It was also the case with rickshaws and rickshaw vans bought by the woman with her loan, even though she was dependent on her husband or some other male to ply them.

In this widening of the definition of what women could own in her own right, the woman borrowers are fully supported by the Bank. Assets bought with GB loans are legally owned by the loanee and Grameen Bank will protect them from theft by male relatives or anyone else. It has happened that an absconding husband or son-in-law has lit out with a "Grameen" cow or rickshaw. When that happens he is pursued by the bank worker, branch manager and a possy of center members in order to get back the asset owned by the woman member.

Does this concept of the woman's ownership rights extend to major assets like land? When the women discuss this they distinguish between different kinds of land. *Waris* land, inherited by the husband, is regarded as being part of the patrimony of the extended family and the men try, where possible to lease or sell this land to members of their *gusti* rather than outsiders. This feeling is so strong that when a man dies leaving no sons there is usually a strenuous attempt by his brothers to get the *waris* land back from his widow. Newly acquired land seems to have a different status. I am talking to Roshanara, a 28 year old woman whose husband died of some kind of heart failure three months earlier. Have his brothers attempted to get control of the field Roshanara is cultivating next to her house? "Oh, no," she replies. "That is not *waris* land. We bought that after we were married."

Most of the land acquired by the Grameen women in these two villages is leasehold and legal title remains with the owner. But several GB women played a role in negotiating these leases, as in the case of Banu and Begum. When Kia took a lease, the landlord came to *her*, because he heard that she was about to get her loan. She and her husband discussed the terms with him. Then the deal was sealed with a chicken curry in Kia's house — a social as well as an economic *coup* for her.

Most GB women are fully involved in the decisions concerning fields leased with their loans. That does not mean that they hold the harvest from those fields separately. In those households where the woman has already wrested a substantial or predominant say over financial decisions in general, and in the absence of any individual goals outside the family, there is no gain for her in holding separate paddy stocks. Similarly, when women sharecropped out their fields, they usually decided what to do with the share that came to them at the harvest.

This is an account from the diary of one of the research team, which is notable not only for the transaction described, but for the surprised tone with which this middle-class male from the city reports it: (This is a large joint family. The Grameen member is the daughter-in-law of Quddus and her husband sharecrops the stepmother's land.)

> Quddus second wife took a 28 decimal lease a year ago and gave it to her stepsons for sharecropping. I asked one of them when she will get her share and what will she do with it. He replied: 'That is her own income for the future of her daughter.' And also Quddus said she will use that money to take another leasehold. I asked: 'Won't she use any of it against the family expenses?' The stepson said: 'No. She only helps sometimes. For example, if we need money for the vegetable business then we borrow from her but we must pay back that money.' It is interesting that people in the same household do business with each other.

However, when a Grameen household bought land it was usually registered in the name of either husband or son, rarely in the name of the woman borrower. Land is expensive and none of our families could buy it without pooling their resources, so that it was unusual for the woman to buy land outright from her loan alone. But even when she did there were often pressing cultural reasons to put it in someone else's name. Chaina, a widow in our sample, bought land entirely from her own resources, but registered it in the name of her son, in order to protect it from her rapacious uncles-in-law. Norjahan and Alia supported putting land purchased partly through their savings into the name of the husband, for explicitly patrilinial reasons. Both of them said that they wanted to make sure that the land would be inherited by their sons — and not fall into the hands of their sons-in-law, since daughters have equal claim on the property of their mothers. The only women in the sample who put purchased land in their own names were those living in *ghor jamai* marriages, where their kin were around to protect that ownership. No woman alone could be sure of that kind of protection from her in-laws.

What women did own in their own names — and this at the insistence of the Grameen Bank — was the land on which they built houses funded by a Grameen Bank housing loan. There were 15 such women in the sample. For a woman without sons or for one whose husband died before her sons were grown, this gave her an essential security. It would be much more difficult for her uncles and brothers-in-law to force her out of the *bari* and back to her father's house.

These then were some of the levers that women could manipulate to gain more influence and control over the lives of their families. They were the cashboxes — they kept the money safe. They operated within a network of contacts which provided them with both information and economic opportunities which offset the constraints of *purdah*. Although a largely female network it was fairly porous to male kin and fictive uncles and brothers. Women could control the income of unmarried sons. Their right to separate ownership of certain assets was widely acknowledged and could be extended to major assets. Their entitlement over land leased with their loans was asserted and acknowledged.

These levers are available to all women in the village, not just to Grameen Bank members. But it was the annual injections of Grameen capital which enabled them to use them more effectively. With such a large chunk of the contents of the cashbox coming from the woman herself, she has over the years become far more than its guardian. The woman's network is more pliable to a woman who can oil it with emergency, interest-free loans to her kin or help out a neighbor with a pot of rice or some extra vegetables.

However, what talks loudest is probably the assets she has been able to buy over the period she has been a Grameen member. Landowners in the village know who are Grameen Bank members and when they receive their loans. It is not uncommon for male members of the *gusti* to approach the woman with an offer of land to lease. A number of elders or *matbar* in both villages had loans outstanding to Grameen women. Legalities aside, the land her husband farms has been leased with her money; the cows which pull his plough are hers and without her irrigation loan there would be no fertiliser to boost the harvest. These inputs into what is normally an exclusively male world give her an influence well outside the sphere which is considered female.

These are new, and economic, recourses. How does a woman reconcile them with what has always been a dependent woman's greatest resource — her relationships within the family, particularly her relationship with her husband? How does she prevent this economic power from becoming a threat to her husband's pride and a source of conflict between them?

A *Lokkhi* Wife

Grameen Bank women are not revolutionaries. I think most of them would be horrified at the idea that they were overturning social structures or challenging religious custom. In a very important sense their rising status makes it more, not less, important that they conform to custom and be seen as "good wives." And so long as they are seen as "*lokkhi*," they can do all the things that the Grameen loans enable them to do, and still be seen by society and their husbands as model wives.

"*Lokkhi*" predates Islam in Bengal. In the Hindu pantheon she is Lakshmi, the goddess of grain, the goddess of plenty. Amongst Bengali Muslims she is a cultural model of great power. *Lokkhi* refers to the wife who is both thrifty and hard working, whose management of the homestead is so competent that there is never want. Lucky is the man whose wife is *lokkhi*. He is respected and his wife is admired.

> *Lokkhi* is especially associated with the particular kind of prosperity *(unnoti)* a married woman brings to the household, such as knowing how to apportion the resources of the family to ensure that the granary is never empty. She is the model of foresight, prudence, economy and is associated with good fortune. She dwells in the houses of those who have order, cleanliness, those who do not quarrel...(Blanchet 1984:42)

Lokkhi is not a loose cannon like Kali; not a threat to order or to the male world. Her qualities are those of a wife and mother and that is the model of womanhood which is cherished in Bangladesh. The concept is also a real face saver for a husband with an active and managing wife. For what is *lokkhi* but a woman in charge, a household manager, to whom her husband has conceded control because she has proved herself to be so competent?

It was Azgar whom I first heard use the term in describing his wife. Azgar, tall and acquiline, with a white beard and his head turbaned in a check cloth, looks every inch the patriarch. Saleha, who is a Grameen member, is his second wife, he explains. With his first there was no happiness and no prosperity. But since he married Saleha they have done well and there is peace and order in his house. So bit by bit he handed the management of the household over to her. "She is a good woman; she is *lokkhi*. In everything I ask for her advice."

Their large *bari* is a picture of rural plenty. You walk into it through a grove of bamboo and a deep fringe of bananas, wind your way between haystacks and cows, dodging ducks, drawn into the inner courtyard by the rhythmic thump of the *dheki*. At one of our first meetings we were taking an inventory of the household assets. We got to the question: "How many chickens?" As if on cue, a hen flew squawking across the *bari* followed by a stream of chicks. We all burst out laughing. "Countless!" Bilkish wrote on the form. Saleha makes more from her *bari* than landless men in the control group make from daily labour. She gets a steady income from milk and eggs, bananas, vegetables and fruit in season, punctuated by sales of bamboo and small livestock. Almost everything they eat they grow themselves.

Saleha has invested her loans in buying cows, part-financing her husband's business hawking clothes and putting her eldest son through college in Ghatail. In the last few years, their surplus, including most of the loans, has gone into Azgar's singleminded effort to reassemble his father's landholdings. (Again, this emotional charge around the *waris* land, the patrimony.) As the only son he inherited half an acre; his five sisters inherited 124 decimals between them. Only one followed the textbooks and gave up her share to her brother. The others wanted to be bought out, albeit at low prices. During the year we were there he completed this mammoth task, by leasing out his own land and paying the remaining 5,500 Taka from Saleha's general loan and irrigation loan. Her seasonal loan taken at the end of the research period was then used to redeem the leased out land. At the end of that period Azgar was farming two acres, including sharecrop, making him the most "landed" of the families in our sample. It is not surprising he thinks his wife is *lokkhi* and defers to her judgment. He also transferred 7.5 decimals into her name during the year.

Saleha is trenchant in her criticisms of thriftless women — me, for example. I contracted her step daughter-in-law to make me a *khata* (quilt), buying three *sari* for the purpose. When I made it clear I wanted, not an embroidered *khata*, but a patchwork, like the village *khata* that hung over the haystacks, Saleha started rolling around the *bari* clutching her stomach and hooting with laughter, calling on the gods to witness this feckless foreigner who would cut up three brand new *sari* to make a *khata*.

Saleha, at 48, exudes the air of a woman of health and energy. At each weekly interview we asked her how much cash she had in hand. One day she turned on me her rather sly, Mona Lisa smile and replied:

"Don't ask me how much Taka I have. I am a farmer. I have wheat and newly ground flour. I have jute. My store is full of paddy. My cowshed is full of straw. What do I need with Taka?" (She didn't say: "I am a farmer's wife.")

There were other men who openly stated that they had turned over the entire management of their households to their wives, because they were *lokkhi*. Banu's husband is a respected man in Ratnogram. He belongs to an influential *gusti* and runs a successful vegetable trading business. But he told David when they were discussing cultivation practices that his wife was no longer burdened with small children and had proved herself so competent that he now left all the decisions to her.

The different women in our sample had negotiated different levels of influence for themselves. The point that is important here is that this was a process of negotiation, rarely of confrontation. When we heard about a fight between husband and wife or witnessed one (when it became public), it almost always meant that the woman had lost the argument. When differences could not be negotiated but broke into open conflict then custom came down heavily on the side of male authority.

The successful negotiations are done quietly and are harder to describe except by their results. And this is the usefulness of the concept of *lokkhi*. Women seeking more control did not have to be seen as breaking tradition or as challenging the authority of their husbands. If they wrapped their power up in the proper forms they could be sanctified by custom. *Lokkhi* legitimised them.

Note

1. This was the proportion found amongst a small sample of GB members. In Goetz and Gupta's whole sample of four credit programs targetted at poor women (forthcoming), they found that for 39% of all the loans taken, the women borrower retained little or no control over their use.

5

Strategies for Survival

Barek stood outside the walled bari of the wealthiest Bepari family in Beparipara and shouted for the landlord. His stomach was churning with gastric pain and he was shaking with impotent anger.

Three months before, the same landlord had approached him and asked for Rofik, Barek's eight year old son. "You cannot feed him. Give him to me. We will look after him well. In addition, I will pay you $300 Taka at *Choitro* for his work." So Rofik went to work, collecting grass for the cows, transplanting paddy seedlings, and fetching and carrying for the family. Although he slept on straw in the *ghani* shed, his parents were in the same *para* and he saw them every day.

Being only eight, he made mistakes. He spilt a pitcher of milk; he lost 27 Taka on his way to the *haat*. After three months of the four month contract they sent him home — with nothing, not even a new shirt. (According to Rofik, they didn't even feed him well.) Now Barek was at the rich man's gate trying to get the promised payment.

"Your son is useless. He cost me money. I am not paying a single Taka for such a boy," the man told him coldly.

Child labour contracts are common in Ratnogram. At their best it is an agreement between relatives and serves as a kind of apprenticeship for a boy in his teens. It usually involves an advance payment — to the parents — and the balance at the end of the contract period. It is a way of maximising the labour available in the household and at the same time getting a lump sum which can be used for investment. It is often organised so that the payment is made during the pre-harvest lean season, at *Choitro* or *Kartik,* and so helps families of landless labourers get through these times of unemployment. At their worst, it involves very young children, like Rofik, working for families who have no interest in their welfare, and no advance payment beyond a promise to feed the child. Frequently, the employer finds some excuse to dismiss the child before the payment is due or renege on the contract price.

But, whatever the risks, selling the labour of their children is one of the strategies for survival amongst the very poor. In our sample of 62 households, there were 10 labour contracts involving children aged between eight and 16 years, both boys and girls. It was a strategy which was uncommon in the Grameen group — only four cases or 12% of the families with children in this age group. It was more common in the control group: six contracts, or 40% of the families with relevant age children. Barek, and his wife Naima, one of these families in our control group, could not say no to an offer to take over the feeding of their elder son, for the simple reason that they could not feed him properly themselves.

Their house is the smallest, but also the neatest, of a dense huddle of straw and bamboo huts that cling to the western edge of Beparipara. They are not Bepari, but only very poor non-Bepari live in this *para*. Barek owns the 3.75 decimals on which the house stands; he sold five decimals of paddy land some years ago when he was ill and could not work; now he is completely landless. The *bari* is too small for Naima to grow anything beyond the usual pumpkin vine or run any livestock except four chickens.

They survive, like all the landless poor, by using the main resource they have — their labour. And this they use in a multitude of ways. When I first met Naima (we were doing a census of the village in order to select the control group) she was clutching some money tightly in her hand. I asked her how she had got it. She achieved the rare feat for a Bengali of blushing. It was her earnings from pushing the *ghani* for one of the Bepari households, work which she desperately needed, but of which, as a non-Bepari, she was deeply ashamed.

When Naima was first married, she worked as a maidservant in a landlord's house, for 1 Taka a day and her meals. But such permanent work is uncommon now. We had expected, because thirty families in this small village had joined the Grameen Bank, which effectively withdrew most of their women and girls from the domestic servant market, that the wages of the remaining poor women who worked in the *borobari* (big houses) would have improved. This is not the case. Women who work as servants are still paid mainly in meals. Some also get between half a kilo and one kilo of broken rice, the equivalent of between four to eight Taka per day, as against a daily wage for men of between 20 and 30 Taka. Moreover, opportunities for women to work year round as domestic servants have declined steeply since rice mills have became common. Even *ghani* work is only available for around four months of the year.

It is only in the harvest months of June and December that women are in demand at the *borobari* to winnow, boil and dry the incoming paddy and to husk and grind the special rice that is used for winter cakes. Women who are called to help with this post-harvest work, which normally lasts a month or so, are better paid than those who depend on domestic labour for their livelihood all year. Adult women are usually given one *maund* of paddy (37.25 kilos, at harvest season value of 200 Taka) and a *sari,* besides their meals. Sometimes they get a cash bonus. Girls usually only get their meals and a dress.

Naima took this opportunity, of course. In the harvest season of mid-1992 she left home for a month to live in a *borobari* in another village, boiling and drying paddy. She ate three meals a day (the only time of the year that she ate adequately) and at the end of the month brought home one *maund* of paddy. I suspect she also earned some cash, but Naima would not admit, even to us, what she was holding in her "secret savings."

Naima, like all poor women, is adept at "expenditure saving" activities. Daily, she gathers edible wild plants from the bunds and banks of the ponds. She collects leaves and twigs for fuel and her sons fish in the village ponds. Naima also mobilises Rofik's younger brother, who is six years old, to help her gather sticks and cow dung from the roads. With these she makes dung sticks, dries them and keeps them to sell "at the crisis time." But her most effective — and invisible — "expenditure saving" activity is going hungry.

It is often "crisis time" in this household. The constant efforts of Naima and her sons, make only very small amounts of Taka; enough to keep them from starving when Barek is too sick to work, but never enough to keep them from hunger. Naima makes three Taka for one shift on the *ghani;* she earns six Taka selling a bundle of dung sticks. Their daily need for rice alone is 1.4 kilos, or 14 Taka. Naima's earnings, including those in kind, only contributed 12% to the total, very low, earnings of the household (9,259 Taka per annum). Naima hoarded a secret store of Taka, and used it at crucial times during the year. This and her efforts to keep the family afloat when Barek was too ill to work, gave her some influence. We classified her as a cashbox-plus. But Barek managed the finances of the family. At the end of the year when Naima wanted to join ASA, an NGO which gives small loans after one year of savings, risk-averse Barek forbade her to go to the meetings.

Their day to day survival depended on what Barek could make from daily labour. But Barek had severe gastric illness and for a total of 52 days during the year of data collection he was too ill to work. "You must eat regular meals," the doctor in Ghatail told Barek kindly. "And good food: milk, eggs." Barek said nothing. How to explain to this man from the university what his life was like. When he was sick he needed money for medicine, or else he would go mad with pain. To get better, he needed good food. But because he was sick he could not work and there was no money for food or medicine.

When Barek was well, he could usually get work. He was known to be reliable, and, like other daily labourers, he had a "patron" landlord for whom he usually worked, and whom he could touch for an advance when he was desperate. When he was sick in March he mortgaged his and Rofik's labour for five days in advance in exchange for money to buy medicine. While he worked that off, they lived on Naima's *ghani* earnings.

When he worked, Barek earned 20 Taka a day when his employer provided him with meals and 25 Taka without meals. During the harvest season, when labour was in demand, he earned 30 to 35 Taka, with meals. The introduction of irrigation and high yielding varieties of paddy in many parts of Bangladesh, including Tangail, has increased the amount of labour needed per cropping acre for paddy. Unfortunately for people like Barek, however, the increase in population and the steep rise in the number of landless men looking for work, has outstripped the creation of extra work (Hossain, Mosharaf 1991:284-289). As a result, real wages for agricultural labourers have declined against the price of rice since the mid eighties.

The BIDS Poverty Trends Study (Rahman 1991), which surveyed districts across all of Bangladesh between 1988 and 1991, found an average wage of 36 Taka per day in 1991, a decline of rice purchasing power of 7% against three years earlier. The wages earned by Barek, and other daily labourers in Ratnogram, at around 25 Taka a day, are considerably lower than this national average. What can Barek's family do with 25 Taka a day? If we take the minimal calorie requirements of Barek, Naima and working Rofik, and count the younger son as half an adult, their minimum rice need per day is 1.4 kilos. Their minimum needs for flour, pulses and vegetables are listed in Table 5.1, at 1992 Ghatail prices. This does not include any provision for oil, sugar, fruit or any protein foods of fish, meat and milk, because Naima's housekeeping rarely includes them unless they can be grown or gathered free. The result is 1,740 calories per adult per day (half for the younger son), about 82% of the calorie requirement of 2112 calories per day set by the World Health Organisation. The cost is 19.32 Taka. Add to that 30%, as the minimum required expenditure on basic non-food needs, and the total comes to 25.12 Taka.

Table 5.1 Daily Food Needs of Barek's Family (3.5 adults)

	Quantity	Taka
	1.4 kg. rice	14
	140 gr. wheat	1.40
	140 gr. pulse	2.86
	91 gr. potato	0.59
	126 gr. veges	0.47
		19.32
30% Basic Non-Food Needs:		5.8
Total:		25.12 Taka

With a daily wage of 25 Taka per day Barek can cover the absolutely minimal needs of his family — for that day. In Malaysia, Malays have a proverb which describes this experience of poverty: "Scratch in the morning; eat in the morning. Scratch in the afternoon; eat in the afternoon." Even if he works every day of the year, Barek can generate little surplus by his own efforts. He has to exploit the labour of his children. Naima has to work very long hours on activities which bring in tiny returns and save money by going hungry, in order to get through the days on which Barek cannot find work.

Barek's landlessness, which makes him dependent on daily labour, the lack of opportunities for Naima to earn more than a pittance, and a tiny *bari* which minimizes other ways of earning income, locks this family firmly into continued poverty. Barek's chronic gastric illness condemns them to recurrent crisis. Barek cannot get access to land to cultivate; unlike Kadeera's husband, Barek has no cows for ploughing and everyone in the village knows he is too poor to buy urea.

But by the end of the year, this young couple had accumulated enough savings to lease in some land; proving once again what the poor can manage to do given even half a chance. They did it in three ways. Barek took contract work rather than daily labour, using the labour of both his sons. Naima saved expenditure by working for meals and paddy. And they frequently cut consumption to well below the minimum. The burden of this mostly fell on Naima, since Barek and Rofik whenever possible ate at their workplace.

Barek avoided going into debt, which is the usual way very poor families cope with the pre-harvest slack seasons when work is scarce. Partly it is hard for him to find anyone who will give him credit. Partly, he was able to get weeding work at a time when many other daily labourers were jobless.

The family's worst crisis came in the wake of the IRRI harvest in June. For nearly a month, Barek lay in their hut, moaning with pain. Every few days he forced himself out to do one day's labour, bringing back 20 Taka before he collapsed again. Rofik was still at the landlord's house, which meant one less mouth to feed. Naima and the younger son went gleaning and gathered 15 kilo of paddy. Finally, Naima emptied her "secret savings" out of the clay pot where they were hidden and took her husband to the district capital, Tangail, for X-rays and medicine. It cost 180 Taka, but for several months after that he was well.

Barek used this time to good effect. At the *amon* harvest, he took on contract harvesting work, with both his sons. For example, he contracted to harvest three *bigha* for 450 Taka. With all three working from dawn to sunset he completed the work in three days and then went back to daily labour, of which there was plenty in this season. He negotiated several planting contracts during the IRRI season. In this way he saved 500 Taka. Together with the 300 Taka Rofik earned on contract and Naima's savings of 200 Taka, they managed at the end of the year to take a lease on three decimals of paddy land. (I should remind readers that three decimals is 3/100s of an acre — an extremely small plot.)

"Next year, God willing, we will eat our own paddy," said Naima.

But this is not a fairy tale of the deserving poor, who get their piece of land and live happily ever after. Their attempts to use every resource at their disposal, namely the labour of every member of the household, right down to the six year old, are certainly heroic. But these efforts are what the landless poor normally do to survive week in and week out for most of their lives. Nor will you meet many landless families who do not have the same intense desire to better themselves — to get the security of a stable income or a piece of land.

The statistical likelihood of Barek and Naima hanging on to their tiny plot is not good. The poor are too vulnerable to disaster to succeed in holding and building their assets, except in rare cases. The story of Kadeera's nest-egg, which she built up over many years and then used up in a hopeless struggle to cure her daughter is an all too familiar tale in the lives of poor households in our sample.

"Rural households in Bangladesh are routinely subject to a variety of crisis which significantly affect their ability to sustain current welfare levels let alone sustain any welfare increases," writes Hossain Zillur Rahman, in the BIDS Poverty Trends Survey (Rahman 1991:94). In the survey years of 1989-90, 66% of all rural households reported facing a natural disaster crisis. Almost half reported facing a crisis of illness and another 25% had to cope with a crisis relating to their personal security (robbery, violence, extortion and rape). All these crisese confront families with a loss; either of property, or by forcing them into large and unexpected expenditure or by putting earning members of the household out of action.

The first reaction of families in the Survey to crisis reflects the strategies used by Barek and Naima. They draw down on whatever savings they have, they borrow from relatives and employers; they reduce expenditure by going without. When these strategies are exhausted, as they soon are for the very poor, families are forced to sell, piece by piece, whatever assets they have. Distress sales in response to crisis partly explain the increasing landlessness of peasants in Bangladesh and the downward mobility of a hard-core of very poor rural people (Rahman 1991:142-158).

Will Barek join the group that is going up through the poverty scale or the group that is going down? In five years, Rofik will be earning an adult wage and his little brother will have just entered the labour market. But in the short term, Barek's health makes it likely that they will go down. Barek was going into another spiral of illness in the last month of data collection. The last time I saw him, he was in pain, unable to work — and shouting, not at a landlord this time, but at Naima.

Barek put some of his surplus from his planting contracts into two *maunds* of paddy stock. Naima sold one of them forward to a rice wholesaler in the next *bari*. He would stock it until *Choitro* when the price would rise by at least 50 Taka. After his cut, the balance, and the profit, would go back to Naima. A good strategy — and one followed on a much larger scale and profitably by both Habibah and Zarinah in Bonopur. There was one crucial difference. Naima's family needed the rice for food. Naima was prepared to risk possible hunger for Taka. Going hungry is one of her survival strategies. Barek needed food. Going hungry literally made him sick. Hence the yelling. Naima, humiliated by his very public abuse, went scurrying off into the Bepari compound to try to get the paddy back.

Coping with Crisis: Benign and Destructive Strategies

In our sample there were 17 Grameen Bank families (43%) who are still below the poverty line in terms of per capita income. There were 18 poor families in the control group (82%). All of these poor families employ various coping strategies in order to survive. They get access to small amounts of Taka, usually for consumption, by informal borrowing. They buy food and materials on credit. They negotiate labour contracts in order to increase their returns. They sell the labour of their children. They take animals owned by richer families and fatten them for a share of their progeny. They sell their land, their house-lots and the tin off their roofs. Women whose hunger overcomes their shame, glean the fields of others. Their children dig down into rat holes and rescue the stolen grain. Some women fall back on the support of their natal families. Some work as servants for landlords. Some become prostitutes. Some beg.

Obviously, some of these survival strategies are more benign, and some are more destructive than others. There is plenty of informal lending and borrowing going on in the village. But borrowing without interest from relatives is a relatively benign way of bridging a lean time. Borrowing from moneylenders, mortgaging land or selling a crop still standing in the field are a net loss for families forced to do so. Selling land is a last-ditch desperation measure and selling the houselot is often the beginning of the breakup of the family and complete destitution.

A man like Barek who contracts to harvest a field for a fixed price, and mobilises his children to help him, can make far more than he would as a daily labourer. But a man who gives a child on a one year labour contract to a rich household because he needs the advance, is risking both the child and the balance of the contract price.

Although the poor Grameen Bank families and the poor control group families seem to be in the same boat in terms of per capita income there are differences in the methods that they used to overcome the various crisese which hit them during the year. Because of their access to credit, the Grameen families on the whole were able to avoid the more destructive strategies which tend to push poor families deeper into poverty.

As we saw above, only three Grameen Bank families had children out on labour contracts. Most of the Grameen Bank children, even in the poorest families, were in school. One of the GB members whose son was contracted out was a divorcee who found her 13 year old mixing with bad company and was afraid that she was losing control of him. So she sent him to work for a relative in another village. The money from this contract was not consumed but invested in leasehold land, which the boy's mother was accumulating against the time her son would return and farm it.

None of the GB families sold land during the year, with the exception of two families who each sold a houselot in order to buy a larger one. Only one Grameen woman was forced to lease-out land during the year to cover a crisis. This was because she was ill with jaundice and was unable to get access to her group fund. Other Grameen Bank families leased out land during the year, but in all these cases they used the money raised to purchase land, adding to their assets.

There were two families in the control group who sold land during the year. One sold land to send a son to Malaysia, then failed to get the necessary immigration papers. Another sold his last two decimals for food. Two other families mortgaged their last pieces of land during the year — one of them lost his last piece of houselot and was forced to move out of the village to squat in the house of his wife's brother.

Grameen families face the same crisese as do families in the control group. They are hit by illness; newly married daughters are "returned" by husbands not happy with either the girl or her dowry; livestock are stolen; a husband or son disappears for a few months. In addition, all poor families face a lean period before each harvest where work is unavailable and the price of rice is high. Two families may have similar levels of income, but if one wife is a Grameen Bank member they can get through these crisese by borrowing from the group fund, taking an irrigation loan, or borrowing from relatives at no interest against the next general loan. The family without such access often have to run down their assets in order to survive.

Dolali was one GB member who was hit by one crisis after another during the year. She seemed quite hapless and depended heavily on her husband, who was semi-crippled and ran a grocery shop from the house. He was also a Grameen Bank member and had always made most of the family income and ran the household. Then, in the space of a month, Dolali's husband suddenly died and her eldest daughter was "returned" after four years of marriage (together with her dowry of 4,000 Taka). How on earth would such a woman manage?

She could not take a group fund loan because she already had one outstanding. So she used up the dowry money and then borrowed heavily from the Union member in Kahpara to cover the funeral costs and her living expenses for two months. She also borrowed five *maunds* of paddy from a fellow group member. None of these loans carried interest and she was able to get them because people knew that her general loan was coming in another month. Then her reluctant son-in-law reappeared and agreed to take his wife back — but only if Dolali would give him back the dowry which she had already spent.

When I talked to her at this time, she was very depressed and helpless. Both her adult sons were working as contract labourers in other villages. The shelves which used to hold groceries were almost empty. When I pulled her husband's account book from the top shelf it spilled a cloud of dust through the bar of sunlight coming through the doorway. Customers want to buy on credit, she explained, and she could not write or remember the amounts. Besides, who could go to buy the goods cheaply from the wholesaler? She still sold some matches and *biri*, but she got her supply from another villager so the margin was very small. She would have to pull her bright 15 year old daughter out of school. The priority has to be returning the dowry, she said, and there just isn't enough Taka.

Dolali spent the next three months juggling all these competing demands. She paid most of the dowry out of her general loan of 4,500 Taka and watched thankfully as daughter and son-in-law took off together for his village. She settled some of her borrowings and gave back the borrowed paddy from the *amon* harvest of her sharecropped land. When she got her seasonal loan she settled the rest of the dowry and her outstanding debts, and put the balance into restarting the grocery shop for one of her adult sons, who finished his contract and came home.

These uses of her loans — paying dowry and repaying borrowings — are against the rules of the Grameen Bank and would have horrified the branch office if it had known of them. (The other center members knew, of course, and were prepared to help her through this crisis.) But by this means the family staggered back onto its feet, without selling or mortgaging any assets. When the school year started, the clever girl went back to school (with the support of her elder brother), despite the misgivings of her mother.

In the next *bari* to Dolali live Forman and his wife Shireen, members of the control group, whose lives I described in Chapter Two. They faced no extraordinary crisis during the year, except the usual lean season unemployment. Nevertheless they ran down their few assets. They are usually short of food and Forman is forced to employ a number of destructive strategies to keep going from day to day. He mortgaged out his only agricultural land of 11 decimals to finance his migration to Dhaka to look for work. When that failed he used the balance for consumption. His chance of getting that land back is extremely slim. Their 10 year old son was sent to another village on a labour contract and the boy was beaten and ran home just before the balance of the 500 Taka was due.

Forman, like most landless labourers, faces at least two lean periods a year when he cannot find regular work. His response is fairly typical. He buys rice on credit and borrows at high rates of interest. This means that by the time the peak season arrives when he can work daily and make a small surplus, it has already been pledged to repay previous borrowings. He managed to get a small plot to sharecrop for the *amon* season, but by the time the crop was ripe he had borrowed 640 Taka against the harvest, while the value of his share came to only 500 Taka.

In Chapter 4, we saw the family of Kadeera, whose situation is much less desperate than either Forman or Barek, caught in the same lean season trap. Sharecroppers usually borrow from the owner of the land they sharecrop, since he has an interest in making sure sufficient fertiliser and other inputs are used on the crop. At the same time Kadeera covered her food deficit during the pre-harvest period by borrowing at high rates from the same landlord's wife. These borrowings were repaid out of the harvest, which meant, in effect, that the landlord took much more than the 50% to which he was entitled under the terms of the sharecrop. Also, although the loans for inputs were given by the landlord "without interest" it is significant that he took from the harvest all the paddy straw, which is usually divided 50:50 or is taken by the sharecropper. "He takes it despite the fact that they have plenty of fuel and I have none," Kadeera commented bitterly.

Slack season unemployment is a routine crisis for most landless labourers throughout Bangladesh. The BIDS Poverty Trends Survey found that nearly half the landless faced a minimum of four months of food deficit per year concentrated in the lean periods of *Kartik* (mid October to mid-November) before the *amon* harvest and *Choitro* (mid-March to mid-April) before the IRRI harvest (Rahman 1991:95-97). Typical strategies to prepare for these expected lean periods include migration of earning adults, farming out of dependents to other households, curtailing consumption and the creation of buffers or stocks (not usually an option of the very poor, although labour contracts are often negotiated so that the payment is made during the lean season).[1]

Poor and a Woman

What these studies do not make clear is how these survival strategies impact on the women of the household.

Both Daria's elder children, a 14 year old girl and a ten year old boy were put out on labour contracts during the year. The boy went to the *borobari* where Shireen's son had been beaten and cheated of the full contract price. Daria and her husband Rahman live in the same *para*; they know the story. "The landlord came to the field where Rahman and Malik were working and asked for Malik. We knew what had happened before, but Malik was so keen to go and earn. He is a good boy and works hard, so we thought they would love him," Daria explains. They treated him well enough for the first few months. Then as the payment date approached they complained more and more about his work. Finally the landlord's sons picked a quarrel with him, beat him and forced him to leave.

Daria's daughter is working in another *borobari* as a domestic servant on a two month contract. After the first contract, her parent's were paid one *maund* of

Daria, a shy and diffident woman, with no surviving natal family and hostile in-laws, who has no power to change the many miseries of her life.

Photo Credit: Nurjahan Chaklader

paddy. For this December-January contract she gets her meals and a set of new clothes. Daria sits in her tiny straw hut and tells us, never looking up from the ground, what this means to her:

> I cannot give her clothes. They will give her clothes. The food is good there; better than here. Whatever they eat they also give to her.

There is a long pause and I wait, thinking about my own 14 year old daughter, whom I long to see, but who is comfortably at home in Malaysia, going to school. Then Daria at last raises her head and looks at me.

> If I could manage enough food, I would *never* give my children to another house. I think about them working there and if they make any mistake the master gets angry and they are scolded, maybe beaten. I know this is common. Then they are unhappy; they suffer. If I were nearby I could hold them and comfort them. But I am not there. Every mother wants her children near her heart, but I cannot be near mine. It is very hard.

What hit the pit of my stomach about this statement is that Daria *expects* her children to suffer; the extent of her hope is to be there to comfort them when it happens.

Daria's hut is sited in the large and prosperous *bari* of the Grameen Bank member we visited in Chapter 3 — Saleha, the second wife who proved to be so *lokkhi* that her husband turned over the entire management of the household to her. Outside the compound are haystacks and cow sheds; inside, the yard is alive with poultry and goats. Saleha's storage baskets are full of paddy and wheat and her *bari* is sharp with the smell of drying coriander.

There is no paddy at all in Daria's hut, only two trays of paddy dust she is keeping for her chickens. Her husband Rahman is the son of the first wife and there is no love lost between him and his stepmother. Eight years ago there was a major quarrel and Rahman's family was ejected from the joint household. "We separated with nothing; not even a pot!" Daria remembers. After that Rahman got no help from his father, not even employment as a daily labourer. He squats on the *bari* managed by his stepmother. Early in the year, Daria planted a pumpkin vine near her hut. This provoked a furious reaction from Saleha, and she was forced to uproot it.

At the end of the year, there was some kind of reconciliation, and Rahman's father signed over to him 7.5 decimals of land and began to give him work. But before that happened this family went through some very bleak times.

Daria is 31 and she has had six children. Two of them died as toddlers of wasting and dysentery. Rahman's family survives (barely) on his daily labour, although what he would like to do is go into business. During the year, he tried a vegetable selling business, borrowing 300 Taka at 10% a month. He lost on that. When work was scarce in July he migrated to Daria's natal village to find work. While he was away, this is what Daria's budget looked like:

Table 5.2 Daria's Budget During Her Husband's Absence

1st Week:

Income: Nil.
Expenditure: Taka

Medicine	2
ASA	24
Total:	26 Taka

(They ate 2.75kg of rice hoarded from the one *maund* earned by the daughter's domestic service.)

2nd Week:

Income: Daria borrowed 200 Taka from a relative without interest.
Expenditure: Taka

Rice 5kg	50
Flour 5 kg	46
Chillie	3
Salt	3
ASA	24
Total:	126 Taka

3rd week:

Income: Daria made 8 Taka selling eggs and 50 Taka sewing.
Expenditure: Taka

Rice 5kg	50
Kerosene	3
ASA	24
Total:	77 Taka
Grand Total:	229 Taka

By this time her daughter had returned from her first contract and Malik was still at home. The minimum calorie needs for grain alone (rice and flour) for Daria, her two almost-adult children and two younger children are 1.91 kg per day, or 40 kg for the three week period. Their actual consumption was less than half of that — 17.75 kg. In the face of her children's hunger, guess who starved?

In the 4th week Rahman came back for one night with 250 Taka (enough to buy 13 days worth of rice and flour) and then went off again for another three weeks. It was a time of eating flour soup with wild spinach and sitting in the dark because there was no kerosene for the lamp. When Rahman finally returned he repaid their borrowings and had exactly 100 Taka left over.

These strategies — farming out their children on labour contracts, Rahman's migration to look for work and curtailing the family's consumption of food and other necessities — doubtless helped this family get through another year. But the emotional and physical costs are borne disproportionately by Daria.

We have seen that Daria does earn small amounts of income of her own. She has a few chickens and sells their eggs. She is a skilled needlewoman and sews *khata,* the patchwork quilts assembled out of *lunggi* and *sari* too worn to wear. During the year she earned 1,726 Taka, or 17% of the family income, through these activities.

We can see how, even when she was virtually starving, Daria kept up her weekly payments to ASA, an NGO which mobilises rural women into savings and loans societies. She regarded keeping that credit line open as one of her few hopes for the future. When the time came for her to take her second loan, however, Rahman forced her to withdraw. She expressed her disagreement to the extent of taking off to her brother's house for five days; but she had no choice but to follow Rahman's decision.

Daria's first loan from ASA had been a disaster. She took 1,000 Taka and bought two goat kids. Both died. Rahman told her that if the second ASA loan had been big enough for him to use to open a grocery shop then he would have agreed to her taking it. But since it was small, he had no faith in her ability to use it profitably, and he did not want the risk of more indebtedness. Although Daria's contribution to the household during the year was almost 2,000 Taka, it had been earned in drips and drabs, and much of it consumed while he was away. He was so little aware of it, that he considered that *he* had carried the burden of her repayment and he was not willing to be saddled with it again. So Daria cancelled her membership, withdrew her savings, bought herself a *sari* and one *maund* of paddy and refused to talk about ASA again.

Naima's contribution to her household was actually less than Daria's — 12% as against 17% — but it was more visible, and Barek's illness made him more aware of his dependence on her scrimping skills. As a result she had a little more say. Unlike Daria, she talked freely in her husband's presence and, except for the last occasion I saw them, Barek treated her with some respect. Shy, self-deprecating Daria had almost no power to change the various miseries of her life; from the leaks in her roof, to the constant shortage of food, to the absence of her children. Her parents were dead and her in-laws hostile. Her own contribution to the household was still too small to be much noticed. When Rahman made a decision which worked directly against her interests there was little she could do about it.

Work of Honor; Work of Shame

Opportunities in the village for women like Daria and Naima to earn cash are very limited. A woman with no *bari* has no space to grow vegetables for consumption or sale or to share-fatten livestock. Several women in our control group could sew *khata* or children's clothes, but there is little demand for these skills. And all the opportunities in the village for a woman to "go out to work" are limited, shameful and seldom paid in cash.

This is a major difference between the world of a poor man and that of a poor woman. A man who has no other resources can exchange his labour for cash. There are very few opportunities in these villages for a woman to do the same. A woman can earn 2.5 Taka for a three hour shift on the *ghani,* but it is considered degrading for a non-Bepari to do such work, and Naima was the only non-Bepari who pushed the *ghani* in Ratnogram. Most of the *borobari* employ a few women during the harvest season to help process their paddy. They are paid in meals, paddy and perhaps a *sari* at the end of 4-6 weeks labour. But there is a great deal of ambiguity involved in this kind of work. Quite a few women do post harvest processing in other houses: eight women in the control group (36%) and nine in the GB group (23%). Those who could clothed this activity in some kind of fictive relationship. They go to "help out" and the payment is a "gift." Alia, the ex-center chief, for example, told me that the wife of the largest landlord in the village, the patron of her family, had called her to "help" during the post-harvest rush. "They call me because I am famous for hard work. My sons did not want me to go, but she is my daughter's *dhormo-ma*, how can I refuse to help her?"

To work straight out as a domestic servant in the house of non-relatives is regarded as shameful and is very badly paid. Two elderly widows in the control group worked all year, doing washing, cleaning and grinding spices in landlord's houses. One received one meal and 20 Taka a month. The other received only her two meals. That this kind of work is regarded as shameful must partly explain why the younger women who do it are so often subject to sexual harassment.

When I talk to Daria about becoming a domestic servant, it is obvious that she would rather go hungry than lose her honour in that way. "I have never worked in another house," she says. "I was the only daughter in my family and they loved me. In my house we used to feed *many* daily labourers."

But the very few opportunities open to women like Naima and Daria to earn a cash income, means that women like them contribute most to the family budget by "expenditure saving" activities. Since they have little room to grow anything, their major "saving" is cutting back on their own consumption of food. This is a silent and invisible contribution and not one that brings them any power in the household.

There is a belief advanced in much of the writing on development in Bangladesh that "increasing landlessness and poverty draws (women) outside into wage employment for economic survival." (World Bank 1990:1) While these accounts recognise that wage employment for women arises out of the breakdown of families and traditional support systems, they carry an implicit judgment that this increased mobility is both desirable and empowering for the women concerned. "Poor rural women in Bangladesh have at least taken the first step to venture out of their homes and make their presence felt in the public domain." (Hashemi 1994:20)

That there are increasing numbers of women entering the wage labour market has been documented in Bangladesh as a whole. But there is little sign of this development among poor women in Ratnogram and Bonopur. With the exception of a group of widows who did earth cutting for CARE, there were no opportunities for women to work for a cash wage in these two villages. The only "outside" work for women were the traditional kinds — domestic service paid in kind, begging and prostitution. The women in the village, not surprisingly, regard such work as dishonourable. The "freedom" of very poor women to work as servants in the houses of others is not a freedom any woman in the village would choose. All it does is take her dependency and subordination out into another household, where she is without the protection and self-respect which would attend the same work if she did it for her own family. The first thing women do when they can "manage the food" is to liberate themselves from such freedoms.

In the North-East of Bangladesh, women are able to hire themselves out as field labourers, at much lower rates than men. Paid field work for women is culturally impossible in Tangail. Women from poor families do work in fields operated by the family if they are fairly close to the *bari*. They help husbands or sons bundle the cut paddy; they collect straw; they mobilise their children to water vegetables. They defend such work as necessary family work, but it would be a mistake to imagine that they feel liberated by it or will not give it up just as soon as they have a son big enough to take over. I was walking through Bonopur one day and noticed Roshonara in the field next to her house cutting wheat. Roshonara, only 28 years old, was widowed only three months ago, leaving her with two young boys. I rushed over, very excited, to take photographs of this independent women actually *cutting* her own crop. She smiled for the camera gracefully enough, but when I asked her later how she felt about it, she said: "Nobody criticises me. They know I am a widow. But when I am out there I am thinking this is not my work and if my husband were here I would not be doing it. Then I feel very upset because he is gone."

Roshonara was fortunate to have a small plot of land and to have retained control of it after her husband died. Most women in our control group had no access to land and very few opportunities to earn income, no matter how much extreme poverty may have "freed" them from the restrictions of *purdah*. It is in this context of very limited opportunity for very poor women that the role of Grameen Bank credit has to be understood. Where women have little opportunity to use their labour power outside of the household, then access to regular credit can open many doors. Although an "enterprise culture" in which women play an active part does exist in the village, women have to have cash in order to participate in it.

What the Grameen loans make possible is self-employment in the woman's own *bari*, employment which is acceptable both to the woman herself and to society, and which she can combine with her domestic and child rearing roles. It enables Grameen women to greatly expand production from their *bari*. But even more important, it has enabled GB women to capitalise the labour of their husbands so that it serves the welfare of the family, rather than the welfare of his landlord employer.

We have seen through the experience of Barek that the system of daily labour in the village gives the labourer just enough for his own subsistence and a life of semi-starvation for his wife and children. With capital to lease in land and pay for inputs a man can labour in his own field for his own harvest twice a year, as well as doing daily labour.

Getting access to land for cultivation cannot be seen as a solely male interest. Land is a woman's issue. Because she plays such an important role in the processing of the harvest, access to land increases her contribution to and her influence in the family. On an even more basic level, access to land gives her food security. All the product of the land comes into her *bari*, she processes and stores it. Since her capital was instrumental in getting the land to cultivate, she will usually have a large say in how it is disposed of.

It is on the basis of this food security, as the paddy piles up in her baskets, that the Grameen women in the village have been able to gradually increase their assets. They have bought or extended their *bari* so that they have more scope for earning income and reducing expenditure through raising livestock and growing vegetables and fruit trees. They have built roomy and leakproof houses where grains and seed can be stored and the health of the family protected. They have bought poultry, goats and cows, both for income and for ploughing. They have leased in land and harnessed their husband's manpower. Some have capitalised the labour of their sons, by buying rickshaws or setting up small businesses.

What is empowering these women is not "going out to work." It is having income in her own hand and assets under her control and the pride she takes in her contribution to the progress of her family. Her relationships with other center members and her link with the Grameen Bank branch office take her into public space in a way which adds to her self-esteem, rather than humiliating her. She has both the self-confidence and the cash to welcome visits from her kin and to visit in return.

In his essay, *Credit for Self-Employment: A Fundamental Human Right,* Professor Muhammad Yunus writes:

> ...employment *per se* does not remove poverty. .... Employment may mean being condemned to a life in a squalid city slum or working for two meals a day for the rest of your life. ... Wage employment is not a happy road to the reduction of poverty. Removal or reduction of poverty must be a continuous process of creation of assets, so that the asset-base of a poor person becomes stronger at each economic cycle, enabling him to earn more and more. Self-employment, supported by credit, has more potential for improving the asset base of the poor than wage employment has. (Yunus 1989:47)

But not all the Grameen Bank families have been equally successful in this accumulation of assets; the Centers in both villages are quite polarised between those who have made it out of the poverty group and those who have been left behind. In the next chapter, I will look more closely at the Grameen families who are still poor and examine the reasons why they have made so little progress.

Note

1. A study which focusses on the interconnected relationships between the provision of credit, and the competition for work and land to sharecrop, all of which tend to the gradual dispossession of the poor of any land, including house-land, which they own, is Jansen 1987. The situation he describes in the Manikganj District from 1976 to 1980 is more bleak than that of Tangail in the early nineties. Irrigation in the areas of our two villages means a *boro,* or IRRI, crop of rice, shortening the slack season substantially. In both our villages there are also some alternative sources of employment for men: a brickfield in one, and government road construction and Food for Work programs in both.

6

Still Poor:
Disaster and Dependency

Rina, a healthy young woman of 30, has been a Grameen Bank member for nine years. In total, over these years, she has borrowed 45,000 Taka. At the end of the ninth year her position is as follows. Value of total assets: 1,590 Taka. Income group: Very poor. Size of houselot: No houselot. Land owned or operated: None. Paddy in store: None. Food supply: Sometimes deficit. Position before joining Grameen Bank: Better than now.

Why have nine years of Grameen Bank membership done so little for Rina? How has all this capital been used with so little result? Rina's story illustrates how "pipelining" her loan to a male relative, her husband's illness and her own dependence have made her poorer. Through a decade of membership her access to credit has done little more than keep her head above water.

When GB started working in Ratnogram, two brothers, both middle farmers owning two and three acres respectively, lived there. One brother was the head of a joint family comprising his four sons and the new wife of one of them — Rina. The other headed a family in which lived his daughter and her husband in a *ghor jamai* marriage. One brother told his daughter-in-law and the other his daughter to apply to join Grameen Bank and told them what to say. So both women told the bank worker that their husbands were landless, which was true, and that they were living separately from their joint families, which was not. Both were accepted as members of the Bank and both simply handed over their loans to the head of the family: Rina to her father-in-law and the other woman to her father, and had no say whatever over how the money was used.

Rina's own family were comfortable middle farmers and she was a protected and cosseted daughter. It was a "good marriage," into a middling landed family, to a boy who was "School Certificate appeared" (he attended school up to Certificate level but failed the examination) and worked as a clerk in a construction company.

Rina did not know what he earned. His salary was paid directly by the company to her father-in-law. Nor did she question handing over her Grameen Bank loans. "We lived in a joint family and he was our guardian. We followed his advice."

She did know how her loans were spent, however. With the first her father-in-law bought seven decimals of land. With the second, of 3,000 Taka, he bought a four decimal extension of his houselot in his own name. He bought more land with the third. With the help of the Bank, via Rina, he increased his holdings from 8 to 10 *bigha* in these early years.

Then Rina's husband fell ill with an eczema so severe he could not work and he lost his job. Nor could he work in the sun or in water, so he could not help cultivate his father's fields. By now there were two small children, so the other brothers complained about the heavy burden and ajitated until the couple were forced out of the joint family.

Now Rina was truly eligible to be a Grameen Bank member. They had no assets; Rina had nothing to show for her first three loans. (When her father-in-law dies, and he is a healthy fifty year old, the land will be divided five ways.)

"My father-in-law gave us nothing, although we asked. *My* father gave us money to build a separate house but we live *utuli* (as squatters) on my father-in-law's houselot." Rina did buy one cow and later sold it. But all her other loans, after the first three, she simply passed over to her husband to fund his business ventures. But his illness continued and he was often unable to go out.

"And so we have gone on," Rina concluded. "When he works he makes good money, but often he cannot work and we spend much on his treatment."

While we are talking, her husband is lying fast asleep on a mat in the shade of the house. He is completely encased in a quilt; only his legs stick out, smeared in green mud, a home remedy made from neem leaves. Currently, he has a job as a nightguard at a nearby rice mill. Earlier in the year he migrated to Rajshahi to work, sending money irregularly. At another time he helped Rina's brother in his rice business. But for almost four months of the year of data collection he was unable to work at all. During that time, the mainstay of the family (now four children) was not Rina's earnings, which are mainly eggs and the odd duck, but the *promise* of future GB loans.

Because of her background and despite her recent experience, Rina still has a conventional view of her housewife role, which limits her activities to chickens, ducks and goats. "My husband is the income earner and I do the household work, that is my duty," she explains piously.

But her husband's illness has forced her to employ other strategies. She leans heavily on her own family. When her daughter was seriously ill and threatened with blindness she decamped to her father's house to have the child treated. She spent a total of seven weeks visiting her home village, with her children, during the year, although, ominously for Rina's future, one of her visits was to attend the funeral of her father.

Rina, a young woman from a fairly prosperous family, survives by borrowing when her husband is too ill to work.   *Photo Credit: Nurjahan Chaklader*

Rina's main strategy, however, when her husband cannot give her the money for food and repayment, is to borrow from relatives and neighbours against the security of her Grameen Bank membership. It is a strategy which depletes her capital before she even receives it and ensures that she remains in the ranks of the very poor. By the time Rina was due for her general loan of 6,000 Taka in September, she had already borrowed 5,500 from various relatives (at no interest) to cover the food needs of the family and her GB repayments. After she repaid these debts, she used the few hundred Taka remaining to cover her weekly Grameen repayments while she was away at her father's funeral. Rina has been creeping more and more into debt over the years, but this was the first time her entire loan had been eaten up before she received it.

Rina is a good example of how a woman without food security must literally eat into future income, which prevents her from building any assets. She understands what is happening, but she cannot see what to do about it.

> The GB loan is capital. If it is used for production then more capital will come, but if not it is useless. But what can I do? When my husband is well he can buy paddy, I husk it and he sells. But he is always sick. My brother gave me paddy, but my husband wasn't working and we ate it. If I had big capital I would get land; that is the best use. But I use all my loans for the children's food and my husband's illness.

"If you use all your loan to repay borrowings for food, and then on top of that you have to pay back the Bank plus 20% interest, how do you benefit? What is the *use* of being a GB member?" I ask her, pushing as hard as I can. A sort of panic comes over her face as it occurs to her that I might have the power to cancel her membership.

"God knows what would happen to us if there was no GB loan coming every year! When we are hungry or my husband needs medicine I can borrow *because* I am a GB member."

The indicator of how much she values her membership of GB is, of course, how faithfully she repays her loans each week. Even in the hardest times, Rina always paid something, and usually she scraped together the full amount.

Four months after her general loan, she got a seasonal loan of 5,000 Taka. This time, because her husband had landed a job as a night watchman and because of gifts of rice from her mother, she was only a few hundred Taka in debt. She repaid this debt; she bought herself a *sari*; she bought a bicycle for her husband to start a business in a nearby bazaar. Then she gave 3,000 to her brother, in exchange for 100 Taka a week for the next year. If this is faithfully paid, it is not a bad bargain for Rina. It covers her principal repayment on the whole 5,000. If her husband remains well enough to use the bicycle profitably she may be able to get through this loan cycle without borrowing too heavily against the next.

It means, of course, that she is dependent on both men to cover her repayments, which on both loans amount to 220 Taka a week. If her husband is ill or her brother fails to deliver the weekly 100 Taka she will go back to borrowing. She has no plans to generate income through her own work. This dependence has not been altered by nine years of membership in GB, nor by her descent into the ranks of the very poor. She is not even very adept at the expenditure saving activities that are second nature to women born poor. In March, when her husband earned nothing at all, Rina was spending around 500 Taka a week on repayment and housekeeping, literally eating her irrigation loan, borrowing, and replying to our queries: "I hope he will get better soon."

It is easy to see the original error of the Bank staff in allowing Rina (and the daughter of the other brother — they joined the same group and could cover for each other) to enter the Bank, when she was living in the joint household of a landed farmer. The household was not poor. Rina did not have any role or voice in the use of her loans. As a young *bo* in her father-in-law's house she had no power. Even her husband had no control over his own income. All income in a joint household goes traditionally into a common pot and so the situation was ripe for exploitation by her father-in-law.

Rina's attitude that it is not her job to earn the income is also, in my small experience of Grameen Bank replication projects in Malaysia and South-East Asia, more common amongst women from less poor families. Never having faced real want or the hunger of their children, such women have not been forced to question their dependence on a male breadwinner. Grameen Bank, and its replications, are targeted at the poorest women precisely because the desperation of such women make them both more adventurous and more resourceful than women who lead easy and protected lives.

For Rina the appropriation of her loans by her father-in-law went on for three years without being picked up by the Bank staff or challenged by her center, presumably because her father-in-law made sure that the loan was regularly repaid. The daughter of the other brother continued to live in her father's house and handed over all her loans to him for eight years. When, three children later, her father began selling the land her loans had helped to acquire and she became concerned about her own future, she tried to take back control of her loans. Her father then forced her out into a separate household, without any assets to show for her eight years of borrowing.

The failure of the Bank and center to enforce the rule that the loanee must use the loan herself did not create the culture of dependence that traps Rina. But it certainly reinforced it. She had no opportunity to learn to use her skills to generate income or break out of her attitudes of helplessness. So when the only income earner, her husband, fell ill, she was particularly vulnerable.

It is not so easy to see what either Rina or the Bank could have done about this calamity once it arrived. Illness which puts the only adult male out of action is a major disaster for any village family. It means a steep drop in income because he cannot earn and heavy expenditure on treatment. For Grameen women engaged in some activity which requires trading at the *haat* rather than in the village, like paddy husking or mustard oil making, it is important to have the "hands and feet" of an active adult male. And most Grameen women, in fact, use their loans as capital for longer term investments like land or livestock, and still depend on the cash earnings of their husbands to cover most of the weekly repayments (Gibbons forthcoming).

Each time Rina has taken a loan she has given "cow/paddy husking" as the loan use. So do eight other members in her center, although in the year of data collection, only two actually husked paddy for sale, for brief periods. Rina only once bought a cow with her loans. The Bank worker, the center chief and the group chairperson are supposed to check the utilisation of the loan, and ensure that the woman is using most of it herself. In practice, however, this is not done. The older the center the less rigorous the loan utilisation check, since members have already proved their ability to use the loan profitably by repaying over a period of years. But the case of Rina and the daughter of the other brother indicates that this loan utilisation check was never done effectively.

Once Rina's husband fell ill, the chances of her emerging out of the poverty group shrank drastically. As we have seen in the last chapter, the opportunities for an assetless woman *on her own* to earn an income above the poverty line are extremely limited in the world of the village. She could have used her GB loans, as have other Grameen members, to gradually increase her assets and with them her capacity to earn a good income. But most of the investment opportunities open to her are fairly long-term. In the meantime, she needs cash to feed her four young children and make her repayments to the Bank. It is difficult for her to generate that cash without the help of her husband.

Because of her husband's illness, Rina has never been able to hold on to her capital. Without food security no family can begin to build up its assets. So long as her husband is too ill to work for several months of the year, she will be forced to borrow for food and repayment and so she will eat up much of her capital before it arrives. Her membership in Grameen Bank can keep her from going under altogether; it cannot pull her out of the poverty group.

The Drain of Illness

If we look at the Grameen Bank members in these two villages whose families still live below the poverty line despite almost a decade of borrowing, we find that most of them have suffered a serious illness in the family in the past three years. In many cases this has put the male earner out of action for long periods, sometimes permanently. It has almost always forced them to liquidate assets in order to pay for medical treatment and/or keep the family afloat when the husband's cash earnings stopped. The disaster of illness struck ten out of the

17 GB families who are still in the poverty group, or 59%. Amongst the GB families who are no longer poor, there are only four, or 17%, who have been hit by serious illness.

One of these women, Gunjara, a mustard oil maker in Beparipara whose husband will probably not recover from a bout of typhoid, I expect to drop back into the poverty group. Her situation highlights the vulnerability of women who finance and depend on a trading business and I will discuss it in Chapter 7. The other three Grameen families who suffered a serious illness but recovered sufficiently to have an income above the poverty line, used their group fund and general loans, as well as help from relatives, to overcome the crisis. Then through subsequent loans they were able to recover their income position, despite a loss of assets.

Why were the Grameen families still in the poverty group not able to do the same? In most of these cases the illness is a chronic, long-term drain on the family's finances and earning capacity, like the eczema of Rina's husband. Or it has resulted in the death or disablement of the male earner. If we take just three of the poorest GB families in our sample: in the poorest the husband is mentally ill and both appropriates and squanders the loan capital; another is semi-paralysed and earns an irregular income fishing. The husband of another is often down with a lung problem, which is perhaps the tuberculosis which killed his father. We have already met Kia, who was forced to return her leasehold land and use all her savings to treat her husband's TB and her own badly burned leg. Another GB family sold all their land to treat a husband who had TB. He died anyway, leaving his widow with two young children and no assets except the houselot.[1]

In Chapter Four we looked at the issue of women borrowers who "pipelined" their loans to male relatives, without retaining any or much control over its use or the proceeds. This does not in itself keep families poor. But there are a disproportionate number of such borrowers amongst the still poor families. A woman who is not an active earner is not contributing a second income to help push her family over the poverty line. And since she is still entirely dependent on her husband or sons, she is particularly vulnerable if he falls ill or dies. There were seven GB loanees in the still poor category, 41%, who were, like Rina, pipelining their loans to male relatives.

When a GB woman's husband falls sick and stops earning and she has few resources of her own, it is easy for her to borrow to cover her food needs and her repayment. Her relatives know that she can repay out of her next Grameen loan. Over time, this borrowing can eat up a substantial chunk of her capital. Moreover, illness is only one of the crises which prompt GB loanees to resort to informal borrowing against future loans. It is one of the benefits of GB membership that a loanee can resort to informal borrowing in a crisis. However, when it becomes entrenched, it destroys a woman's capital before she even gets it and keeps her poor. Amongst the Grameen Bank families who are still poor, there were seven, or 41%, who had borrowed more than half the amount of their general loans before they received them. After payment of Group Tax, and repayment of these informal borrowings, there was not enough capital left for investment and the remainder tended to be spent on consumption, repayment and moneylending.

No Safety Net

It is possible to argue that Rina is actually worse off as a Grameen Bank member, since she cannot use the loan productively, but carries the burden of repayment with interest. As we have seen, Rina herself strongly disagrees. When her husband was in Rashjahi and no money had arrived, she lived on flour and sweet potatoes in order to make at least part payment to GB, in order to keep that vital (to her) credit line open. And one only has to look at the situation of Halimah, in the control group, who also has a sick husband, to appreciate the difference that Rina's GB membership makes.

Halimah's husband has syphilis. Her explanation for this illness contains a certain justice. When she was pregnant with their only child, she suffered badly from water retention and could not have intercourse for several months. Her husband told her that if she "puffed up again" he would divorce her, so after the birth she had a ligation. She thinks his disease is a punishment from God for his lack of understanding. But in her opinion, God has gone a bit overboard; the punishment has gone on too long.

Liton is too weak to work consistently. (Halimah tells me that he is too lazy. There is no happiness in this family.) He is also mentally unstable; he gambles with borrowed money and cannot hold a job for long.

Liton inherited a large 16 decimal houselot on which he used to grow bananas and a variety of vegetables. This he has mortgaged against borrowings and lost bit by bit over the five years of his illness. A year before we began our research he borrowed 3,000 Taka against the last 2 decimals on which their tiny straw house stands; a sum he has little chance of repaying. Meanwhile he operates a sharecrop of bananas on the 16 decimals which he previously owned. By the end of the year he had lost that last two decimals — and with it his remaining foothold in the village. He quarrelled with his "patron," from whom he had borrowed and to whom he lost his land, because he could not get a VGD ration card.[2] The "master" had nothing more to extract and so no reason to keep him on as a client. He told Liton: "I am already doing you a favour by letting you live on *my* land." By the end of the year the house was deserted. The couple with their son had moved to Halimah's natal village to live with her brother.

During the year, Halimah did all she could to earn income. She share-fattened a goat and raised share chickens. She did a lot of the work on the bananas. She tried, but mostly failed, to get work in *borobari* as a servant. But she earned very little. In her home village Halimah could more easily get work as a maidservant at one of the big houses, where she used to work before she was married, although this was still limited to harvest seasons. In the last resort her brother would feed her. Meanwhile her son, now ten years old, did some daily labour with his uncles, and put his earnings into her hand. After visiting them in her brother's house, however, I had my doubts about how long Liton, who refused to work and occasionally slipped back to Bonopur to gamble, would be tolerated. It seemed likely that this family unit would disintegrate under the pressure of its extreme poverty.

The 1992 net income of Rina's household came to 9,747 Taka. Halimah's household earned even less at 7,454 Taka. Rina was short of food for most of May, while her husband was working in Rajshahi. When he returned sick in June and could not work, she took a loan from her group fund to tide them over. Halimah's family was short of food all year, never eating more than cold leftovers in the morning and one cooked meal at night. In March and April they were literally starving, eating only one meal of flour per day. Seven times during the year, before they moved permanently, Halimah took her son to her brother's house "visiting" so that they could eat.

Both women leaned on their brothers because they could not depend on their husbands. But Rina had something to offer — part of her loan — and she retained her home and some autonomy. Halimah had nothing to offer. She lost her home and was forced to throw herself fully on her brother's charity. How long he would bear the burden is a matter of doubt. It seemed likely that Halimah's family, like many forced down into the ranks of the homeless poor, would break into its separate pieces.

Rina's eldest three children are all in school. Halimah's ten year old is already out in the fields doing daily labour.

Poor women with chronically sick or disabled husbands, and no other resources, are more or less doomed to a rapid descent into the ranks of the desperately poor and homeless. GB women in this position have the safety net of their loans. But unless they have been able to build up their assets and their skills by playing an active economic role themselves, all their membership can do is to prevent pauperisation.

Notes

1. The threat of illness to the progress of Grameen Bank families may be lessened by an experiment now underway in the Tangail and Dhaka districts. The Grameen Trust has begun a pilot health scheme in six branches to see if they can directly tackle the health problems of GB members by providing a medical service from the branch office. Each Health Center is staffed by an MBBS-trained doctor, a trained paramedic and a laboratory technician. The Health Center is supplied by the Trust with a range of basic

drugs. Three sub-centers located in the Branch area are run by paramedics, all women, who live in the village, give basic health care, primary health education and refer patients when necessary to the Health Center, which is in or near the Branch Office. Attached to the paramedic is a female health assistant, usually a School Certificate holder from the locality, who makes house to house calls to discuss the health problems of the borrower's families.

Members join this scheme by paying a three Taka annual fee for a medical card which includes all members of the family. They pay a two Taka prescription charge for each visit to the doctor and the market cost of whatever drugs are supplied.

2. The Vulnerable Group Development scheme is a government program which gives rations of wheat to disadvantaged groups, mainly widows, in return for small savings. The scheme uses donor food aid, and is distributed through the Union Council representatives.

7

Women on Their Own

It is generally accepted that the most vulnerable group of women in rural Bangladesh are those without any adult male, sick or healthy, in their households. Women of any income group who are widowed, divorced or abandoned are likely to suffer a drop in status and economic well-being. Women who find themselves alone in the poverty group, where there is no surplus to be shared with a widowed mother or divorced sister, and few ways to sell their labour, are in a peculiarly precarious position.

As Shamim Hamid rightly remarks in her essay "Female Headed Households:"

> Female headed households in rural Bangladesh are being formed not through women's emancipation or through any desire or economic capability on their part. They are being forced to manage the households through a combination of economic, demographic and social factors which hold no advantage to them in any form. They are the end products of a pauperisation process and represent the poverty situation in its most acute form.(Rahman 1991:169)

Given the vulnerability of this kind of household it is remarkable that of the six female-headed households in our Grameen Bank sample, four had come right out of the poverty group. An examination of how they did it has some lessons for the future of the Grameen Bank. As the two million members of the Grameen Bank get older, there will be increasing numbers of widows amongst them. Whether they can sustain the progress they have made when they are widowed is an important question for the future.

There are 11 Female Headed Households (FHH) in our sample, six in the Grameen Bank group and five in the control group. The differences between these two groups is striking. All of the five FHH in the control group — those without access to credit — were very poor. Their average net per capita income was 3,314 Taka per annum. All five are widows. Two are beggars; two work as domestic servants. The elder of these sweeps and scrubs at a *borobari* for one and sometimes two meals a day — a payment the landlord's wife regards as kind-hearted charity. The other works two houses, for a meal at each and 20 Taka a month. These four elderly women live precariously; they are often hungry and desperate; they have little family support and their lives have no dignity. Two of these widows have adult sons living in the same *bari*, but have been repudiated by them. The fifth FHH in the control group is Roshonara — a recently widowed woman in her twenties with two young sons. Although she is still poor, she has a small amount of land inherited from her husband, she has a patron in the Union member who has got her a VGD ration card and at whose house she works in the harvest season and she receives considerable support from her mother and brother.

The GB widows and divorcees are economically much more secure than those in our control, although they still *feel* vulnerable and physically insecure. But the difference between their fruitful struggles to survive and the hobbling descent towards death of a beggar like Bachiron is clear for everyone in the village to see.

We met Bachiron in Chapter Two, when Shireen, her daughter-in-law, closed her door down on her. Bachiron lives in a hut next door to Shireen and Forman. It is like a very small cow shed. One wall is missing, and one of my first memories of her is the morning she woke to find that a dog had stolen the only food she had — half a pot of cooked rice. She is in her seventies and bent almost double with arthritis and hobbles about on swollen bare feet with the help of a stick. But she walks to her natal village about one kilometer away, where she still has distant relatives, begging from house to house for food, every day that she has the strength. When she cannot go out, she starves — unless one of her daughters visits with some rice. (Her two daughters were married without dowries and both are now divorced with small children. One works as a live-in servant in Ghatail and brings some food to her mother each month. Another is doing domestic labour for Bachiron's nephew, paid in meals. Sometimes she brings her evening meal and shares it with her mother.) Her son, Forman, gives her no help at all.

Bachiron was brought up in a landed family and married to the son of a wealthy farmer. In the village where she now goes begging, her father was a respected figure. "We had bullocks and cows. We never had to buy rice; there was always plenty. At harvest time we would feed 20 or 30 daily labourers!" she recalls dreamily. "It's because I was happy then, that life now is so hard."

Her husband had many brothers, so he inherited only one acre and that was sold in the face of various disasters. The last 20 decimals was given to Forman when he married, because they then lived in a joint household. When Forman repudiated his first wife and married Shireen, his mother quarreled with the newcomer. When her husband died, she was finally forced to move out into her tiny shack. But economics is the groundrock of the quarrel between these two women. Shireen says bitterly: "They only gave us 20 decimals and nine we had to sell. How can we feed her? We don't have enough for ourselves."

The days that Bachiron was too weak to go begging increased progressively during the year. Her grey hair grew wilder and her only *sari* more ragged as her back bent her closer to the ground. In the spring I was sitting talking to one of her neighbours when she fell to the ground in a kind of fit, shaking and moaning. Although every family has a mat, someone brought an old sack for her to lie on and then, after a long interval, a pillow. When she came to, our research assistant was massaging her hand, and Bachiron whispered: "Soon I will die. But I want to die in peace, saying God's name, not in this suffering."

All the women in the village are uneasily aware of Bachiron's painful passage. She is a kind of bent and stumbling cautionary tale of how they might end up themselves. In the same *para* is a GB member, Dolali, whose grocer husband died suddenly during the year. She is determined to delay as long as possible the division of her husband's land. When she bought a two decimal extension of the houselot "for her sons" she registered it in her own name. "If I divide the land and give it to my sons it will never come back into my hand. Look at Forman's mother," she said.

Driven from Her House

The poorest and most insecure GB member in Ratnogram at the beginning of data collection was Parul, a 50 year old widow with no sons and four daughters. She was often irregular with her repayments and the whole Center regarded her as a "problem." But she was struggling successfully to secure her position and by the end of the year she had pulled herself out of the poverty group.

Parul had never been able to use her Grameen Bank capital productively in her previous eight years of borrowing. Some she used to pay dowry. Some was bullied or cajoled out of her by male relatives. She had borrowed a total of 21,600 Taka during her decade of membership; her assets at the beginning of the year of data collection amounted to 1,670 Taka. She survived by doing work considered degrading by village women — she pushed the *ghani* of one of her neighbours and she worked as a maidservant for several *borobari*, in exchange for food. All her daughters were married, with dowries that increased in size with the length of their mother's GB membership. The last, and best-dowried, was "returned" very pregnant at the beginning of the year, adding another mouth to be fed out of Parul's very slender annual net earnings of 9,979 Taka a year. Her position seemed pretty hopeless.

Basic economic survival was fundamental to Parul as to all the very poor. But she, along with other women who lived alone with only daughters or small children, had an equally pressing concern, that of physical security and social acceptance. When I finally heard all of Parul's story, I was able to understand more clearly how the village world pressed on her to the extent that her very presence in it was an achievement.

Parul was widowed 20 years ago, when she was 30 years old and her youngest daughter was still a baby. Her husband left her 20 decimals of land in two plots and a 7 decimal houselot with a large house on it. Since there were no sons, her husband's elder brothers were determined to get the property out of the hands of this outsider and back into the male line of the family.

They moved forcibly into the house, building a partition at one end into which Parul and her daughters were pushed. "I called all my neighbours to help, but no-one would help me."

Later, they tried to marry her off to a man in the same *para* who was looking for a second wife.[1] Parul went on strike. She refused to eat or bathe and sat outside the house wailing. This time her neighbours told her: "If you stay here they will force you to marry. Go back to your father's village."

This was exactly what Parul wanted to avoid, knowing that whatever her husband had left her she would lose if she left the village. However, she had no choice. She left her three eldest daughters and all her livestock in their care as a signal that she would be back and she went to her father and uncles and asked them to call a *shalish* to assert her rights to the house and land in Ratnogram. Over the next two years Parul confronted five *shalish* and all ruled in her favour. While they did not order her brother-in-law to vacate the house, they told him that she had a right in the village and he should "take her back." (Such is the traditional construction of dependence.)

As frequently happens when *shalish* judgments go against the more powerful, the rulings were ignored. Finally, Parul, desperate at her exile from her daughters, returned secretly.

> I crept into the house like a thief while they were away at the *haat* and I hid behind the partition. All night I stayed there and only in the morning did they discover me. Then my elder sister-in-law pulled me out of the house by my hair and beat me. My brother-in-law grabbed the *bota* (a curved knife) in a rage and came to hit me with it, telling me to get out of his *bari*. My daughters were screaming and I was crying for help, but no-one came. I fled to the Thana police.

The police told her to go to the *matbar*, and if they did nothing then the police would come to the village. So she walked back to Ratnogram, on her own.

> I went from door to door of all the *matbar* crying for help. They called a *shalish* and this time the whole village was strong against my brothers-in-law. [This was probably because she had shamed the village by going to an outside authority and nobody wanted the intervention of the police.] They were forced to take me back. But they never accepted me and were always thinking about how to get me out.

While Parul was living with her father, her brother-in-law had registered one of the lots of paddy land belonging to her husband in his own name. This was easy to do since it had been a gift from father to son and not registered. Meanwhile, he cultivated both lots and Parul worked on his *ghani* in return for food for her children.

All these dramas took place before Parul became a member of GB. This stabilised her position in the village. "They liked me better because I was not always asking for money. When I get my loan, my brother-in-law asks *me* for money."

That, of course, is the problem. Parul has won acceptance of her place in the village only at the price of handing most of her capital to her brother-in-law. While she has gained some security, in economic terms she comes off second best. About six years ago, for instance, the brother-in-law sold the house which had been the subject of so many *shalish* and built himself another. He helped Parul build the tiny house in which she now lives, although she paid for the half-tin roof herself from one of her loans. Parul buys small livestock — mainly sheep and chickens with her loans. She has also paid dowry from 1,000 to 3,000 Taka each for the marriages of her four daughters. But much of her capital has gone to her brother-in-law, through a combination of cajolery and threats. He repays in drips and drabs, when she begs him for it, enough for repayment, but not for investment. In the same way he has sharecropped the 10 decimals which remain in her ownership, but never gives her full share.

He is the head of the extended family and traditionally, Parul must obey him. For instance, when I asked her (in my naive period) why she didn't trade mustard oil from *para* to *para,* she replied: "If I do that the family prestige will drop. It is not socially acceptable and my brother-in-law will never allow it."

But she now feels stronger in relation to him than she did before.

> If he asks for my loan and I refuse, he gets very angry. But he won't beat me nowadays. Before I was weak; I was *nothing.* Now I am stronger. If he beat me now all the Center members would come and support me. If I was a GB member when my husband died, my brother-in-law would never dare to drive me from my house.

In the last few years Parul has gradually asserted her independence from her brother-in-law. Recently, she leased her land (the plot her brother-in-law had been cultivating) out to someone in the next village. I suspect she did this to raise the dowry for her youngest daughter, but it is also a way to protect it from any attempt to change the ownership registration. She has also tried to protect herself from her brother-in-law's demands by giving part of her loans to one of her sons-in-law. He repays in full, plus 30%, at the times she cannot get work. She has stopped work altogether on her brother-in-law's *ghani;* when she works for Gunjara she is regularly paid.

134

Parul, the struggling widow with three daughters. Here she looks very fiesty, in a *sari* borrowed from Norjahan, talking to Professor Yunus on his visit to the village.
Photo Credit: Helen Todd

When Parul got her general loan in 1992, she did something she had never done before — she invested all of it in a productive asset. She bought a second-hand rickshaw, planning to hit three birds with this one stone. She hoped to lure the son-in-law who had "sent back" her youngest daughter to come and build himself a house on her houselot, simultaneously getting the husband back for her daughter and physical security for herself. The rental he agreed to pay to her would cover her repayment, while he would take the responsibility of feeding his wife and baby.

In this plan all the threads of Parul's life come together — the welfare of her daughters, her own physical security and economic survival. As it happened, this son-in-law pulled out at the last minute, accepting a well-paid labour contract in another village, the proceeds of which he promised to use to build his house on Parul's houselot. He further signaled his renewed commitment to wife and baby son by beginning regular payments for their upkeep. In the meantime, another son-in-law agreed to rent the rickshaw and when we left he was paying Parul 100 Taka regularly every week, enough to cover her repayment of 80 Taka a week and buy four days supply of rice.

The qualitative difference this arrangement made in her life can only be understood in relation to her desperate struggle during the rest of the year to feed herself and her daughter and keep up her repayments to the Bank. Like the other women we have discussed, who have to attempt to live by selling their labour, Parul's earnings were meagre and usually paid in kind. For a long lean period between July and November, when the *irri* paddy drying was completed and all the *ghani* were silent, she had no work at all. She sold eggs, bananas and beans, two ducks and ten chickens. She took a group fund loan and her elder daughters helped her with gifts of rice and salt. But they ate little and she was often short on her repayment.

Once she began getting the rental from one son-in-law and remittances from the other, Parul's expenditure on food promptly doubled. She had no problem with repayment. She was still dependent for this income on the muscular legs of the male who rented the rickshaw — but she was far more in control and respected in her relationship with her sons-in-law and less likely to be cheated, than she had been in relation to her elder brother-in-law. The rickshaw rental, and the remittances from her youngest daughter's husband, together with her earnings from *ghani* work, domestic labour and occasional sales of goats and poultry, pushed her per capita income just above the poverty line.

Making It as a Widow

There is a world of difference between the serene security of someone like Saleha, the *lokkhi* wife in Kahpara, and the anxiety which haunts the lives of even the most successful widows and divorcees in our sample. Parul shared her tiny house with her goats at night, because as a woman on her own she could not risk tethering them in her *bari*. Chaina, now in her late forties, heads one of the most successful families in our sample. But she still lives in an environment so hostile that it was only alone in our room in the area office, two miles from the listening ears of the village, that she was willing to tell me about her struggles.

By all objective measures, Chaina has made it. Her large *bari*, fringed with a flourishing brinjal garden, houses two cows and a cacophony of hens and ducks. She has turned her only son, now 20, into a farmer cultivating four *bigha* of paddy, wheat and potatoes. Except for a brief period at *Kartik*, her paddy baskets were always full. During the year she bought a new field and an extension to her houselot. But her life as a widow has been a continuous battle.

Chaina's husband died when she was 28, leaving her with two toddlers, two plots of paddy land and a five decimal houselot. After his death, one of his uncles fraudulently registered one plot in his own name. The other uncle cultivated the second plot himself by force, taking all the harvest. The uncles combined to argue that her title to the houselot was not legal (her husband had bought the land from his uncles) and to drive her off it. How could a young widow combat forces like these?

Firstly, unlike Parul, she had a son, so her uncles-in-law had no legal claim to her husband's land. Second, her brother, who was in the military and had some clout , helped her take the case of the fraudulent registration to court. Some three years and 7,000 Taka later she won the case and the land was legally registered in her name. She immediately leased it out to a powerful family who were *dhormo uncle* (religious uncle) to her son in order to protect it. "I will put my plough into this land!" her uncle-in-law threatened when he lost the case.

Third, she had a patron — a minor landlord, a distant relation, who helped her to register both the houselot and the second plot of paddy land in her own name. Her husband's only brother, who lives next door, was also supportive (he had his own quarrel with the uncles) and once the land was registered he helped her to cultivate it. Only then did the uncle stop cutting by force all the crops which grew on her land.

Since becoming a GB member Chaina has bought and sold a number of cows, both for milk and fattening. But her main focus, especially since her son became old enough to farm, has been to gradually build up the amount of land cultivated. The plot she leased out to protect it has now come back to her son to sharecrop. She has extended her alliance with her landlord patron, from whom she has obtained three *bigha* to sharecrop. From her brother-in-law she leased in 15 decimals and bought another five. In the year of data collection she bought another 10 decimals of paddy land and a two decimal extension of her houselot, raising the cash from her general loan and from leasing out most of her remaining land. This she will redeem with the GB loans which she will receive in 1993. She now owns half an acre. When she redeems the leasehold she will be operating, with her son, one and a half acres.

Chaina is the only woman in our sample who earns a regular daily cash salary like a man. She works for CARE, cutting earth in the fields and spreading it on the rutted rural roads that lead into the village. Every 10 days she walks to Ghatail and gets her pay of 280 Taka which she uses for repayment and food expenses. The Grameen loans and her surplus harvest income she uses as capital. It is this combination which has enabled her to build up her assets and escape poverty.

For Chaina, CARE provides what a husband provides for the married Grameen women — a regular cash income, the lack of which forces other widows to use up much of their Grameen capital in crisis consumption, or to invest it via a male relative getting only half the income. (Parul gets rental from her rickshaw, not the full value she would gain if she pushed it herself.)

Although it is 18 years since Chaina was widowed, her son is now adult and she looks prosperous enough, she is still not secure. No less than four years ago she had to fight off another attempt to take her land, this attempt closely connected with the social disapproval of her CARE work.

An absentee landlord told her to drop the shameless work for CARE and come and work in his house in Ghatail as a servant. Apart from the fact that she would have to live away from the village and get paid only in meals, Chaina did not like the look in his eye.

"He is a bad character. Greedy. He tries for whatever is going. The whole village knows it."

Although he badgered her, she refused. He was furious. He decided to take a seven decimal piece of her land which adjoined his own. He roped in the two uncles and a gang of local youths attached to the *dol* opposed to Chaina's patron, and turned up in force in her *para*, calling her to confront this crowd in the uncle's house. Her brother-in-law, who is semi-paralysed, had the title in his trunk. He passed it to her in panic saying he couldn't defend it against such a gang. Chaina put the land title under her quilt and lay down on it. The youths raided her brother-in-law's house, as he expected, but failed to find the title. None of them dared to actually break in to Chainah's house (*purdah* has its advantages) so they grabbed her son instead, then 16, and forced him to sign a blank transfer form. Then they left, yelling threats against herself and her son, if she refused also to sign.

Since then she has kept her land titles locked in her patron's safe. The recent purchases, and the disputed field, she has registered in her son's name.

That is safer than in my name. Since then I have managed [the hostility of] the village by marrying my son to a girl of that landlord's *gusti*. Although he tried to disrupt the marriage, he did not succeed, and now he has to be very polite to me. Although my son is very young to be married, it was the only way to strengthen our position.

For Chaina, alliances and patrons and the support of her brother and brother-in-law have been crucial, and she has used all her skills to manipulate them for her protection. She also has an obedient son, a cash income from CARE, and credit, both to keep these relationships well oiled and to finance a steady build-up of assets. These are the factors that Chaina has managed in order to survive and prosper in a threatening environment. The Grameen capital has been a vital resource, but it has been handled with remarkable skill and courage within a network of relationships.

A Frightened Grocer

Credit alone, without this enabling environment, or the kind of management skills than Chaina demonstrates, does not seem able to shift a female-headed household out of the poverty group. Sofiah's husband died of TB in 1989, after all of their assets had been sold in an attempt to cure him. At first she tried to make an income by using her GB loan to build a small grocery shop onto her house. Her front door, as is always the case, faced into the *bari*. The back wall, which faced a lane, was without windows, to protect their privacy. She dealt with the problem of *purdah* by installing her small son in a lean-to shop facing the lane and giving him instructions through an opening she cut in the back wall. Twice, however, the shop was broken into during the night and the stock stolen. She then demolished the lean-to, rethatched the back wall, and moved her goods inside the house, where she could trade with other village women. One night she woke to find a man inside her house, helping himself to the *biri*. She recognised him, but nothing came of her complaints to the *matbar*. From that experience she decided it was safer to stop being a grocer.

In the year of data collection, Sofiah, the ex-grocer, had no less than nine different sources of income at various times of the year. She sold bamboo, eggs and bananas from her *bari,* she share-fattened a goat and several chickens, she lent some of her capital at interest, she worked for brief periods in a *borobari* husking paddy, she and her daughter gleaned the fields for a full two months after the harvest, and she had a half share in a VGD ration card.[2] She leaned on her natal family. When she ran out of money for food she visited her brother. She borrowed from her sister and other relatives for repayment. Her daughter spent part of the year "helping out" at an uncle's house in return for food. All these varied activities brought in only small amounts of Taka, although they made up 69% of the household's net income. The rest was earned by her 15 year old son from collecting broken glass and metal in Bonopur and the neighbouring villages in exchange for sweets. He was sickly, however, and in the wet season he earned almost nothing.

At the end of the year, I met Sofiah walking in one of the lanes with a huge bundle of sticks in her arms. She was laughing and excited. The Union election and the season of winter cakes had come neatly together, and a relative had arranged for her son to set up a cart in town, to sell tea and *pitta*. Sofiah put up the capital and made the *pitta* and they had two good months. Then it folded and her son went back to broken glass collecting.

Sofiah was well down in the poverty group, earning only 3,494 net per capita per annum, and her position was precarious. Her GB loans helped to capitalise her son's broken glass and *pitta* businesses, but these were not generating enough income to cover her repayments. She was often irregular and only settled her general loan by borrowing heavily from her brother. After she had repaid him, there was not enough left for investment. She had been in constant crisis since her husband's expensive illness, and then his death. As a result, much of her capital was consumed before she received it by her borrowings to feed her two children.

What emerges from these three very different experiences of Parul, Chaina and Sofiah, is that all of them have used their credit to mobilise the "hands and feet" of a son or son-in-law. The reason widows find it so difficult to survive is that they cannot trade in the larger markets or work in the fields. But once Parul had a rickshaw, she could find a relative to rent it — and Chaina with her land holdings and sharecropping fields can easily command the labour and loyalty of her son. You could say that no women could survive "alone," without a male, in rural Bangladesh. But what the successful survivors amongst the Grameen Bank widows have worked out with male relatives, is not a relationship of dependence. It is a trade. The reason Sofiah is going under is that she has consumed most of her capital and has nothing left to trade.

Widows in the Future

The life history of women in Bangladesh as a whole is different from that of men, and shows marked ups and downs. The BIDS Poverty Survey (Rahman 1991:989-91) shows that women usually marry in their late teens (average age at marriage is 17.6 years) to a man at least ten years older, and their first two decades of married life are likely to be a struggle. They will soon separate from the joint family and will bring up a number of children, dependent on the earnings of a husband who has not yet inherited land or accumulated any assets. Her lot will improve only in her forties, when her 50+ year old husband has probably inherited or accumulated some assets and has some surplus. The BIDS Survey found that the majority of women in their twenties and thirties belonged to poor, food deficit households. In their forties a higher proportion belong to stable or surplus households, although the proportion, at just over 30% of the total female population, is still low.

As we have seen in Chapters 2 and 3, the access of the Grameen women to credit and the use that most of them have made of their loans has lifted their average incomes as well as their influence in the family far above the women in the control group. This access has enhanced a natural life cycle advantage for women moving into their forties.

But, unfortunately, this life cycle advantage for women does not continue for long. While the proportion of men who achieve a stable or food surplus position peaks in their fifties and continues with little change until they die, women begin a slide downwards in their fifties which continues until their death. Women in their fifties begin to be widowed in increasing numbers. By the time Bangladeshi women reach their 60th year, half will be widows. For many this will be the beginning of an abrupt descent into poverty and powerlessness.

If access to credit can enhance the natural life cycle advantage of women in their forties, will it be able to mitigate or even prevent the downturn which awaits them in their next two decades? While it is impossible to provide an accurate answer to this question, it is important to ask it, and to look at the conditions under which GB women could sustain their income gains and protect their assets once they are widowed.

The average age of the GB women in our sample in February, 1992, was 39 years. Already 17.5% of them were widows, higher than the national average of 12% for that age group.   Another 7.5% were divorcees. In another decade, according to the statistics of widowhood in Bangladesh as a whole, 35% of these women are likely to be widowed. Since the divorcees are unlikely to remarry, this means that a substantial group of 17 women in our sample of 40, are likely to be widows or divorcees by 2002.

All the stories in this chapter have shown that this group is vulnerable, even those who have made a success of their lives. We have seen from the life histories of both Parul and Chaina, that young widows, with or without sons, can face an attempt by their male in-laws to repossess the land and even the houselot left by their husbands. Despite their rights under Islamic law, at village level they are regarded as outsiders sitting on the patrimony of the *gusti*, and can be forced out of the village to return empty-handed to the charity of their father or brothers.

Older widows with adult sons are not likely to face this kind of threat. However, once their sons marry and form separate households, and in a climate of scarcity, their daughters-in-law can lobby to limit or stop any support given to them by their sons. This was the fate of the beggar, Bachiron.

At the minimum, most GB members are likely to escape both dispossession by their in-laws and abandonment by their sons. GB members who have taken housing loans have a security which is beyond most village women, including those from wealthy households. The house in which they live is legally registered in their own names, and *so is the land on which it stands.* Even if they are widowed it would be very hard to dislodge such women from their home. Any male relative who tried would find himself up against the official weight of the Grameen Bank, which has a mortgage on the house until the loan is paid off. Amongst the 40 GB women in our sample 17 had taken housing loans and owned at least part of their own houselot as a result. More are expected to do so as their economic status improves.

GB women are also unlikely to be abandoned by their sons, since they make an important contribution to their family. Some widows in our sample, like Parveen, pass most of their loans over to their sons to invest. Some use at least part of their capital to generate an income so that they are less of a burden to support. In these two ways GB women have a safety net against the time that they become widows, although it may not save them from a decline in their current levels of living and they may, like Parveen, have little control over their lives.

Those GB women who have invested in productive assets, and kept these assets under their control, are the ones who will be able to sustain the improvements which GB membership has made in their lives. Chaina's case shows this clearly. A woman like Habibah, the de facto center chief of the Bonopur center, who has strategically kept ownership of at least a third of each major field in her own name, so that "nothing can be decided without my consent," will have no trouble with widowhood, whatever her relationship with her son's future wife. Others who have put their loans into acquiring leasehold, even though they have no legal paper, usually control the use of that land and the produce comes into their hands for processing. The only change that is likely when such women are widowed and their sons form separate households, is that they will sharecrop this land out to their sons. Although they will get only half the product, they will also be feeding only themselves.

This was explicitly planned by Banu, the woman whose two daughters work in factories in Chittagong, who told us: "Even if my sons' *bo* turn out to be no good I can sharecrop out my land for income and for food."

Other productive assets bought with GB loans — like rickshaws — will bring at least a rental income to a GB widow, even if there is no-one in her household who can operate it. Such assets are also protected by being registered in her name under the rules of the Bank, which will take action officially in the event of theft.

There are, however, some GB members who have accumulated few assets and who are still largely dependent on the income made by the daily labour of their husbands. There are others who have invested their loans in activities in which they are dependent on their husband's participation. These women are likely to suffer a steep drop in welfare if they are widowed.

One of the most prosperous partnerships amongst the Grameen women in Ratnogram was Gunjara, a 35 year old, round-faced, sly-eyed beauty and her 65 year old husband, Fulubepari. Fulu was a striking presence when we first met him, tall and straight, a red Haji cap setting off his white hair and long white beard. His opinions were orthodox but trenchant and he had a mocking wit. He was the man who pursued Parul when she was first widowed and to avoid marriage to him she decamped to her father's village. Gunjara, thirty years his junior, is still in awe of him and says little when he is around.

Gunjara and Fulu were in the mustard oil business. Gunjara made the oil, pushing the *ghani* herself with two paid helpers, one of whom was Parul. She worked very hard. When I first talked to her she was walking backwards around the *ghani* shed, pushing the *ghani* with her back, while both hands were occupied feeding the child on her hip from a plate of rice. Fulu sold the oil she made, or exchanged it for crops in season in all the villages around Ratnogram. He was a clever trader and in the first three months of data collection their joint efforts were pulling in over 1,000 Taka a week. Fulu also operated 90 decimals of land, 40 of his own and 50 sharecropped, which kept them in paddy throughout the year with a surplus for sale.

He used to operate much more. Fulu's first wife inherited nearly two acres which she sold to buy land in Ratnogram, some in her name and some in Fulu's. She became deranged when her eldest son disappeared into the fighting during the Liberation war. (He survived and is still in the army.) Before taking a second wife, Fulu "settled" with the first by signing over all but 40 decimals of the land in his name to his three sons. Then he plucked 15 year old Gunjara from her village in another district and brought her to Ratnogram. They lived behind a partition in the house of the youngest son — who is older than Gunjara. Fulu traded oil, but he had very little capital and Gunjara worked on her stepson's *ghani*. She gave birth to a son and two daughters, all of whom died. I need hardly say she was very unhappy.

Membership of Grameen Bank has worked a sea change in her life. With Gunjara's first loans they bought their own *ghani* and put capital into expanding the oil business. Gunjara was one of the first GB members to take a housing loan and built a large house, which now queens it over the smaller houses of the first wife and two stepsons in Fulu's *bari*. He has gifted to her the five decimals on which this house stands. She gave birth to three daughters, all of whom survived. She bought a bullock. By early 1992, they were amongst the second largest mustard oil traders in Beparipara (after Nurul and Norjahan) and one of the most prosperous GB families in Ratnogram, well out of the poverty group.

Then in June, Fulu fell ill with typhoid. He remained bedridden for months, unable to trade or farm his land. When we left the village in early 1993, he was still hovering at death's door.

Fulu's illness suddenly exposed Gunjara's vulnerability. The mustard oil business collapsed. Gunjara could make the oil, but she couldn't sell it. She tried to make a contract with the only *borobari* in her *para*, but they were buying the cheaper milled oil. "How can I go any further? I am a woman," she said in despair. In March, before Fulu's illness, the couple made and sold 4,797 Taka worth of mustard oil. In December, when Gunjara was making oil and selling it from her house, she made 344 Taka.

Fulu fell ill just as the *aus* crop was being planted and so they missed that season. *Amon* was planted late using hired labour so production was low. Although the landowner from whom he sharecropped was initially sympathetic, after Fulu had been out of action for six months he took back his half acre. Fulu continued to farm his own 40 decimals, using hired labour, but without the sharecrop the family will harvest around 28 *maunds* of paddy in 1993, compared to 45 *maund* in a "normal" year.

When we look at how this family coped with the crisis of Fulu's long illness, we can see how some of their strategies worked against the long term interests of Gunjara. Gunjara got her general loan of 8,000 Taka in April intending to put part of it into the mustard oil business (which she did) and buy a cow with the balance. Fulu was still well and business was booming. She never bought the cow. The shallow tube well operated by her two stepsons, which also irrigated Fulu's land, broke down in the driest time of the year and she was prevailed upon to lend them 5,000 Taka for the repairs.

When Fulu collapsed and income stopped, they sold Gunjara's bullock. Gunjara used this cash and the business capital that Fulu had in hand, to cover her repayments to GB, medicine and doctors, and the daily labour needed in the fields. They ate paddy stored from the harvest and Gunjara sold paddy stock, eggs and hens when she needed to buy other food items. The sons pitched in with some gifts and helped supervise the cultivation of their father's fields. The last of the bullock money went to repay Gunjara's outstanding arrears on a group fund loan, so that she could take another of 2,000 Taka. This she used to take her husband to a reputable hospital in another district hoping to cure him.

In other words, protection of the land and its production is the first priority. So Gunjara's capital was used to solve a sudden production crisis — the breakdown of the tube well. Then, faced with the crisis of Fulu's illness, the family first ran down its liquid capital and savings — a large part of which was Gunjara's capital. Then movable assets were sold — Gunjara's bullock.

In Fulu's own words, these are the steps they would be forced to take if the crisis continued: "After the bullock, if we had not got the GB loan, I would have to lease out some land. Then I would be forced to break my pride and worry my eldest son. Finally, if he didn't help, I would have to sell land."

When we returned in November, Fulu was sitting on a pile of straw in the *bari*, still wearing his jaunty red cap, but gaunt and aged. His wit was as sharp as ever, but it seemed unlikely that he would ever carry the heavy cans of mustard oil from village to village again.

"My husband is old. He will not help me again. These six months since he was ill have hardened me and I am thinking what I can do," Gunjara said when we could talk to her on her own. From her we learned that the stepson had repaid some of the Taka he had borrowed and had given her a lease on 15 decimals of his land in exchange for the rest.

In addition, Fulu had gifted to his three daughters 5 decimals of land each.

This decision is best told in Fulu's own words, because it illustrates both the nuances of his relationship with Gunjara and his realistic fears for his daughters.

> One night I thought I was going to die. I said to my young wife: 'What will become of you and your daughters? I must do something and the only thing is to give them some land.' I know she wanted it, but she didn't show it. She just said: 'That would be good, but it depends on you. Think about it carefully.'
>
> It was my duty as a father. In my absence, my sons should take the responsibility for the marriage of my daughters. But only with the inheritance would they be interested in arranging good marriages and paying dowry, in return for the girls signing over the land. Gunjara will be alright because I have given her the five decimals. Without that my sons might seize the big house.

In November, when we talked to Gunjara about how she might earn an income on her own, all she could think of was the same tired old pair, paddy husking and poultry, that other GB women have abandoned or do only as a sideline, because returns are so small. By February, she had taken a seasonal loan of 6,000 Taka and gone into business with her stepson. He uses the capital to buy large amounts of mustard seed, 15 to 20 *maunds*, at every *haat,* which he mills and sells. The profit they share. Meanwhile he buys seed for Gunjara which she grinds on his *ghani*. (Her *ghani* is broken and Fulu has been unable to fix it.)

"I am not his employee," she stresses. "That oil is my oil. I work for myself and hire my own helpers." The month that this deal was in place Gunjara received 810 Taka as her share of the profit, which covered her repayment on that loan plus 47%. In addition, she sold mustard oil she made herself, mustard cake and *bari* produce worth 979 Taka during the same period. Her thinking was producing results.

What will become of Gunjara when Fulu dies? His land will go to his sons and his houselot will be divided between them and his first wife. Gunjara will retain control over the 15 decimals now owned by her young daughters and over the 15 decimal leasehold. That should be enough to feed her and her daughters until they are married. It will be difficult to dislodge her from her house since she owns it in her own name, together with the land on which it stands. Her capital will continue to make her an attractive business partner to her stepson. She is in a much stronger position than Parul was when she was widowed in her thirties with four daughters and no sons.

Nevertheless, her income will drop, even further than it has with Fulu bedridden, because there will be less paddy surplus to sell. Unless her stepson is willing to help her, she may have to sharecrop out her land and take only half the harvest. Fulu's illness has caused her great anxiety. His death will make her even more vulnerable and she will have to calculate every move, as Chaina does, with an eye to her physical security and economic survival.

One of the greatest dangers to Grameen women is not widowhood alone, but the impact of the illness which often precedes the death of the husband. As we saw with Fulu's illness, families cope with this kind of crisis by running down stocks and savings and selling assets. The first things to go are movable assets; livestock, brass pots, rickshaws. In Grameen households, these are precisely the assets most likely to be owned by the woman. The next step is to return any leasehold land and take back the capital. As we have seen, many Grameen loans are going into acquiring leasehold land. The last thing to be touched is owned land, and even that is mortgaged first or sold by degrees. But the first to be mortgaged or sold would be land purchased by the couple, to which the GB loans or profits may have contributed. Last would be the *waris* land inherited by the husband. Last of all, and only in the most desperate circumstances, would the houselot be sold.

This is what happened to Gunjara. The assets which were run down in answer to Fulu's illness were Gunjara's assets — her capital, her bullock, her group fund savings — in order to protect the land which will be inherited by her stepsons and to which her daughters have no claim.

Too Great a Risk?

In terms of its wider social objectives, I believe that the Grameen Bank has failed Parul and many of the other widows by not insisting that they use their loans themselves. For ten years she recorded her annual loan use as "*ghani*-mustard oil making". Even a cursory look at her *bari* reveals that she has no *ghani*, nor has had in the last decade. An effective loan utilisation check would have soon uncovered the fact that she was not using most of her loan and that it was being "borrowed" for most of the decade by her brother-in-law. What makes this worse is that he is a Grameen Bank member of the male center. His wife is a member of Parul's center. It should have been possible for a bank worker close to the ground to put pressure on him through the center to stop the exploitation of Parul. The power balance between a widow and the elder male of the *gusti* is inherently unequal, and the Bank has the weapons to redress it.

Such a course would have meant confronting the norms of patriarchy current in village society. An elder man loses no honour in the eyes of tradition by appropriating the income of his brother's widow (or his son's wife, in the case of Rina), since he can claim that she lives under his roof, under his protection and he feeds her and her children in a crisis.

But Grameen Bank by policy has never been confrontational in the context of power politics in the village. It sidesteps conflict where it can and withdraws when faced with open hostility. This strategy has allowed it to disarm potential political and religious opposition. It has also made it possible for staff to work in rural areas where there is no police presence and where the only law and order that exists is administered by the male elders of the village. The alternative strategy of mobilising the power of the group to confront the men who exploit women has been attempted by other NGOs in Bangladesh, with some success according to their own descriptions (Kramsjo & Wood 1992; BRAC 1980), although they do not spell out the costs to staff and borrowers of these confrontations.

It is my own conviction that the Grameen Bank has become such a powerful presence in rural Bangladesh and the "trickle out" effect of its lending has had such widely beneficial effects, that it has the political support it needs in the village context to play a more proactive role on behalf of its women members than it does at present. As I will show in Chapter 8, the existence of Grameen Bank groups and centers has already changed aspects of gender culture, not only in Grameen families but amongst their neighbours as well. And on issues on which the Bank has decided to push hard — like family planning and clean water supply — it has made a dramatic impact.

The wider social programme of the Grameen Bank — the economic empowerment of women and the spin-off impact of that on the welfare of themselves and their children — depends on the woman retaining control over her own loans and the assets they buy. If this control were enforced by the centers and insisted on by the Grameen Bank staff it would certainly undermine the culture of dependency which makes women like Rina so helpless and widows so vulnerable. The fact that an ever larger proportion of the membership of the Bank will become widows in the future, and can sustain their current progress only if they are active earners and in control of the assets bought by their loans, makes this an issue of urgent concern.

In order to deal with it, however, the Bank will need to look into both the management and attitudes of its front-line staff, and deal with some of the negative consequences of its overwhelmingly male composition.

When Parul took a loan to buy a rickshaw to rent to her son-in-law it was the first time in nine years that she had used her entire loan for a purpose which was of benefit to herself. The proceeds went immediately into better food and consistent repayment. But the Bank worker initially refused to approve the loan on the grounds that since Parul obviously could not ply a rickshaw she must be "pipelining" to a male relative. Bank workers, who service up to 10 centers, or 300 women, and who are transferred frequently, judge who uses the loan by the loan activity. That is why declaring "paddy husking" as the loan use is such a safe bet, because men do not husk paddy. But as we have seen in previous chapters, putting a loan into a "male" activity like land-lease or rickshaws says little about control, and Bank workers would need to know a great deal about their members to make fine judgments on who is in charge and who benefits.

Apart from these practical difficulties, the attitudes of the bank staff affect how they handle women like Parul or Rina in the centers. The commitment of the founders and senior staff of GB to the wider social goals implicit in giving credit to the poorest women and particularly women who head households on their own is of long standing. Grameen Bank founder and Managing Director Professor Yunus, writes:

> The women who have been abandoned by their husbands, leaving a few children with the mothers who have no place to turn to, who feel that they have nothing to lose, stand solidly against all odds.
>
> A large number of impoverished women are those who have been abandoned, divorced or persecuted by their husbands. Our society is reluctant to admit the notion that such women may have separate identities and independent potential. (Gibbons ed 1994:67/30)

Grameen Bank, after a rapid growth spurt at the end of the eighties, now has 11,800 staff, all recruited from this society which is reluctant to admit the possibility of women's autonomy. Some 9,460 of them are non-graduate field-level staff who manage the day to day conduct of the Bank's business in the villages and fully 91% of them are men.[3] In their daily work and in their career prospects with the Bank, the bottom line is loan disbursement and loan repayment rather than the hard-to-quantify issues of women's status and welfare.

Also, if Taka talks within the household, in the way I outlined in previous chapters, Bank assistants are likely to be *more* traditional in their attitudes to women than the husbands of GB members, and that is certainly my personal observation. Bank assistants are good catches, in village terms; "service holders" earning a regular salary; *their* wives do not have to earn and are unlikely to make much contribution to the family budget.

Some bank workers and officers I got to know in Tangail believe that women on their own were simply too much of a repayment risk to be Grameen Bank members. They were reluctant to admit women without husbands into the centers and they were impatient with those, like Parul, who were already there. Although we were not studying the Grameen Bank staff and these comments are simply anecdotal, I noticed how some field staff and officers reinforced the culture of dependency in their work. One branch manager described to me how he pursued defaulters by going directly to the male relative "responsible" for the woman concerned and shaming *him* into paying her debt — a process he described as "chasing him up and up the tree" until he agreed to settle. In the case we were discussing, the defaulter was a widow in her forties and the branch manager was harassing her brother in another village. This approach, of course, denies the woman's own responsibility and the responsibility of her group and center, and reinforces the notion that women throughout their lives are both the property and the burden of their nearest male relative. To counter the *staff* attitudes which work against women borrowers own loan use and control is likely to be a harder task than changing the attitudes of borrower husbands. It is, nevertheless, a prerequisite to getting the Bank to put itself officially behind the struggles of women like Parul to take charge of their own lives.

In the previous chapters I have looked at the contribution of the women in our sample to the income of their families and how central a position they have managed to negotiate for themselves. I have looked at the reasons a substantial number of GB families are still poor and the strategies that female-headed households use to overcome the obstacles that society puts in their path. In all this, however, I have delayed discussion of the role that membership of the Grameen Bank center plays in their lives, apart from the credit which comes through it.

Yet this grouping, where they are members in their own right, outside of the pecking order of their kin group, could be considered to be as important a source of self-esteem and empowerment as any economic gains from their loans. This is the belief of many commentators on the Grameen Bank. In the next chapter, I want to examine how this grouping actually works in these two villages and what it means in the lives of our 40 women members, in an attempt to separate out myth from reality on this highly intangible issue.

Notes

1. We first heard about Parul's struggle to stay in the village from this man, but he omitted his part in the story! Fulu *did* find a second wife, Gunjara, who appears at the end of this chapter. Gunjara and Parul are in the same group and Parul worked on her *ghani* in the first half of the year of data collection.

2. The Vulnerable Group Development scheme did not exist in Ratnogram, which was a small village without a Union member and of no great importance in local politics. Bonopur, in contrast, is a very large village and elects a union member and the Union Chairman. The VGD scheme is an integral part of the political patronage system; in fact, the Chairman "split" each VGD card into two, so that he could spread the gravy further. That is how Sofiah ended up getting a shared card which entitled her to 10 kg of wheat per fortnight. The ration was always short weight, however. The poor women of Bonopur would walk back to the village from the distribution centre and weigh their share and make salty remarks about the morals of the powers-that-be. Sofiah was also offered a place in the CARE program that employs poor women, usually widows, cutting earth to make rural roads. But she was told by the Union Chairman that the officer in charge required a bribe of 2,000 Taka to include her name, so nothing came of that.

3. Women are even rarer at the graduate officer level of Grameen Bank. There are only 156 female officers or 6.7% of the total. These figures are for August, 1994.

8

Group and Center: Solidarity and Self-Interest

Our education into the workings of the Grameen Bank centers at the village level began with a strike. All 30 women in the Ratnogram center simultaneously stopped payment on all their loans. In the same week, the male center in the same village also came out on strike in support of the women's action.

I never unraveled all the causes behind this action, particularly the participation of the male center. But the catalyst was the Bank worker's refusal to process Kia's general loan proposal. Kia, the *dai* and my best informant in Beparipara, finished full payment of her previous loan in mid-January. She paid her interest on February 9 and submitted her proposal for another loan of 4,000 Taka. The proposal, for "*ghani*-mustard oil making" was approved by her group and center and then blocked by the Bank worker. His grounds were that the interest owed by another Bepari member, not in Kia's group, had not been paid.

All of the members thought this decision was unjust. (During the week this crisis persisted we were stopped all over the village by indignant little bunches of women, spitting fire.) Eight members, including Kia, marched the two miles to the branch office to complain to the branch manager. But it was a loan dispersal day and they were not able to see him. The Bank worker, finding them going over his head, scolded them and threatened to stop all their irrigation loans, which are disbursed at this season of the year, if they persisted.

"He talks to them like cows in the field. No respect!" commented my research assistant indignantly.

At this, their resentment against the Bank worker erupted. All the women decided to stop payment that week. The men's center, which also had loan proposals delayed, decided to join them. It was the fasting month; it was almost *Choitro*, the hungriest, dustiest, most irritating month of the year. Tempers were short. At the next meeting of the men's center the verbal fireworks came within an inch of a punch-up and the Bank worker was forced to beat a fast retreat into the house of Alia, the ex-center chief.

In a few days, the branch manager and his senior assistant arrived in the village and met with both centers. Some of the grievances were aired. Kia's loan was approved, along with several other delayed proposals. Members resumed repayment.

The refusal of the women members to be cowed by the Bank worker's threats was impressive. After a decade of membership in the Bank they knew exactly how it worked. They knew that a full-scale strike by both centers would immediately command the full attention of the branch manager — and his superiors, the program officer and the area manager. They knew that an unjust decision by a Bank worker could be overturned by their collective protest. On both counts they were right. In the midst of this crisis, as we talked to women members in all parts of the village, they gave us a very clear sense that they *are* the Grameen Bank at village level. Bank workers change every year; they have seen many come and go. Some are better and some are worse than others; they love the good ones and tolerate the bad ones with admirable courtesy. But despite all the saluting and "sah" ing, which I mentioned in the preface as a first impression, no Bank worker can force an action on an experienced center when they oppose it together. The culture of the center is already long established and they can run their affairs themselves regardless of the character of the Bank worker.

In another sense, however, although the outcome was a triumph for the women and removed the immediate threat to their loans, nothing fundamental was solved by this crisis. The underlying problem, which was a scam involving interest payments, continued for the rest of the year. There was a logic behind the Bank worker's refusal to pass Kia's loan proposal. But neither the Bank worker, nor the center leaders wanted the real problem to come out, so they kept quiet about it when the branch manager came to the village.

The principal amount of the general loans is repaid in 50 equal installments over the year. Only then is the interest of 20% calculated, on the basis of a declining balance. Theoretically it comes due in the last two weeks of the annual loan period. In practice, however, most members don't pay their interest until they are ready to take their next loan, which could be weeks or even months after they have finished repaying the principal amount. Although it should be recorded by the Bank worker when it is paid, there is no way a branch manager can spot a delay in recording this payment. Moreover, interest payments in mature centers like these, where members are on their 8th to 11th loan cycles and are borrowing from 6,000 to 8,000 Taka, are quite hefty — ranging from 300 to 800 Taka. Payments on group fund loans are also intermittent, so that delays in recording them cannot be spotted at the branch.

In the particular case which provoked this strike, a member had left the center to take a job in Chittagong. She had paid the principal amount of her loan but the interest payment was still outstanding. More than three months before the strike, she had sent the interest payment to her brother. He gave it to Kia who took it to the center meeting and handed it to the center chief, in the full view of all the center members and the Bank worker. Three members were short on their repayment that week, so the 280 Taka was distributed amongst them by the center chief for repayment and not recorded as interest paid by the Bank worker.

This practice had started as an "private" arrangement between the former center chief and a few members with repayment problems, a couple of years before. It was done without the knowledge of the Bank worker so that the interest amounts withheld could only be rolled over for a week or so before they had to be officially paid and recorded. By the time we arrived in the village the practice was widespread, interest payments were not recorded for longer periods of time, and the Bank worker was in collusion with the center chief in managing what had become a quite complicated system of double accounting.

Nobody was corruptly pocketing this money, as far as we could tell, although the potential for abuse was certainly present. Those members who were "helped" in this way did eventually repay, most from their new loans, which eroded their capital and sustained the weakness which had generated this rather dubious solution.

Center members were ambivalent about what was happening. Everybody was grateful to have access to somebody else's interest money when they were short on their repayment. Members knew they should help each other with repayment if necessary, and this seemed a painless way of doing it without members having to dig into their own pockets (untie the knot at the end of their *sari*). There was also the "clean" record of the center to be maintained. This was important to keep the center eligible for special types of loans, like housing loans and seasonal loans. It was also of importance in the promotion prospects of the Bank worker. "Sometimes people like Parul come to the meeting with not one Taka! If the center chief can help them it keeps the good name of the center," explained one member.

But there was a general feeling that the practice had got out of hand. For the rest of the year it certainly generated many quarrels. Loans were being delayed for several members because their interest had been paid but not recorded. At least two members did not get an irrigation loan at all in 1992 because the arrears and interest they had paid remained unrecorded for more than a year. Gunjara, who paid off the 800 Taka still outstanding on her group fund loan so that she could get another to treat her husband's illness, had to wait three months before it was recorded and she could take her loan.

Members of the Bepari group and the group from Khapara complained that *their* interest payments were being taken by the center chief and used to help *her* cronies in Musjidpara. It was noticeable that those whose interest payments went unrecorded for long periods, so that their loans were long delayed, were the least powerful members of the center, like Parul. Powerful members, like Banu, the aunt of the center chief, were never subjected to this practice. Nor was the prosperous Bepari family of Norjahan, because her husband Nurul had the alarming habit of waiting on the road to complain to the Bank worker as he wobbled his way to the Center hut.

Mistakes were inevitable — our *lokkhi* farmer, Saleha, ajitated all year because her recorded interest payment was 28 Taka less than the amount she had given to the center chief.

It is likely that the Bank worker stopped Kia's loan to put pressure on the Center to clear up the mess before it got *him* into trouble.[1] But he chose the wrong target. Everybody had seen Kia pay the interest to the center chief, and she was universally liked by the other members. The Bepari group were furious at being made the scapegoat of a system which mainly benefited groups from Musjidpara — with the connivance of the Bank worker. But the reason everybody was willing to act in unison was that everybody felt that *their* loans were equally at risk of being delayed or stopped if this decision was allowed to stand.

After the strike, the system of rolling over interest payments continued unabated. It never produced another moment of collective unity. On the contrary, arguments about who benefited from the system and who was hurt due to delayed loans tended to exacerbate the divisions that already existed in the center. These arguments reached a crescendo at the end of the year when the seasonal loans were introduced. Members who had not repaid their irrigation loan from the previous year were not eligible for this new loan, and several irrigation loan interest payments had been absorbed into the "black" repayment window operated by the center chief. None of the Bepari group, except Norjahan, qualified for a seasonal loan for this reason.

The center chief came under fierce pressure to return the payments she had taken, so that these members could get seasonal loans. Many members were now refusing to hand repayments through her and were insisting on seeing them recorded at the meeting where they were repaid. Then came the news that the Bank worker was to be transferred. He advised the center chief to quickly settle all outstanding unrecorded interest payments "otherwise there will be trouble." At the same time he approved her seasonal loan, which enabled her to do so.

In this way, without the intervention or even the knowledge of the branch office, the center managed to clean up a mess which was threatening its members' access to a new and attractive loan.[2] At the beginning of the year, during the strike, members clearly expressed their feeling that they *are* the Grameen Bank in the village, in defiance of the Bank worker if necessary. It was a logical extension of this feeling that several also expressed the feeling that the Center *should* solve its own problems and there was no need to involve (or inform) the officers of the Bank.

This is Alia, the ex-center chief giving her views on this issue — a complex mix of protectiveness towards the center, a badmouthing of the current center chief, a fear of open confrontation and a way of expressing her anger at the Bank worker in a way which is culturally acceptable.

> This interest money belongs to the Grameen Bank; it is not good to use it this way. If we have problems we should solve them some other way, not by using the Bank's money. When I was center chief we did it a few times without the knowledge of the Bank worker. But now with R [the current center chief] it is happening all the time! When the Branch Manager came to the center meeting after the strike, R did all the talking and the rest of us stayed quiet. Even now, I don't want to go to the branch manager, because we should solve our own problems in the center — and we don't want to fight with the center 'Sir'. But when he was leaving and he asked me to forgive him,[3] I replied: 'No, I will not forgive you, because these interest payments are still not settled.' Now I am advising the new center 'Sir': 'Take the interest payments when they are paid, and if any members ask you for them, you answer them strongly.'

We were lucky to have a particularly weak Bank worker in this village. It enabled us to see the workings of the Ratnogram center, more or less independently of the official hierarchy of the Bank. Or, to put it more bluntly, how thirty illiterate, em*purdah*ed, poor women ran the Grameen Bank at village level, despite its salaried representative.

How did such women, who had no previous experience of public life and to whom "service holders" like the Bank staff used to be a distant and superior species, come to have this conviction that they *own* the Bank — at least at the level of their village?

Owning the Bank

"We are Grameen Bank members. We have much power and we are valuable people," stated Habibah in her usual blunt fashion when we were discussing the affairs of her center in Bonopur. She had been center chief from the time of the center's near collapse and resurrection in 1987/88. The center hut has been reerected inside her *bari*. When, in 1991, the Bank began enforcing its rule that the center chief must be changed each year, Habibah bowed to the inevitable and selected as her successor the aptly named Baby, who was a new member and had slid in with more than half an acre of land because of Habibah's patronage. Baby went to the workshops (branch-level seven day workshops for center chiefs are held around once a year), but all the decisions remained in Habibah's hands.

Habibah made this statement about the value and power of Grameen members in the village in the context of explaining how she selected new members for the center. Bonopur was a large village with many poor households who were not members of the GB center. There were many supplicants for the few vacancies. Habibah vetted them, discussed them with a cadre of trusted group leaders, and then with the Bank worker. Her selections (there were three new members admitted in the year of study) were accepted as members by the Bank. (I discuss her criteria for selecting new members on pp177-8.)

This was fairly typical of how this center was managed. The Bank worker who serviced the Bonopur center was very competent and treated the women members with respect. But he had few problems — the Bonopur Center ran itself. There were no open divisions or conflicts here as there were in Ratnogram and Habibah maintained an admirable unity and discipline. "She is our leader. From the beginning she has been strong and wise and we obey her," explained a member, one both more educated and wealthier than Habibah herself.

It had taken years for this autonomy and sense of ownership to grow. We knew that this center had almost collapsed four years before. Moreover, it belonged to the Shajanpur Branch which was infamous amongst the 1,041 branches of the Grameen Bank, because its record was so bad that the Managing Director, Professor Muhammad Yunus, had ordered it closed down. ("Put a lock on it!" was what he actually said, enraged at both its record and the apathy of its members during a visit to the Branch in 1986. He was later persuaded by the branch staff to give it one last chance.)

In our research team was the former Branch Manager, Kajul Chowdury, who had succeeded in turning the branch around. So we spent some time talking to the members of the center about its history and their personal reactions to its near collapse. Through this we got a picture of the process by which an outside institution came to be owned and controlled by its members.

In 1987, Zarinah, the ambitious young woman who appears in Chapter Three simultaneously building a house and buying land, had been a member of the Bonopur center for three years. Although she admits now that she had enough income to repay her loan, she was already 49 weeks in default. By May of the next year, she was 88 weeks behind in her payments and had long ago stopped going to center meetings. So had nearly everyone else. Kajul remembers the first center meeting he attended in Bonopur as the newly arrived branch manager, with a very embarrassed bank worker standing in a central place and yelling. After a long time, they conducted the meeting with the three members who turned up. There were only five members still paying; most of the others had been in arrears for more than a year. The center appeared to be dead.

Zarinah remembers that year: "My husband was angry when I went to the meetings. He said: 'All these NGOs come and go. They offer something, then they disappear. If you don't repay this Grameen Bank Taka it doesn't matter. What do they really do for us anyway?'"

That is a logical, and probably thoroughly justified, reaction to the fits and spurts of 'development' aid, and the 'here-today-gone-tomorrow' NGOs that have been thrown at rural Bangladeshis over the last two decades. Even on the rare occasions that something actually trickled through to the poor, 'the poor' have usually been the objects of an agenda set in the Western capitals of the aid agencies which is largely irrelevant to their needs.

But by the end of 1988, Zarinah had paid off her arrears and was back at the meetings, with the full support of her husband. So were 20 other members, most of whom had also cleared their arrears and were again members in good standing. Only eight members did not return to the center and still have outstanding debts to the Bank. What had happened in those two years to change the minds of the majority? Zarinah remembers:

A new bank worker, Firoza, came to every house and talked to us, husband and wife. Her behavior was very polite and nice, no pressure. She said don't worry about Taka yet, just come to the meeting and see what the others are doing. Then she persuaded us to start paying something small, so that the interest payment on our arrears didn't grow too big. Then a few members cleared their arrears and got new loans. When we saw that we wanted to clear our arrears and get new loans too. So I paid mine in one shot by selling a goat and took my fourth loan.

During the '88 flood, the GB staff came in boats to see if we were O.K. They gave us wheat and an emergency loan. That convinced my husband, because at that time moneylenders were charging huge interest rates.

Another member, who was also a 'grand defaulter,' said:

Indiscipline was so bad in those days that people didn't even bring their passbooks to the meeting. We didn't think this Grameen Bank would last. Then during the big flood, the Bank helped us with wheat and rice, *all of us,* even the defaulters! You know, sister, how Khatimon had a miscarriage during the flood and the branch manager saved her life?[4] At that time Habibah was going back and forth to the branch office getting news of Khatimon and help for the members. After that most people went back to the center and those who thought that it would disappear started to take it seriously.

Firoza, now working in another area, remembers with satisfaction some very long days in Bonopur.

Our Zonal Manager was stressing 'after hours' work. This meant house-to-house visiting. I tried to understand the members' real problems. I talked to them about what they wanted for themselves and their children in the future. I found five members who were really committed and serious who wanted the center to survive, so we worked together persuading members to come back to the meetings and pay just one Taka into the savings fund. Some members decided that this Grameen Bank will live after all and so they paid their arrears. Immediately we gave them new loans and that was a big boost to the others.

The most difficult problem was those who had lost their capital because of illness or misuse by their husbands or sons. When they started attending regularly we helped them with group fund loans and special loans, which they used to settle their arrears and begin regular repayment. In this way they could get a new general loan and restart their projects.

One of the group of five motivators remembers how they operated:

We used to meet in my house or Habibah's house and discuss case by case how to rehabilitate members who had lost their capital. We used the group funds so they could quickly settle and get new loans. We went to their houses and discussed how they could earn income and keep up their repayment.

Habibah, whose energy and strength led this process, comments:

We had to prevent members from borrowing from moneylenders to pay their arrears. This is a bad practice because the interest is high and eats up their capital. That's why we used the group fund. Although there were many with arrears, the arrears were not large, so they could clear with a small group fund loan and get a new general loan, pay back the group fund and then we used that money again to save the next member. The male center collapsed in this village, so many women members thought GB would not stay here.[5] I told them GB will stay only if we are good members. Even some GB staff were doubtful about this village because of the record of the male center. But we were determined to keep a GB women's center in this village.

That was the process. The Bank staff responded to the repayment crisis by an effort to get closer to the members and understand why they had stopped attending and paying. They made new capital available on a selective basis. During a disaster — the major flood of 1988, which destroyed many houses, crops and livestock throughout this area — they provided real help in the form of grain, emergency loans and a month long suspension of repayment. But most of all they continued to work in the village. In a world of fly-by-night NGOs, the Grameen Bank stayed in place, despite serious setbacks. They were on the ground at the most important time — when it was covered with water.

The psychology of Grameen Bank repayment rests on the certainty that as soon as one loan is cleared, another, larger loan will be available. Doubts about this reliable, regular access to future credit, which lay behind the repayment crisis of 1987-88, were cleared by the persistence and responsiveness of the Bank staff. Then, in 1989, the branch office building went up in Shajanpur — a brick and mortar symbol of the permanent presence of the Bank.

An equally important process was taking place among the women in the center. A small cadre of members took on the responsibility of motivating the others. They went from house to house persuading the other center members to return. *They* worked out the strategies for rehabilitating each member. The group and special loans were made available by the branch office, but the women decided who should get them and on what terms. The revival of the center would not have been possible without their efforts. In the process they made the center their own. This cadre of capable and active women, led by Habibah and reflecting her confidence, are still the leaders of the center in Bonopur. Since 1989 there have been no serious repayment problems in this center, although there are a handful of members who are sometimes irregular. As a result, 30 women in this village have had continued access to increasing amounts of credit and more than half of their families have risen into the ranks of the middling-prosperous. It is this very visible progress, and the central role that these women have played in bringing it about, that has made them "powerful and valuable people" in the society of the village.

From "Just Credit" to "Credit-Plus"

What I have described here are two groups of women committed to the survival and continuance of the centers which give them access to credit. Is it possible to go any further than this and see them as a solidarity group, two cells in a collective movement which now embraces more than half the villages in Bangladesh? Is it a "sisterhood" in the feminist sense, undermining the patriarchal structure of the village and the broader society?

To examine these questions it is necessary to go back to the origins of the Grameen Bank and set it into the context of other NGOs which emerged at the same time, and with which it is now often compared.

In the seventies two streams of idealism came together in Bangladesh and irrigated a rapid growth of NGOs. The war of liberation blooded a whole generation of student activists and intellectuals, who had been particularly targeted in the brutalities inflicted by the Pakistani army. After the war, frustrated in the political arena and, as leftists, increasingly under threat from the security apparatus of the military regime, many turned their idealism and energies to NGO work in the countryside.

Coming in from the West and funding many of these NGOs were what might be called the minor donors (they refer to themselves as the 'Like-Minded Group'); both NGOs and government agencies from smaller countries with strong social-democratic traditions: Sweden, Norway, the Netherlands, Denmark and Canada. Inspiring many of them was the political activism of the sixties in Europe, and the third world movements of mass literacy inspired by Paulo Freire's 1970 book, *The Pedagogy of the Oppressed*. This argues that social change can only come through organising the poor directly to undertake collective action to confront and overturn the structures which oppress them. Many Bangladeshi intellectuals took these ideas enthusiastically on board. NGOs, the best known being Proshika and BRAC, fanned out through the villages organising collectives of the landless, men and women, and "conscientising" them through various kinds of informal education so that they would understand the structures they had to fight. Credit was also offered to these groups so that they could achieve some material autonomy from the landlords and moneylenders who were their class oppressors (Khan 1989; Kramsjo and Wood 1991; North-South Institute *Report of the Like-Minded Group* 1985).

But the resonance between the minor donors and the post-Liberation generation of activists did not extend easily into Bangladesh's semi-feudal villages, where life is still largely organised around patron-client clusters. Although there are many individual cases of success in organising landless poor to claim *khas* lands and ponds and effective collective protest by rural workers being cheated or underpaid on Food for Work schemes, the revolution these landless associations were supposed to spearhead did not happen. Many of those young Bangladeshis involved as 'animators' became as disillusioned with the Freire approach as they had been with the Awami League. S.A. Khan, a convinced Maoist, who spent five years organising landless associations in the Comilla district, writes:

> 'Consciousness raising' group discussions were held in an attempt to assist the landless in 'systematising' their thinking and to discover for themselves the reasons for their poverty and misfortune, i.e. class oppression, which would in turn lead the landless into 'class action'.
>
> However, I was perplexed at the time by the ease with which the landless assumed a 'class' perspective in discussing their situation on the one hand, but on the other, by their unwillingness to act as a 'class', let alone rise up in a fit of spontaneous class fury. After very little time, their discussion hinged around concepts of 'us' (*bumihin*) and 'them' (*borolok*). Given that all the landless groups thus organised (36 groups involving about 400 individuals) collapsed as soon as the project ended, it would appear that the provision of credit was the main attraction. In order to gain credit, they were willing to undergo superficial 'class' indoctrination. They soon realised that the more 'revolutionary' they appeared in rhetoric, the greater their chances of receiving credit. (Khan 1989:125-6)

Similar experiences have led most NGOs following the Freire approach to beef up their provision of credit and de-emphasise their conscientization activities over the last decade. BRAC, for example, has reduced the "functional education" component of most of its women's groups from one year to as little as two months before they become eligible for loans.

Nevertheless, in the 1990s, the complex of ideas referred to above is still a potent influence within Bangladesh and in the donor community (Kramsjo and Wood 1992, and the revision of the Report of the Like-Minded Group, 1990). It influences both the critics and the admirers of Grameen Bank. Added to them is the voice of feminist writers who see collective action by women as fundamental to their empowerment. Summing up this literature, Judith Bruce writes:

Few who have studied women's position would conclude that fundamental change for women, and, by extension, better prospects for their children, can be based solely on increasing their individual earning power. Feminist theorists have identified collective action as a primary step for women in achieving personal power and status in the public domain. Sanday's cross-cultural analysis of female status identified four indicators of female status, the most important of which — superceding female material control — is the existence of female solidarity groups. (Bruce 1989:987)

Of all the NGOs that emerged from the foment and disillusionment of the first decade of liberation, the Grameen Bank Project was probably the most minimalist in its approach. The young professor in econometrics was no Marxist; he was looking for concrete ways to help people in a village he already knew well. He, and quite a number of students working in his Rural Economics Program, had already been working for two years in Jobra, in the wake of the 1974 Famine, trying out ways to increase production and involve poor sharecroppers, including a share management system for a deep tube well (a success) and joint cultivation between students and farmers (a flop). The idea of small loans rose directly out of the expressed need of some Jobra women stool-makers who were bonded to wholesalers because they had no capital to buy their own bamboo (Yunus 1987; Counts forthcoming).

The Grameen Bank method grew experimentally with the needs and responses of poor families in Jobra, continually batting off this reality, dropping the ideas that failed and going ahead with what worked. It was informed by Professor Yunus' critical reaction to the development success story of the previous decade — the Comilla cooperative — which turned sour when it was adopted wholescale by Government and kidnapped by landlords. GB, therefore, was targeted to the very poor and its groups kept small enough for the poor to retain control of them. Underlying the whole experiment was Professor Yunus' revolutionary belief in the creative energy and enterprise of the poor and their reliability in the handling of money. It is partly this belief — that the poor already possess survival skills and can handle money, so that training is not a prerequisite to credit — which has kept GB minimalist.

Initially, the Grameen Bank Project was just credit and was offered to men and women. It slowly evolved its current structure of five-member groups and five-group centers, but the main function of these solidarity groups was to maintain credit discipline, not much more. When it expanded from Chittagong to Tangail district in 1979 the Project added workshops in social development for women members and in 1984 a national workshop formulated the 16 Decisions.

Around this time, mainly in response to increasing repayment problems within male centers, the Grameen Bank Project began a shift towards recruiting mainly women members, which would by the end of the decade make it a woman's Bank, with 94% of its members women, disbursing 93% of its loans to women and with 75% of its shares owned by its members. [6]

In some ways, then, there has been a convergence between the 'conscientizing' NGOs like BRAC and the Grameen Bank, with BRAC putting more emphasis on credit and Grameen Bank moving from "just credit" to "credit-plus" by putting more weight on social development through the 16 Decisions. I will discuss the 16 Decisions in more detail in Chapter 9, but I doubt this convergence has gone as far as some commentators have suggested (Chowdhury 1991; Schuler and Hashemi 1994). GB group training for prospective members lasts just five days. (If they pass. If they do not, it goes on until they pass or give up.) They are required to memorise the 16 Decisions in order to be admitted to the center, and I imagine that they do so, at least initially, for the same reason that S.A. Khan's groups learned their revolutionary rhetoric — to get the credit.

In addition, the 16 Decisions is not a particularly revolutionary document; neither is the training manual for the women's workshops. [7] Most of the Decisions are a practical guide to better health, sanitation and child care, a sort of Mrs. Beecham's Better Housekeeping for rural Bangladesh. The decision which advocates the most fundamental change — the ban on dowry — is, as we shall see in Chapter 9, the least observed. However, some believers in social change through collective action, who also admire the Grameen Bank, see the social development program as resulting in a solidarity movement which has of itself awakened and empowered its members.

Fuglesang and Chandler, who bring from Norway and Canada the idealism that characterises the minor donors, found that the center meetings and broader Grameen Bank gatherings reminded them of: "the Norwegian Labour Party's youth phalanx, the "Framfylkingen" in the Thirties... the same inspiring speeches, the same reiteration of the issues in the slogans, the concern for solidarity and the sense of awakening together." They describe the Grameen Bank as a 'peoples' movement:'

> Quite literally, it means to stand together and to move together, to have an intention together and to act in pursuit of that intention. This is literally what a people's movement is all about. Such a formation is expressed both in a physical or spatial arrangement and in the thinking, the feeling, the attitudes and behavior of the participants, right down to their body language. Most significantly, it is a social design in which people participate by making themselves socially and economically accountable to each other. It is a people's movement. (1993:86,39)

It is now time to come down from these general assertions and ideas and test them against the actual workings of the two centers in Ratnogram and Bonopur.

Are they part of a 'peoples' movement'? How much of the empowerment of Grameen women is coming from their participation in their groups and centers? In this context, I will also look at two recent studies of empowerment which compare Grameen Bank women with women in BRAC and other NGOs which, unlike Grameen Bank, explicitly aim to empower women through 'conscientizing' procedures.

Group Myth and Reality

When I began investigating the dynamics of the groups and center in Ratnogram I spent a lot of time in the *bari* of the former center chief, Alia. She is a soft spoken woman in her late forties, who has managed her family of two sons and two daughters for years, with little help from her much older husband, who is now too weak to work and was always, according to his mother, "a bit loosebrained." Alia was center chief for many years until the rule to change these positions annually was enforced in 1991. Though illiterate, Alia is a poet, like so many Bengalis. As center chief, she attended several workshops and she composes songs about Grameen Bank, which she sings in a perfectly pitched, plaintive, reedy voice.

She likes to talk about the history of the center. This is one of the stories she told me:

> The Khans are newcomers to this village. They came just before the Liberation War and they bought up a lot of land here — mostly by foreclosing on mortgages and cheating! As you know, Khan tried to cheat Amir (the husband of Renu, a GB member in Alia's group) out of his paddy land and his houselot by making him sign a paper he thought was for his contract wages. Some years ago, Khan came into Amir's *bari* with a gang of thugs to drive the family out of this houselot and knock down their house. There were 12 of them and Amir was only one. Renu came crying to my house in a panic. Quickly we called the whole Center and our families and we went to Amir's *bari*, nearly a 100 of us! I confronted this Khan, who is a fierce and evil-tempered man. I told him:
>
> 'We are thirty women and thirty husbands and thirty sons! Do you want to pull down the house of our member?'
>
> When he saw us and heard us he just turned and went away. He has never dared to try again.

This is a wonderful story of center solidarity and empowerment. There is only one problem with it. It never happened. When I checked it with the family concerned and the other members of the center, it became clear that this confrontation had never taken place.

I heard many stories of this kind during the time we were in Bangladesh, some from GB leaders in the villages, but most from officers and field workers in the Bank. All of them illustrated the unity of the center in the face of threats from evil landlords or the scorn of *mullahs*, and the lengths to which members would go to help each other in trouble. A field worker, talking about the disastrous flood which hit Tangail in 1988, told me this charming tale:

> In one of my villages many houses were washed away and children were drowned. One GB member was very worried about another member of her group. So she made a raft of banana stems lashed together and paddled to her group member's house to see if she was O.K. There was no-one there. Even more worried, she paddled back to her own *bari*. There to her relief, she found her friend, also on a banana raft. 'I wasn't at home, because I had to come and see if *you* were all right,' her group member said.

These stories serve an important function. They illustrate and reinforce the 16 Decisions, which serve as a framework for the social development policy of the Bank, such as: "We shall not inflict injustice on anyone, neither shall we allow anyone to do so" and "We shall always be ready to help each other. If anyone is in difficulty, we shall all help her." These stories are the very stuff of the workshop program, which brings center chiefs and sometimes group chairpersons together for motivation and training. It is not surprising that someone with the poetic imagination of Alia and the experience of several workshops should possess a fund of them. But I grew increasingly skeptical of how much they represented reality.

Amir was, in fact, in dispute with the Khans over his houselot, and a complex case about it had been dragging through the courts for more than a decade. Amir was getting legal advice and other help from M, the main landlord in the village, who himself had several land disputes going on with Khan. Amir and his wife were both Grameen Bank members and this may have strengthened his position against Khan, (it certainly gave them the money to fight the court case) but Amir himself denied this when we talked to him about the case.

The *bari* in which we so often sat while Alia talked about the center had also been the subject of a dispute between Alia's father-in-law and the family of the Khans. Khan initially bought it, but failed to pay the full price so the sale lapsed. It was then resold to Alia's family and registered in their name. But when they began to build on it, Khan protested and sent men to build his own hut on it to forcibly establish his ownership. This drama certainly happened, with Alia trying to pull out one of the house pillars they had just erected, Khan's men forcing it back in again and all falling to the ground amidst general uproar. But I could never find a center member who remembers coming physically to her support as she remembers. The crowd that gathered in her support were mainly members of the father-in-law's *gusti*.

A village *shalish* ruled in favour of Alia's family. But what is of more significance than the details of this drama, is the fact that soon after the *shalish*, Alia and her husband built a GB house on the houselot and so did Begum, her sister-in-law. In addition, the center hut, which serves both the male and the female centers, was built on this land, which put it forever beyond the thuggery of a fairly minor landlord like Khan.

Membership of the Bank has given poor families extra resources in both income and status and ownership of assets, like houses, which the Bank staff will protect under challenge, which certainly strengthens their hand in conflicts. Parul, for instance, the widow with the bullying brother-in-law, got more respect and gradually more autonomy as a result of her GB loans. Without them, he would probably have continued his campaign to drive her out of the village. But these conflicts and their development and resolution over the years — with the GB members strengthened by more income, more assets, more self-confidence and the potential backing of the Center — are part of a gradual and subtle process. They never become the army of marching women which so fires the imaginations of Westerners living behind walls in the leafier suburbs of Dhaka. Overt confrontation is too risky for the women involved.

Family Comes First

After a year of watching how members related to each other, I became just as skeptical about compliance with the 14th Decision that members should all help others in difficulty. Members *did* help each other with repayment, since default of one member threatened the new loans of the other members in her group and the good name of the whole center. But even this help had distinct limits. More general help for members in trouble was rare.

When members were in temporary difficulty over repayment, other group members did sometimes bale them out. For instance, Alia went through a very bad time in the middle of the year when she became seriously ill and remittances from her rickshaw stopped. One of her group members took a group fund loan and lent her half of it so that Alia could meet her repayments. Alia could not take a group fund loan herself because she already had one outstanding.

Swapna, a young divorcee who lives in her father's bari, told me proudly:

> Our group is very strong. If one of our members does not have enough Taka for repayment, we help them. We also help each other in other ways. For example, when R had a fever I went to her house to bathe her head and sometimes we call each other to help cook when many relatives are visiting.
>
> When I have to make a decision I usually discuss it with my group as well as with my father and uncle. Like when my son was offered the labour contract I talked to R, and she said it is good to let him take it.

Swapna does belong to a strong group and none of them had repayment problems during the year. She herself has a good income from milk and from sharecropping out her leasehold land. Her group contained the center chief and her aunt, Banu, who had plenty of surplus. In other words they very seldom had to help each other out. One of her group members had problems, but they were not financial. Her husband had periods of madness, during which he used to beat her. Her group never intervened on these occasions.

I got a different picture when I talked to members of the center who were *frequently* short of Taka. Rina, the woman whose husband had excema and could not work for months at a time, had this to say about her group and center:

"They do not help me with repayment. They should, but they have no more Taka than me, so how can they? When I am short of repayment I ask my brother or my in-laws. After all, they are my family; they are closest to me."

In Bonopur, Sofiah, the widow with the failed grocery shop, justified the lack of help from her center in the same way. "They also are poor. They cannot help me with Taka. But they advise me to borrow outside and settle my arrears so that I can get a new loan. I go to my brother's family when I am short. They can help me more."

In fact, there are many members in both centers who are not poor and Rina and Sofiah are much worse off than other center members. Also when Sofiah borrows from her natal village, she often has to pay interest of 20% per month.

On another occasion during the year, a member of the Bonopur center discovered that her husband had absconded with all the money in the house, including her repayment, on the morning of the center meeting. When she did not turn up at the meeting someone was sent by the Bank worker to see what was wrong. They found her in tears. One member, not in her group, lent her 50 Taka; Laili broke her secret clay "bank" and took another 70 Taka to make a part payment of what she owed the Bank. The next week she sold some paddy stock to repay the 50 Taka and sold a chicken to meet her repayment. For the next six weeks her husband did not reappear and she had no idea where he was. She sold vegetables and eggs and paddy and with this managed to feed her two children and the deluge of relatives who descended on her with their sympathies. She also managed to pay 100 Taka or more each week of the 160 Taka weekly installment she owed to GB, without further help from the center.

She harvested the paddy crop her husband had left standing in the field by working with her brother and small son. She arranged the ploughing and hired the labour to plant one field with mustard, but the other she gave out on a sharecrop, fearing that she could not manage the paddy planting herself. "Every week feels like a month to me," she said. It did not occur to her to call on the center for any extended help in this crisis. Like most women she turned first to her own family.

Women in the village traditionally depend on their in-laws, with whom they share a *bari,* the wider *gusti* to which their husbands belong and on their own natal family, which is usually in a village within walking distance. Grameen women are not much different in this respect. When we analyse the interest payments, for example, this dependence on family becomes clear. As I pointed out above, interest payments on 8th to 10th term loans are substantial and are usually paid in one lump sum before a proposal is submitted for a new loan. Only about a third of the Grameen women could come up with these sums from cash savings. Most (64%) borrowed to make the interest payment and then repaid this borrowing out of their new loan. It was easy to borrow this money because people knew it would be quickly repaid and so most of these informal loans were without interest. Some members, however, like the widow Chaina, had such poor relations with their kin group that they were forced to borrow from moneylenders. Others borrowed from employers or wholesalers who extracted a disguised interest.

FIGURE 8.1 Source of Borrowing to Pay Interest on the General Loan

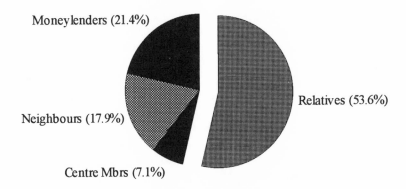

Note: 25 members out of 39 borrowed all or part of the interest payable on their general loan (64% of the sample). One member paid her interest before the start of data collection and had not finished her loan by the end, so is not included in the sample. Some members borrowed from two sources to cover their interest.

Altogether 15 of the 25 who borrowed to pay their interest did so from relatives and five others from neighbours. Neighbours usually belong to the same *gusti* or clan group. Only two borrowed these fairly large sums from other center members; in one case from the center chief who was also her aunt. Six members borrowed from moneylenders — defined here as any lender, whether relative, neighbour or employer, who charges interest. These figures make very clear the preponderance of family networks in raising these sums over group and center members.

It seemed that the women who got help from their groups and centers were those who needed it least often. Those members who were often in trouble were the least likely to receive it. There is a logic in this. Group members who lent 50 Taka to Swapna, for example, to meet a shortfall in her repayment, could be sure not only of getting it back, but of Swapna having the ability to reciprocate when they were in a similar predicament. Members who lent to Rina had no such certainty. Rina was chronically short of Taka. She could not reciprocate such help and anyone who lent her money would probably have to wait until she got her loan before she could repay them. Members were unwilling to give frequent help to members who would become a burden on them.

This was true even in cases where a major crisis hit someone they saw as a 'good member.' When Fulu got typhoid and Gunjara was suddenly stranded without anyone to market her oil she got no help from her group to overcome this particular problem, even though both Norjahan's husband and Kia's father were major mustard oil traders. Gunjara asked Norjahan for help in marketing and was refused.

This Bepari group was usually very cohesive. Early in the year, when all was well, Gunjara quite often helped Parul with food and lent her small sums for repayment, because Parul worked on Gunjara's *ghani* as well as being in the same group. Kia also occasionally helped Parul with rice. Once I saw them sitting with their legs outstretched, one behind the other on the ground, like children playing trains, cleaning each other's hair, joking and laughing, and I wished I had brought my camera to record this moment of "group unity."

At the end of the year, when Fulu had been bedridden for many months and Gunjara was trying to make an income selling oil from the house, the research team made a point of buying whatever mustard oil we needed from her. This got us into trouble with Norjahan, who complained that we never bought her oil any more. One day, I made my way across Beparipara toward Gunjara's house to buy a quantity of oil to take to Dhaka — a purchase I had arranged with Gunjara in advance. First Kia intercepted me, pulled me by the arm into her father's house and insisted that I buy oil from his stock. Then I passed Norjahan standing scowling in her doorway before I finally made it into Gunjara's *bari*. When it came to Taka, it was every woman for herself.

In these two villages, the groups and centers pulled together in unity when their access to loans was at stake. Otherwise, the more primordial loyalties and support networks of family, *gusti* and even *dol* usually took precedence.

In no sense had the center displaced these networks. They were still central to the survival of each woman's family. The sharecropping arrangements and opportunities for daily labour still seemed to follow the old patron-client patterns, except that GB families were now in a position to buy and lease land from their patrons and even lend them money. How this might have changed the basis of the relationship can be illustrated in the life of Swapna.

A woman like Swapna — a young divorcee with a small child and no assets, "returned" by a dissatisfied husband to burden her father, is the bottom of the social heap. Like most women in that position, she went to work as a servant at the house of a landlord, long hours paid only in meals. Now a decade later, the same *borobari* still calls her to "help" in the peak season, but since she is now in a position to refuse, they have to pay her more than her meals — in *maunds* of paddy and a *sari* for each season. This rich household is now her regular customer for milk from the cow she has bought with a GB loan. Before her 1992 general loan was due she borrowed 800 Taka from this landlord to pay her final installments and interest — then she leased in one of his fields for 5,000 Taka with her new loan. The landlord needed the money to repay some of *his* borrowings.

We did not collect systematic information about the relationships between GB families and their *gusti* or to their landlord and political patrons, although incidental evidence, like the above, indicates how fundamentally they are changing. In 1986 a BIDS scholar asked the landlords and *matbar* how they thought the Grameen Bank centers in their villages had affected their relations with their tenants and labourers. One of his findings, that GB members were dropping out of patron-client clusters, contradicts our observation that they were simply turning these relationships to new and more equal uses (Atiur Rahman 1986b). However, an anthropological study on how the presence of Grameen Bank in a village is changing its wider economic and political structures has still to be done.[8]

Politics in the Center

In Ratnogram, the six groups which form the GB center are themselves divided according to *para*. One group is Bepari, which is a caste as well as a geographical area. One is from Khapara, two are from Musjidpara and the other is mixed. The tension between these groups surfaced periodically. When Kia's loan was denied and *before* all the members decided to collectively stop payment, I was cornered in Beparipara by Kia and Norjahan. Gunjara and Parul left the *ghani* and came running. Norjahan's black eyes were blazing and Gunjara was spitting fire.

"The center chief and her members from Musjidpara split the interest money and now a Bepari is getting the blame. That is typical! The power is always with them; the center chief is always from Musjidpara; all the benefits are given to them; the Bank worker sides with them..."

This anger was quickly buried when the center swung behind Kia, but it surfaced again at the end of the year when seasonal loans became available. Both the Bepari group and the Khapara group complained that the center chief was only supporting applications from the two Musjidpara groups and delaying loans from qualified applicants from the other *paras*.

When the Ratnogram center was set up in 1982, it also reflected the factions which existed in the village. All the village studies of Bangladesh indicate that rural society is divided into patron-client clusters, with the poor hitching their survival to a landlord patron who could give them access to work, sharecropping contracts and consumption loans. He needs them, not only for their labour, but for physical security and political support.[9]

In Ratnogram there is one major landlord, M, and his relatives live in various *borobari* in Musjidpara. A woman member of this family, a landlord in her own right, has a large walled compound at one end of Beparipara. The Khans, who came from a neighbouring village around 25 years ago, are involved in legal disputes over land with several members of M's family. Khan's attempts on the land of the woman landlord have led to several violent incidents and house burnings. M was quite supportive of the idea of setting up a GB center in the village ten years ago, and the family of Alia, who was center chief for many years, are among his clients.

None of the poor families associated at that time with the Khans as sharecroppers, labourers or maidservants became members of the center. (Several of them are in our control group.) And, as we have seen above, Khan made claims on the houselot of Alia's family on which the center hut now stands and is still pursuing a legal case to take over the houselot of another GB member.

This standoff is changing, however, as various Khans worm their way into the queue of landowners with their hands out for GB capital by leasing their land to GB members. Two members leased in land from the Khan family during the year, reporting in one case that Khan needed the money for another of his legal battles against M!

However, only Chaina, the widow who works for CARE and who has fought successfully to keep various predators from taking her husband's land, is seen as being part of the Khan *dol*. Chaina is not a "client" of Khan in the same way as three members of our control group — who live in the shadow of his house, labour in his fields and work as servants in his house. Chaina lives in Khapara and married into a *gusti* with several educated and prosperous members, one of whom is now a member of the Union Parishad. But Chaina's struggles to protect her land have forced her to forge alliances outside. Since her brother's death, she has gone to Khan for legal advice and he has become a *"dhormo uncle"* to her son. He has helped her with legal registration of some land lots. And after the raid, when a gang of men forced her son to sign a land transfer form, she has kept her titles in Khan's safe. She borrows, at steep interest rates, from Khan's wife and in the year of data collection, she took an acre of Khan's land to sharecrop.

Chaina is not popular in the center, nor with the Bank worker, and she gets little support from them. Like many survivors, she has no tolerance for the social niceties that paper over the evils done to women like her. She has a sharp and sarcastic tongue. And she has reason to be bitter. One of young men in the gang who tried to force her to give up seven decimals of land, who raided her brother-in-law's house in search of the title and who threatened to return and beat up her 16 year old son, was the son of one of her group members.

I could never decide how much Chaina's isolation in the center was due to her personality and how much to her other allegiances. I heard a number of snide comments about her CARE work and she was criticised for bringing her payment to the center meeting and then leaving for her workplace. Since the meeting often started late and would meander on for a couple of hours, attending all of it would have meant that Chaina missed a day's pay. The fact that the absentee landlord who tried to cheat her out of the seven decimals was able to raise a gang of youths in his support seems to have been related to both her flouting of *purdah* and to her status as a client of the Khans. (Two of M's sons were also in the gang.)

The result was that Chaina's loans were often delayed, despite the fact that she made her repayments regularly and was making very successful use of her loans. At the end of the data collection, more than half the Center had received seasonal loans, but Chaina was still waiting. Chaina cultivated more than an acre of land and depended on these special loans to buy the inputs she needed. Delay forced her to borrow. Since tension with her in-laws made benevolent loans from them impossible, she borrowed from moneylenders at very high rates of interest.

Chaina's case may be unusual. But it does show that loyalty to *dol* can shape a Center and even destroy the unity of a group. There was no solidarity in this group, where the son of one member could threaten the most basic interests of another. This lack of cohesion was reflected in the state of their group fund. None of the members of this group had been able to take group fund loans for over two years, since a third member had failed to settle her group fund loan and was deaf to the pleas of the rest of the group.

Far from Equal

In their recent book on Grameen Bank, Fuglesang and Chandler write:

Throughout the Grameen Bank the prevailing attitude is that the group must progress as a whole. If one member is lagging economically behind and another is forging ahead, the prospering member's loan may be delayed until the others achieve the same standard. ...[Field staff] use every occasion to reinforce the message: 'You must go forward together and help each other.' (1993:100)

This simply does not happen on the ground. The 30 GB families who make up the center did not start as equals. Some inherited a little land and a houselot; others had nothing. Some women had the labour power of several males; others had only themselves. Over the decade of borrowing some had better luck or more acumen. Others fell sick, their cows died, they were robbed, they paid dowries for their daughters. Credit is only one of the resources women use to improve their economic status and women with more resources make faster progress.

Even if it were desirable to hold back someone like Norjahan because she shares a group with someone like Parul (who as an embattled widow with no sons is never going to "forge ahead"), any Bank worker who tried to enforce this kind of idealism would face a revolt from thirty angry women — a *collective* revolt to defend their *individual* interests.

The centers are now quite polarised. As can be seen in the following pie chart, of the 40 GB members in our sample, ten of them earn almost half the total income of the sample. The bottom ten earn less than 10% of the total income. The differences between the top ten and the bottom ten, not only in income, but in housing, food security, prospects for their children and their position of status and respect within the community, are very marked. This polarisation is not caused by the functioning of Grameen Bank credit. The distribution of income amongst the control group, although the total income is much smaller, is similarly skewed. In fact, the share of the pie of each quartile is almost identical with that of the Grameen group.

FIGURE 8.2 Distribution of Income Amongst Grameen Bank Sample (N=40)

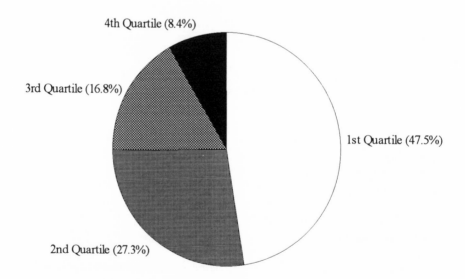

If this polarisation is not caused by credit, it certainly has an impact on the way the center works. In Bonopur the leadership is firmly in the hands of the top few income earners, particularly Habibah, whose attitudes shape both the selection of new members and the treatment of poor members in trouble.

The solidarity of the *bumihin*, the poor, against the *borolok*, the landlords, is not an idea that has any appeal for Habibah. Once when I was checking her various landholdings I joked to her that she was already a *borolok*.

"Of course I'm a *borolok*," she shot back, "and I shall be a bigger *borolok*. I didn't join this Grameen Bank to be poor."

Like many self-made capitalists, Habibah believes that the very poor are lazy, weak and stupid — otherwise they would have made the same progress that she has. This makes her quite intolerant of the less successful members within the center. There were five members in this center who were seriously irregular in their repayments during the year. Most caught up before the 52 week loan period was over by borrowing from outside and making lump payments of their arrears — a practice which depleted their loan capital. Sofiah, the widow and ex-grocer, was the most irregular. Beyond advice to go and borrow from her brother she got little help or support from her group or center. As we saw in Chapter 7, she, her young daughter and 16 year old son undertook no less than 10 different income earning activities during the year. Such was her desperate scramble to feed the family she turned to anything to make a few Taka.

But this is Habibah on the subject of Sofiah:

> The woman is lazy and her son is weak spirited. When she applied for her general loan the Bank worker was reluctant because she is often irregular. But we supported giving her a last chance. Now look at her — she has not paid for five weeks and she is out gleaning again.

When I wanted to include Sofiah in a group discussion held at Habibah's house, Habibah screwed up her face and said flatly:

"Corpse."

Similarly, there was much criticism of Parul in the Ratnogram center, not from her group who helped her the most, but from the other members. I was talking to Swapna, a woman on her own like Parul, but living securely in her father's *bari* and accumulating land for her son to cultivate in the future. Parul has no sons and therefore no secure future and she lives in a threatening environment dominated by her evil-tempered and exploitative brother-in-law. Swapna was describing the strength of her group, and without any prompting from me she brought up Parul as an example of a weak and foolish member. "She just gives her loan to others. Her brother-in-law asks; her sons-in-law ask; she just gives. Nobody else in the center does that."

I asked her what she thought Parul should do and how the center could help her, since everyone in the village knew the character of her brother-in-law.

"She can be strong and refuse. At every center meeting we advise her," came the smug reply. Then, as an afterthought: "When they pressure we are not there, so what can we do?"

In a particularly bad week in Parul's year, she was called to a rich neighbour's house to help fry *murri* (puffed rice), work which would supply her household with this delicacy for a few days. She skipped the center meeting to do this work and sent only half her required payment. In her absence, she came in for a chorus of criticism. It is hard not to sympathise with her when she commented bitterly:

"I have no sons, no husband. I work hard, but they cannot imagine how I have to budget this Taka and what I have to do to get it."

Dropouts and Replacements

Eight members of the Bonopur Center have dropped out since it was formed, most of them during the crisis that almost caused the collapse of the center. As far as we could reconstruct from interviews with Habibah and other members, this is what happened to them. Five of them followed husbands or sons away from the village, sometimes permanently and sometimes for long enough to make the center reluctant to trust them with new loans. One was divorced by her husband and went back to her own village. Two others, both very poor widows, were asked by Habibah to leave because they were irregular in their repayments.

What is interesting is what was done about their arrears. Two of those who left the village had no debt with the Bank. But three very poor members, who could not handle the repayments, arranged with other women to take over their place in the Center — and the payment of their arrears. These new members paid, respectively, 1,128 Taka, 1,200 Taka and 2,200 Taka. The old irregular members paid off their debts to the Bank, clearing the books and then dropped out, leaving the places free for the newcomers. This was a private arrangement in the sense that the debt is still owed by the dropout to the new member. But the center knew and approved it by accepting the new member. One of these arrangements took place during the year of data collection; the others in the preceding year. The current official center chief is one of those who bought her way into the center and is very much a client of Habibah's.

There are still three members on the center's books who long ago dropped out but who still owe money to the Bank. One of them actually came back to the village during the year we were there, after a year in jail on a false murder charge. She begged Habibah to allow her back into the center. Habibah played her along in the faint hope of getting back the interest: 998 Taka that she still owed to the Bank. But Habibah was sure that as soon as the woman's husband, who was also in jail, got out, they would disappear from the village, and she had no intention of letting her back in the center.

Under the Bhidmala (Constitution) of the Grameen Bank, this buying out of defaulting or irregular members is not allowed. If a member drops out without repaying, it is the responsibility of her group to pay what she owes. Only the share in the Bank (each member buys one share in GB worth 100 Taka, which is how the members own the Bank) can be sold by the old member to the center and then resold to a new member. Obviously, getting new members to pay the arrears was more popular with the groups than coughing up the money themselves. But equally obviously, those new members who were able to pay off the arrears of old members could not be from the ranks of the very poor.

Anyway, Habibah's criteria for the selection of new members explicitly excluded the poorest women in the village.

> They should not be landed, but they should have some land — some house land and some vegetable land. They should not be extremely poor. Most important, they should be hard working, not just the wife but also the husband. They should be experienced in goats and poultry and grow some vegetables.

This excludes widows and divorcees, women with sick or foolish husbands, and the completely landless. It is quite some distance from the advice the founder and Managing Director of the Bank, Professor Muhummad Yunus gives to his staff, which is to go to the remotest village and motivate the very poorest women in that village, particularly targeting widows and divorcees. In an old center like this one, where the progress women with credit can make is apparent to the whole village, bank workers do not have to motivate women to join; they are queuing up. Nor do they have to depend on the most desperate women to brave social criticism to join, as they did when GB was new here. GB women have status in the village and the less poor are very keen to join.

Conversations with the Branch staff put them closer to Habibah's definition of the rules. One told me: "We look for people who have some *profession*. They must have a source of business, like trading, or tailoring or cows. Landless, yes; but not *hopeless.*" (Trading and tailoring are male activities in Bangladesh.)

One of the founding principles of group formation in the Grameen Bank is that members should be of the same economic and social status; they should be 'like-minded groups' — and that they should select themselves. This ensures a reasonable level of equality in their dealings with each other. Habibah's criteria for admitting replacement members is in keeping with this principle, except that *she* selects them, and the new members are 'like-minded' with the more successful members, not the bottom quartile.

The three new members who were admitted during the year were all qualified by the rules of the Grameen Bank. None owned more than half an acre of land or other assets to the value of one acre. But they also met Habibah's criteria. One of them was a middle-aged woman with two cows of her own and seven goats that she was share-fattening. They had a 10 decimal houselot and her husband farmed 20 decimals of vegetable land as well as a 15 decimal sharecrop. She had tried to join a new center in the neighbouring village, but since her husband had an outstanding loan with Janata Bank, she was disqualified. Now that the Government had forgiven that loan, she had been lobbying Habibah for a chance to join this center.

"This is a good loan. If I borrow from the moneylender it takes time and quarreling and the interest is high. With this GB Taka I can raise more livestock, make more profit and buy land."

Another, who was in our control group, had few assets — her own houselot, three goats and some chickens. But her husband sharecropped two *bigha* and he was certainly a hard worker; at the end of the year they had a per capita income just above the poverty line, mainly because of his labour. What also tipped the scales in her favour was that she was a childhood friend of Habibah; both of them had *ghor jamai* marriages and grew up in Bonopur.

In 1991 GB Headquarters told its Branch offices that they could expand existing centers from six groups to eight, at their discretion. Bonopur is a large village and there are many more poor households outside the Grameen Bank than there are within it. When we did a rough census of the village in early 1992 to select the control group we counted over 60 households who were very poor, judging by the dilapidated state of their houses. None of these households were members of Grameen Bank. So this center seemed an obvious candidate for the new ruling. But Habibah was dead against any expansion.

"I say we have enough now. Newcomers will only create trouble. Before we had many defaulters, but we overcame that and now our members are good members. We don't want any more problems. If these poor people want to join Grameen Bank they should start a new center," she said. That was the solution that the branch office was considering when we left.

It is probably inevitable that as centers mature and their members become more prosperous they should become less tolerant of the very poor and should be reluctant to admit them to their centers. After the near collapse of this center it is also not surprising that Habibah should be reluctant to have newcomers messing around with the unity and discipline which had been so painfully restored. But however understandable, these attitudes have negative implications for the poverty situation of this village. The members of the Bonopur center, with access to more capital through the seasonal loans, will certainly become more prosperous. If this remains the only center in the village, it will become a privileged club from which the majority of the poor families in the village are excluded.

This would be accentuated if the center drops out its poorest members. We have seen the impatience, even intolerance, with which the few irregular members were treated. Members were not prepared to permanently bail out a member who was not able to generate enough income from her loans to repay regularly. Although Bank officials stressed the obligation of group members to help each other in trouble, they did not expect them to take on the burden of permanently supporting a woman who was incapable of helping herself.

Grameen Bank is not a welfare program. It rests solidly on the ability of poor women to use capital for self-employment to improve their own incomes. It is implicit in the principle that group members select each other, without any intervention by the Bank, that people in the village know who can make good use of credit and will themselves filter out those who are unable to use it. But where does the center — and the Bank — draw the line?

One of the saddest women in our control group sample was a beggar in her early fifties who was once, seven years before, a Grameen Bank member. In a single year she had lost her only son and her husband. All their land had been sold to meet the cost of medicine for her husband before TB killed him. She had always "pipelined" her loans to him. After his death, she withdrew from the center, feeling she could not use the loan herself, a feeling the center shared. But was she truly a welfare case, incapable of using capital? Or could she, once she had got over the shock of two bereavments, have learned to stand on her own feet? And how "voluntary" really was her withdrawal?

The least successful members at the time of our study were the most desperate to retain their membership. I could not foresee that any of them would voluntarily withdraw. Nor do I think that the Ratnogram center, despite its lack of sympathy with Parul, would try to force her, or Rina, to withdraw. In the Ratnogram center, leadership was more diffused and it was not the monopoly of the more prosperous members. Kia led the Bepari group by force of personality although she was still struggling to recover from the illness of her husband and herself. Alia, the ex-center chief, wielded a lot of influence, although she was still poor and herself went into arrears at mid-year.

In the case of Sofiah, however, the Bonopur Center was moving towards shedding her as a problem member they were all quite tired of. Neither Habibah nor Sofiah's group were likely to support her next loan application, and without access to loans there would be little point for her to continue her membership. This, and the criticism of other members, would probably cause her to 'voluntarily' withdraw.'[10]

The implications of that last statement are central to my conclusions in this chapter. If Sofiah cannot get another loan, there is no point her continuing in the center. She belongs to the center in order to get access to credit; it has other functions, but these are peripheral for her. They would not bind her to her group and center once the credit window is closed.

Credit Plus What?

The fundamental meaning of these two centers is not a collective one for their members. They go to the meetings and keep the discipline in order to keep open a regular line of reasonably priced credit. For the same reason, to keep their eligibility for loans, members would help others with repayment, so long as they did not ask too often, and pressure each other to follow the rules and keep the good name of the center. Their purpose is not a group purpose but an individual one, firmly rooted in self-interest and based squarely on their primary loyalty to their immediate family.

These centers are cohesive and self-confident enough to take collective action to protect their access to credit, as they did during the strike, including against the officials of the Bank. The small group of motivators in Bonopur, who were farsighted enough to see what *continued* access to credit would do for their families, were willing to brave criticism and spend a great deal of time to keep the center alive when most members had abandoned it in 1988. The centers are also capable of solving their own problems when these threatened future loans. But I never saw (or heard about) any collective action by either center which was not related to the individual, economic self-interest of its members.

We have seen how the members of a close-knit, warm and supportive group like the Bepari group in Ratnogram split immediately into competing individuals when it came to selling their oil, even though one member desperately needed a market and the others were doing fine. We have seen the limits on how far members are prepared to go to help each other and how they normally turn to their own families for help in a crisis.

The centers also mirror the divisions and factions that exist in the village. This is particularly striking in Ratnogram, where the groups are divided by *para* and caste, and where only the adherents of one *dol* have become members.

Given all this it is difficult to see the centers as a 'people's movement' in the Freire sense. Denied credit, members will drop out. If the loans stopped to the center, it would disintegrate into its separate parts. Despite the social development program, the centers have not developed any agenda beyond credit to individuals that would keep them together.

This is not to say that the Grameen Bank is not having an impact on the local power structure or making quite radical changes in patron-client relations. But I would hypothesis that the changes that are being made in local structures are rooted in the changing economic relationships which tie the patron-client clusters together. It is certainly not my impression that any members saw the center as a 'countervailing power' base for the poor against the landed rural elite, as claimed in the writings of Atiur Rahman (1986a; 1989). Far from showing class loyalty, many GB members aim to become *borolok* themselves. The Bonopur case shows that a long-established center with many members already out of the poverty group, will tend to become exclusive against the demands for entry of the large numbers of poor who remain outside it.

The centers have the organisational potential to act politically as a lobby or a voting block. Grameen Bank headquarters counted 400 GB members who became Union Parishad members during the 1992 elections and centers were encouraged to discuss the local candidates and vote together for the best (or least worst!). But this is a power which I think the women members do not yet see the point of using.

As a 'female solidarity group' these centers are certainly capable of functioning as a collective. But they rarely do, except to protect their loans. Although no such events happened in either center during the year of data collection — nor could members remember any such incident which could be verified — the women claimed in discussions that they would defend each other against violence.

I think in extreme cases of oppression of a woman member — dispossession of her house or land, particularly if it is a GB house, theft of property bought with a GB loan, any attempt to physically drive a widow out of the village or severe physical beating by a husband — the center and the staff of the Bank would come to the defence of their member. This probability no doubt acts as a constraint on husbands, in-laws or landlords prone to this kind of behavior. But I think a more important constraint is the economic resources that GB women have accumulated and the self-confidence that she has developed in her relations with others.

In the day to day negotiations within a marriage or in the interaction between GB families and their *gusti*, the landowners for whom they work or from whom they lease or sharecrop land, the center as a solidarity group has little or no function. As Swapna so aptly put it:

"When they pressure, we are not there. So what can we do?"

The bargaining power that a GB woman has in relation to her husband, or that her family has in relation to the wider family and the village power structure, is an economic empowerment, more than it is a political one arising from the backing of the other 29 women in her center. Although the 40 women in the GB sample are all center members and have equal access to its liberating potential, they are by no means equal in their influence in the household. As we saw in Chapter Four more than two-thirds of the GB women are central or dominant in their households, while a third of them are still marginal in the decision making process. It is the woman's economic contribution to her household, through her loans and what she does with them that explains most of this empowerment — although not all of it.

Similar results have been obtained in a much broader survey which compares the impact of Grameen Bank and BRAC on women in six villages in 1992-93, looking at their level of empowerment (Schuler 1994). In this study, women who were members of the two credit programs scored much better than a control group of non-members on various empowerment measures, including ownership of assets, ability to make independent purchases, decision-making and freedom from beating by their husbands. What is striking about these results is that they show that Grameen Bank members are more empowered on most measures than are BRAC women, despite BRAC's explicit training in consciousness-raising amongst its women members. Grameen women were more likely to own assets and make independent purchases, more involved in household decisions and suffered less beating than similar BRAC women. They were slightly less mobile than BRAC women, and had about the same level of political and legal awareness.

The authors of this study conclude, as I do here, that these differences can be largely explained by the differences in members' contributions to family income. Seventy per cent of the GB members contribute substantially to family income compared to only 39% of the BRAC members and 20% of the non-members in a non-GB village. However, when these authors add economic contribution to their regression analysis, the effect of simply being a member of Grameen Bank declines, but does not disappear. They conclude:

"..credit programs affect women's levels of empowerment by strengthening their economic roles, and in other ways as well." (Schuler and Hashemi 1994:71.)

To get a handle on these "other ways" in which the center works to strengthen women, it is not much use to look at collective actions. This study, like mine, found that collective actions by either GB *or* BRAC women to counter injustices or oppose oppression against women were "extremely rare," although some women were campaigning for candidates in the Union Parishad elections.

What the women themselves talk about when they discuss the impact of center membership is how interaction with other women in the center and their mobility as GB members has made them 'braver' and 'smarter' as individuals. They are 30 women (from the previously powerless poor) who meet weekly in their own center hut and have done so for many years. For most of them it is their only contact with other women outside of the prescribed pecking order of their kin group. At the center they are called by their names. (Within their husband's *gusti* they are known as "so-and-so's *bo*" or "so-and-so's *ma*," their names almost disappear.) They have a separate identity as a group member. They are expected to make loan proposals, defend them, answer questions from male bank workers, and generally speak up for themselves as individuals. It is important to realise that there is no comparable group in the village of any class or sex, except for occasional meetings of the male *matbar* in the *shalish*. Although some women are more dominant in the center than others, both in terms of their personality and their economic status, these women have emerged from the ranks of the poor. They are not automatic leaders by virtue of being wives of the rural elite.

Center meetings are not particularly participant; they are generally pretty tedious, as money is counted and recounted and entries made manually into passbooks. But they involve a ritual of saluting, sitting in rows and chanting slogans which binds the women into the group and gives the meeting a feeling of legitimacy. Schuler and Hashemi comment:

> Grameen Bank's weekly meetings, the chanting, saluting and other rituals are important in creating an identity for women outside of their families... The program gives women socially legitimate reasons to move about and to associate with one another in public spaces... Ironically, Grameen Bank's more regimented approach appears to be more effective than BRAC's in strengthening women's autonomy. (1994:73)

Many observers have commented on the self-confident body language of GB women compared to other women in the village. And it is easy to spot a GB woman by her erect posture and direct look, a posture enforced by the saluting ritual, just as you can tell a non-Grameen woman by the way she chews the end of her *sari* when you ask her a question.

The center meetings have an important social meaning to most of the members. Many of the women told me that they felt 'uneasy' and 'lonely' if they missed a meeting. And although it often took the whole day to walk to the branch office and back for a loan disbursement, for the member herself or in support of one of her group, I noticed how most relished this chance to go to town and talk with GB members from other villages. Sometimes the group would venture further, into the shops that sold cloth, thread and household utensils, although they never went into the *haat*. On the nights after these visits they would be the center of attention as the extended family sat around eating *paan* and listened while they told 'Bank stories.'

When I analysed the mobility of the Grameen Bank members compared to the control group, just looking at visits to kin outside the village (usually visits to their natal village) there is not much difference between the two groups. GB women averaged four trips to visit relative outside the village during the year. The control group visited more; an average of 4.7 trips, partly because there were several very poor women who constantly visited their fathers or brother's houses for food. But when I looked at all visits, including those to the branch office and other public institutions, the GB members made an average of 10 trips outside, compared to only 5.5 by the control group. The exposure and self-confidence that these outside experiences give to GB women is one of the factors behind their direct look and ability to speak out.

Termites in the House

What we found in these two villages are two groups of women, the majority of whom are empowered as individuals principally because of their economic contribution to their families, and to a lesser extent through their greater freedom of movement and interaction with other women in the center. We did not find that they were empowered through collective action. In addition, a broader study than ours asking similar questions has found that GB women are more empowered than BRAC members, which explicitly aims at empowerment through training women to recognise and oppose male oppression.

The findings of another study called "Who Takes The Credit," (Goetz forthcoming) which looks into whether women retain control of their loans, makes a similar discovery. This study found that Grameen Bank women are more likely to use their loans themselves or at least to retain significant control over them, than are women in BRAC, Thangemara Mohila Sebuj Sengstha (TMSS) or the RD-12 component of the Government's Rural Poverty Program. This study found that 62% of the GB women retained full or significant control over their loans and only 10% had only limited or no control. Only 28% of the BRAC women (N-106) retained significant or full loan control, while 45% had only limited or no control. In other words, Grameen women have more power to protect their loans against males in the family.

The findings of this study seem out of line with both its ideological position, which is critical of the minimalist approach and the rapid expansion of credit to women, and its recommendations, which are more training, more literacy classes, more technical support, access to markets for women, collective enterprises and measures to guarantee women's ownership of productive assets. Only the last seems to me to have any value in enhancing women's control, although all of them together would certainly slow down the expansion of credit opportunities to poor women.

Of the two approaches discussed earlier in this chapter — the minimalist credit approach of Grameen Bank and the more integrated, consciousness-raising approach of most other NGOs, it seems that credit alone is more effective in empowering women within their families. Outside of the family, neither GB nor BRAC, according to the Schuler/Hashemi study, has succeeded in mobilising solidarity groups into collective action, against either the class enemy — the rural elite, or the gender enemy — the patriarchy.

In terms of poverty alleviation and the individual empowerment of women this is a very significant discovery. The minimalist approach is cheaper than any method which combines credit with training. It has a more rapid economic impact on the individual member and it enables the organisation to reach much larger numbers of poor women at less cost than integrated programs. This is why Grameen Bank has so far reached two million families, with 94% of its members women, while BRAC has reached half a million women, over a longer time period.

If we look at the wider social structures which oppress women and destroy choice, they all seem quite intact. Patrilocy and early marriage still send young brides into strange villages on the lower rungs of hierarchical households. Law and practice limit their ownership of property. Husbands are always older, usually more educated and can divorce their wives at the drop of a *talak*. Domestic violence still exists. The dowry system makes daughters an economic burden. Public spaces and institutions — the *shalish*, the mosque, the bazaar and the *haat* — are off-limits to women. In terms of the feminist ideology, if the centers are not the kind of solidarity groups that seek to confront and overturn these structures, they cannot bring about fundamental change for women.

But they have. In the area where women live out their lives — their *bari;* in the relationships which are crucial to their welfare — their marriages and kin groups, Grameen Bank women have become powerful enough to protect their own interests and those of their children. Within their families, these women *have* undermined the patriarchal structures which threaten them, in ways I have described in previous chapters. Increasing numbers own the family home, for example; they negotiate land leases and jointly decide on how household earnings should be spent. They eat together with their husbands; they send their daughters to school and walk through the village chaperoned only by their GB passbooks to attend meetings. But they work more like termites than through the tidal wave of collective action. They are adept at using traditional levers to legitimise these non-traditional actions.

GB women work through negotiation and subterfuge because they are negotiating about power. Authority, which resides in village institutions like the *shalish* and is sanctioned by the village practice of Islam, still wears a male face. But in fact and practice the power of termites is hollowing out male authority in the household.

Notes

1. The field workers of the Grameen Bank are the lowest level of the Bank hierarchy and its main contact with the two million members of the Bank. The next level up — the graduate-level officers of the Bank, branch managers, program officers and area managers, are often in the field. But a branch services 50 centres and an area office 500 centres. So any one centre will see a Bank officer rarely. (The Ratnogram centre was visited once to my knowlege by the branch manager in the course of the year, in response to the strike.) The main contact between the centre and the Bank staff is through the field worker. He attends the weekly centre meeting, takes the collected payments back to the branch office, processes the loan proposals and is responsible for the loan utilisation checks. See Holcombe 1995 for an analysis of the personnel policies of the Bank.

2. This solution was certainly helped by the practice of transferring Bank workers fairly frequently, usually after one year. This limits his closeness to the members he serves, but it also puts a severe limit on all kinds of natural evils, like favouritism and corruption. While the practice described here was not corrupt, it was certainly improper, and in the end created more problems than it solved.

3. It is customary to ask forgiveness for any wrong you might have done when you are saying goodbye.

4. At the height of the flood, Khatimon, who was around six months pregnant, started bleeding. Her husband managed to get her by boat to the main road where he intended to take her to the hospital in Mymensingh, in the next district. That was impossible, the

transport system had collapsed. They got as far as the bus station at Modhupur, but by this time Khatimon was almost unconcious from loss of blood. Here Kajul, the Branch Manager, spotted them and took them immediately to a mission hospital in Modhupur, where Khatimon was treated and recovered.

5. The male centre, established before the womens' centre, took a collective loan to buy a shallow tube well. They fell out over its management and finally sold the well, divided the proceeds and then absconded. Most people in the village expected GB to withdraw in the face of that setback.

6. These figures are important because Shelley Feldman in *Report to the Like-Minded Group* (North-South Institute 1985, 1990) keeps repeating the accusation that Grameen Bank reinforces the ideology that womens' economic activities are secondary by giving larger loans to male members. This did not have much substance even when it was first made in 1984; male members had larger loans then mainly because they were older members. The preponderance of women makes the argument irrelevant now. The individual woman and her group decides the loan size, within a ceiling set by the Bank, which rises with each year of membership. The fact that women are more cautious makes them better borrowers and has ensured that they can repay and sustain their membership over time — which has not been the case for many earlier male members.

7. This manual is reproduced in Fuglesang, 1993:274.

8. See Gibbons forthcoming, on the flow of capital, through leasehold, from GB members *largely* to middle or large farmers, a reversal of the pattern described by Jansen a decade earlier. The political implications of this change must be considerable and are still not explored.

9. The most useful account I found of the interlocking interests involved and how they have changed since Liberation is Shakeeb Adnan Khan 1989.

10. I would assume a tendency for older Centres to shed their least successful members. These members, who are still very poor, are no longer of equal status with women who have been able to use their loans to escape out of the poverty group. If they are irregular in repayment they threaten the access of their fellow group members to new loans. Statistics of the overall drop-out rate within the Grameen Bank show a rising number of dropouts from 5% in 1985 to 15% in 1991, but the dropout rate is higher amongst centres which are less than three years old (Khandker 1995:60-62).

9

Centered on the Children

> Poor women have an intense drive to move up; they are hard working, concerned about their human dignity; concerned about their children's present and future, willing to make personal sacrifices for the well-being of the children. In Grameen Bank, with 74% [now 94%] of our borrowers being women, we find it much more easy to address a whole gamut of social and economic issues with a high level of effectiveness. (Yunus 1989:48)

Senior officers in the Grameen Bank (and the Grameen Bank replicators in other parts of Asia) make no bones about the usefulness of targetting women in order to improve the welfare of the family as a whole, particularly the children. Women's centeredness on their family and children is fully exploited in GB's motivation work, reinforced in their training and in the workshop program and enshrined in the 16 Decisions. A GB replicator in the Philippines, describing motivation work there, recently wrote: "We talk about their dreams for their children. Teardrops fall, and we know that the first battle is already won." (FAXNET 8)

The success of GB is, in part, dependent on the self-discipline women cultivate when they deny themselves food, do without warm clothing and put all their energies into the welfare of their families. It is these "virtues" which ensure that the loans are not squandered on consumer luxuries or blown in teashops, but secured into assets. It is this discipline which carries over into the weekly routine of attending meetings and making repayment. It is this self-abnegation which ensures that the income generated by their loans goes immediately into better food, better health, clothing and shelter for their children. There is no guarantee that putting money into the hands of fathers would have the same result.[1]

Nor would any of the women in our sample have any quarrel with this approach. They are maternal altruists to the last woman. I quickly discovered that there was no point looking for any cracks in the *ideology* of maternal self sacrifice. What I needed to look at were the *practices* that were bathed in this virtuous glow, but which actually worked against the interests of the women and their girl children, and see if they were changing. We also needed to test the assumption that putting credit in the hands of women would improve the welfare of their children, by seeing if there were measurable differences between the Grameen children and the children of the control group in terms of health and education.

We devised a health survey to gather information on maternal health and the health care of children. We measured the children under ten to get indicators of their nutritional status. We enquired into food entitlements and contraception and the education of girls and boys. Finally, we held a series of group discussions on the contentious issues of schooling, marriage and dowry to get some insight into how attitudes as well as practices were changing amongst the Grameen women.

Taller and Fatter

As the easiest way to measure nutritional status, we measured the heights and weights of all the children born to Grameen Bank mothers during the time they had been members of the Bank and compared them to same age children in the control group. The detailed results are in Appendix 2. There were 68 children aged ten and under in our sample of 62 households; 40 amongst the Grameen Bank families and 28 in the control group. The numbers in each age cohort are too small to be statistically significant, but the tendency we discovered went in the expected direction. The Grameen children are a little bit taller and quite a lot heavier on average than the children in the control group. When we compared these measurements with the international standards used by the World Health Organisation for children in the same age groups, both groups still look nutritionally deprived, although the GB children are better off than the control group children.

What surprised us was that the Grameen Bank children turned out to be slightly taller and heavier than the average Bangladeshi child of the same age. The country-wide nutritional survey done by the Bangladesh Bureau of Statistics (1991) covers all income groups and all areas of Bangladesh and finds that the higher the per capita income of the family the less likely are their children to be malnourished. The poor score lower on all measures than the non-poor and the rural poor lowest of all. But our sample of Grameen children, who come from families who were, pre-Grameen, in the poorest rural group, are now nutritionally better off than the national average.

This can be explained, partly, in terms of income. Grameen families earn more on the whole than the control group and so have more resources to spend on better food. These resources are also augmented by the Bank in very concrete and practical ways as part of the process of implementing its Sixteen Decisions.

But this explanation — more Taka, better food, healthier children — goes only half way towards understanding why the Grameen children are nutritionally better off than the national average. What is crucial to the welfare of these children is that at least part of this income is in the hands of the mother and that she has a powerful voice in deciding *how* the resources of the household should be used. This enables her to direct the benefits of better income to the welfare of those who matter most to her — to her children.

A Question of Control

During the year, the son of one of our Grameen members died. When we left, the son of a control group family was on the point of dying. A look at these two families, at their response to illness and at the role of the mother in the management of the illness, is instructive in showing this crucial difference between the Grameen mothers and the mothers in the control group.

All the time we were working in Bonopur taking the measurements of the children, Faruq, the son of Sobhan and his second wife, was lying outside his grandmother's house on a mat, too wasted to stand.

The father of this family, a landless labourer, has three wives. The first and her children were long ago discarded and driven out of the village. The second also left — but after a year of starving in her natal village where her eldest daughter died, she returned with her remaining three children and moved in with Sobhan's mother. The third wife, Moriom, the one currently in use, was enticed away from her first husband by Sobhan about four years ago, with two children from that marriage (the daughter subsequently drowned in a pond). The real attraction, by Moriom's own account, was a nest-egg of 4,000 Taka she had saved and which Sobhan quickly found and stole. She now has two more children by Sobhan, one born during the year we were there.

Faruq, the eldest son of the second wife, was seven years old and 99 cm high — the height of an average five year old in Bangladesh. But he weighed only 13 kgs — under the WHO standard that is the weight of an average two year old. His middle upper arm circumference was a mere 9.6 cm, well below the cutoff point of 12.5 cm for serious malnourishment. But one did not have to measure Faruq to see he was close to death. What flesh he had was stretched over the frail bones of his shoulders and all his upper ribs stood up through the skin. His belly was swollen to balloon size. His mother lifted him onto a stool to feed him and the bones in his backside were as sharp as knives.

"He has been sick like this — all puffed up — for two months. I begged my husband again and again to call a doctor, but he said 'No Taka.' He brought some medicine from town but it had no result," Faruq's mother said. (This means that Sobhan went to a quack doctor with a private pharmacy, described the symptoms and got some syrup and pills, which is cheaper than going to an MBBS-trained doctor.)

The next time I went to the house Faruq was lying on the ground completely covered by an old *lunggi*. There was an ajitation amongst the women. His mother uncovered his head and I saw that all the flesh had dropped back against the bones of his face. I thought that he was dead. His mother crushed an onion in her fingers and mixed it with a drop of mustard oil and rubbed it around his nostrils. Faruq twitched slightly and lapsed back into unconsciousness. His mother covered his head with the cloth to keep the flies off him and sat over him crying.

A week later I went back with a government doctor.

He has kwashiorkor. This is the end result of a long process of insufficient food leading to protein deficiency. That makes him vulnerable to diarrhoea and respiratory infections which further weakens him, until now he is deficient in almost every body building nutrient. With proper feeding he could be on his feet in three weeks — with tube feeding even faster. But we don't have the facilities here; only in Dhaka.

Faruq turned his head and stared at the man talking this strange language. The doctor pressed the swollen tissues on his legs, leaving the clear imprint of his fingers behind. Then Faruq coughed and cried in distress as the doctor sat him up.

We filled his prescription for injectable saline and vitamin and mineral supplements at a private pharmacy and left them with the Union Member to supervise the injections. We also left cash with him to cover the cost of the milk, eggs and fish that Faruq needed. It was not that we did not trust the mother to care for her own child. But we knew from previous events and from a year of observation that she simply did not have the networks to organise the injections, nor could she protect any cash or goods we left with her from falling into Sobhan's hands. Filling the prescription cost 330 Taka — a small sum which the mother had no earthly hope of raising.

As we left the village with the doctor, we stopped at the third wife, Moriom's house to look at Faruq's two year old step-brother, Fazlul. He weighed 8 kg, only 60% of the WHO reference weight; his arm measurement was 12.4; his stick-like legs could barely hold up his pot belly. He was wasted — his weight for height was only 82% of the reference.

"He's got worms. They've probably *all* got worms. They all have to take tablets or he will just get reinfected. It's just *ignorance*," the doctor said, irritated.

It is more than that. Faruq's elder sister had died a year earlier, after an illness which followed the same pattern. The chances of any of these children getting the high protein diet they need to recover from recurrent attacks of worms, diarrhoea and respiratory infections, is almost non-existent, when Sobhan's family have for years been living on the edge of starvation. This family was so chronically short of food that they made no attempt to stock it. Sobhan simply bought 2.5 kilo of rice each day that he had work. He gave 1kg to his second wife and her three children and 1.5 kg to his third wife, Moriom, and her two children. He ate with Moriom. He and his brother each gave 7.5 kg a rice per month to their mother. When he had no work and. could not borrow, he bought no rice and the entire family of nine members starved.

The minimal grain needs for the four adults and five children (6 after Moriom's baby was born) in this family were 22 kgs per week. Their average consumption was 17.5 kg a week. Apart from chillies and salt, Sobhan rarely bought anything else for his two wives. They scrounged for cauliflower stalks in the winter and wild leaves in the summer. They ate fish occasionally, and meat once a year.

It is impossible to really understand the suffering caused to these three women by this routine, long-term deprivation of food. What can be seen and measured was what it was doing to the children. When I pick up Fazlul, one of the few children in the village passive enough to allow me to do so, he is pitifully easy to carry. Although he is nearly three, he is as soft and clingy as a baby.

Neither of Sobhan's wives have any control over the family income. Moriom told me bitterly, shortly after giving birth:

> Anything I could do to make income, if it produces Taka, he will take it. He is a bastard. [She uses a word so crude that Nahar refuses to translate it.] If I have money in my hand and he divorces me, then I would survive. But if he divorces me now, I cannot live on this earth.

Sobhan's drop into the ranks of the extremely poor, dragging his two families with him, is a familiar enough story. But what was really killing Faruq, his sister before him, and also threatening Moriom's two year old, was not just the lack of Taka for food. It was the helplessness of the women to exercise any control over how the resources of the household should be used. In the same week that we took the doctor to examine Faruq, and gave money to the Union Member to provide special food to the dying child, Sobhan got back 800 Taka from his moneylending three months earlier. The original money had come from selling the remaining two decimals of his mother's land — illegally, without her consent, to a thug in the village who was willing to protect his purchase by force. Sobhan spent this 800 Taka on a calf, which he gave to Moriom to fatten.

Several Grameen women are married to feckless or incapable husbands, and some have no husbands at all, but all of them have some income as well as access to loans for emergencies. They have the power to direct this income to the welfare of their children. It is impossible to imagine a Grameen child dying, like Faruq, of starvation and neglect, without treatment, while the mother knelt over him weeping helplessly like Sobhan's second wife.

On the other side of the village, in a *bari* busy with cows and ducks, lives Eliza, a Grameen Bank member whose two year old son died in June of the year of data collection. When he was seven days old he had a kind of seizure and ever since he had suffered from water retention and had failed to grow properly, Eliza said. Eliza took him regularly to a private doctor in Gopalpur and was spending 50 to 60 Taka a week on various medicines during the months that we were recording her expenditure. This Western doctoring was backed up by herbal treatments from the *kobiraj* (homeopathic doctor) and spiritual help from the *hujur* (spiritual healer who recites verses from the Koran and blows "whew"). There was not a single medical practitioner of any kind in the area that Eliza had not tried several times. In May when the child's condition worsened, Eliza got our research assistant, the bank worker, the branch manager and the area manager all involved in the effort to save his life. After visiting her house, they authorised a group fund loan of 2,000 Taka and arranged for the child to be admitted to Modhupur hospital. He improved for a few weeks and then suddenly he died. Eliza grieved; but at least she knew that the child had not died of neglect or lack of treatment.

Eliza's household's annual income puts them just below the poverty line. But Eliza holds the cash income from their vegetable land, her milk and egg sales and her husband's rickshaw driving and the couple decide together how it should be spent. Neither of Sobhan's wives have any access to the cash he earns and they have no earnings of their own.

Eliza's other children are healthy. They are a little short for their age, but their weight for height is within the normal range. When her middle son developed the swollen belly and pain that indicates worms, she took him to the government hospital in Gopalpur for the necessary medicine and he was cured. Her four year old daughter is so plump with well-being she looks as though she has been patted together out of chocolate butter.

When I ask Eliza if she thinks boys need more food than girls, she looks at her daughter, who is sitting on the bed stuffing her face with *murri,* and she laughs.

"Girls should be fed *more* than boys," she replies. "Later they will go and live in another house and they may not get enough. So now I feed her as much as she can eat."

Eliza also looks after herself. After her son died, she "forgot" to take her contraceptive pills and now she is pregnant again. She eats strengthening food in preparation for this new child — milk from her own cow, vegetables from her own large garden and fish. "Especially I eat *saak* (spinach). That is the best food. I heard that at the workshop."

Nearby, her neighbour and fellow center member Halimah, has also done her

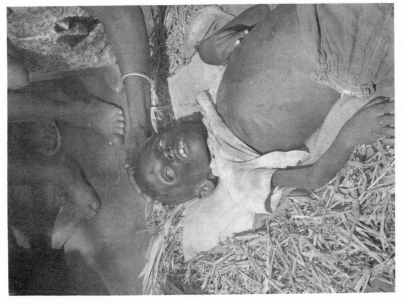

Faruq (right) close to death after years of inadequate food and lack of medical treatment. In Ratnogram (left) healthy children of Grameen Bank members helping with the goats and going to school.   *Photo Credits: Helen Todd; Nurjahan Chaklader*

share of grieving over lost children. She has had six children, all before she joined the Bank, and three of them died. One died of tetanus after 7 days, a common fatality caused by cutting the cord with unsterile equipment. Another died at three years from diarrhoea and wasting. The third child died suddenly of a fever.

"None of them got treatment from the doctor, because we were too poor. Sister, I tell you, if we had Grameen Bank Taka at that time, my children would not have died."

Four years ago, Halimah's husband contracted TB. The complete course of treatment cost them 9,000 Taka. But they were able to raise these funds by taking two general loans (Halimah's husband is also a GB member) and a group fund loan and by selling part of their houselot. Her husband was completely cured. He is now a successful trader and the family is well out of the poverty group. Without access to the GB funds for his treatment, Halimah would probably be today a widow.

The Health Environment

Our health survey showed that the 62 families in our sample experienced a great deal of serious and/or chronic illness and spent substantial amounts of their income on medical treatment. The illnesses which had resulted in death or illness severe enough to almost bankrupt the family included TB, typhoid, jaundice and gastric ulcer. Diarrhoea, associated with wasting, was a widespread killer of children. Many of the women in Ratnogram had goitre. As I have shown in Chapter 6, illness was a major reason many Grameen families were still in the poverty group. On the whole, however, the Grameen families enjoyed access to better health care and lived in healthier surroundings than did families in the control group. In this, the dissemination of information about nutrition and hygiene through the workshop program and the 16 Decisions seems to have played a motivating role.

Doctors and Quacks

In this area of Tangail there exists a suprising wealth of medical expertise. Every three months in Bonopur the Union Member's house becomes a clinic, staffed by three government doctors, who immunise children and offer various forms of family planning and prenatal care. Children who need it get worm treatment. As a result, children are immunised and tetanus and eclampsia is much less the killers of women and their new-born children than they used to be.

In Ghatail and Gopalpur, there are district hospitals with large staffs of qualified doctors. There are also private MBBS trained doctors in both towns. By the standards of the village poor, however, these services are expensive. Since government hospitals have minimal supplies of drugs, government doctors can do little but write prescriptions which their patients fill at private pharmacies at their own expense. As a result, poorer families often go directly to the pharmacies and get their diagnosis and advice from the shopkeeper or *huturi* (quack) doctor that runs them. Or they save money by buying only a half course of the prescribed drug. Our survey showed that GB members were more likely to consult private MBBS doctors for most illnesses, despite the expense. The control group more often went to the cheaper *huturi* doctors. Of the GB families who were admitted to hospital during the year, all bypassed the government hospitals and went to a private hospital in Modhupur.

Training Through the Sixteen Decisions

The constant reiteration of the 16 Decisions and their dissemination through the workshop program of the Bank has had an impact on the health environment of the Grameen families. Seven of the 16 Decisions, which sum up the social development program of the Bank, aim to improve the health of the member's family. (The full text of the Sixteen Decision is in Appendix 3.) They are:

* living in weatherproof houses
* growing vegetables and eating them
* planting fruit and nut trees
* drinking tube-well water
* using pit latrines
* planning for small, healthy families
* keeping children and their surroundings clean

These are concrete and practical objectives and GB women are largely implementing them, as shown in Table 9.1. All of the families in both of the villages under study have access to tube-well water for drinking, although some women have to walk further to get it than others. Those families who have their own tube-well in the *bari* also use it for washing clothes, preparing food and for bathing, all of which are more hygienic than bathing in the village ponds.

GB women have other advantages in the implementation of these decisions. Most GB members own their own houselots and these are generally larger than those of the control group families, which makes it feasible for them to plant vegetables and fruit trees. The Bank also gives practical help to members to encourage them to implement these decisions, most notably, the housing loan. Members in good standing can borrow up to 25,000 Taka to build a large, simple but sturdy house, supported by flood-proof cement pillars and covered with a tin roof. It is spacious, dry and easy to keep clean. Members who take a housing loan are required to purchase along with it the cement parts of

Table 9.1   Implementation of Health-Related 16 Decisions

Item	GB (N=24)	Control (N=16)
Drinking Tube-Well Water	100%	100%
Using Sanitary Latrines	21%	0%
Growing Vine Vegetables (*lau/sim*)	96%	63%
Growing Field Vegetables (*begun/saak*)	50%	6%
Practicing Family Planning	78%	85%
Children Immunised	85%	65%
Av. No. Trees Planted	11	3

a sanitary latrine, still a strange and unnecessary piece of equipment in the minds of most villagers.

GB women can get a special tube-well loan to install this essential source of clean water in their own *bari*. The Bank distributes vegetable seeds to members at one Taka a packet and also tree seedlings. Workshop participants are often given gifts of seeds, tree seedlings or iodised salt to take back to their villages.

The results of our survey into the implementation of the health-related Decisions (Table 9.1) shows wide differences between the different decisions as well as between the Grameen families and the control group. All drank tube-well water. However, sanitary latrines were unknown amongst the control group. The only Grameen families who had them were those who had taken housing loans and had been required to buy them.

Growing vine vegetables, like marrows and pumpkins, over the house or over trellises inside the *bari* is very common in the villages. All but one of the GB families grew them, but only 63% of the control group families, mainly because several did not own their houselots.

But growing green vegetables and crops like brinjals or tomatoes is rare amongst the control group, although half the Grameen families grew them. The difference in cultivating fruit and nut trees is equally striking. The control group women could point to an average of only three trees planted in the last five years. The GB women had planted an average of 11 trees in the same period.

As we have seen, everyone in Bonopur has an immunisation service on their doorsteps and a doctor coming to the house every three months to check that the children are getting their injections. All the relevant age children of GB members were immunised, and all but one of the control group households. In Ratnogram, where children had to be taken to another village for immunisation, 85% of the GB children were covered but only 43% of the control group children.

Contraceptive Choice

It seems odd that more control group women are using contraception than GB women. But the results are skewed by the fact that many of the older women are firmly convinced that large families are an excellent thing. These women are overrepresented in our small GB sample. This is because many of the over 40 Grameen women have husbands and so got asked about contraception. Most of the older women in the control group are widows and were not asked. The control group, on this issue, was a younger, and so more family planning-oriented group.

It helps that all women in both villages have access to contraception devices of several kinds, including ligation and menstrual regulation, if they want it. Knowledge about contraception is almost universal amongst the women. The regular presence of family planning workers in villages where you almost never see any other kind of government extension officer is a striking witness to the single-minded preoccupation of Western aid agencies with limiting the fertility of Bangladeshi women.

The rates of contraceptive use in these two villages, amongst both GB and control groups are much higher than the national average of 38.5%. Two recent, broad-ranging studies have shown significantly higher contraceptive use amongst GB members, at 53%, than amongst a matched control group, at 36%, and an even higher use — 63% — amongst long-term borrowers (Kamal 1992). The second study linked contraceptive use strongly with empowerment and found that GB women had higher rates of use than women in villages where GB did not operate. There was little difference between the BRAC women and the comparison group.

What is interesting about this study, since it probably partly explains the very high prevalence of contraceptive use in our two villages, is their finding that non-members living in GB villages *also* had high rates of use. They describe this as:

...a diffusion effect, the result of changing fertility norms in Grameen Bank villages. ... When women see others using contraceptive methods, their fear of serious side-effects and of being criticised for violating social norms is reduced. In addition, when more women use contraceptives, women who would like to use them are more likely to know someone who could help them get access to methods. (Schuler 1994:73)

I was mainly concerned about whether the women were able to decide for themselves how many children they wanted and when. I was also looking for women who wanted no more children, but who were unable to use contraception because their husbands or in-laws opposed it on religious or customary grounds.

Of the 32 still married women of reproductive age in the sample, there were only two who had no control over their reproductive lives. One was Moriom, Sobhan's third wife, the mother of the seriously malnourished boy the doctor said had worms. Her lack of control over her fertility is of a piece with her complete lack of control over the family budget and her inability to earn even the smallest income. She had an older son from her former marriage, the malnourished boy just mentioned and a baby son born during the year of data collection. The baby was an accident, she said. Since she was still breast-feeding the second son, she thought she would not conceive. She wanted a ligation after the second son was born, but Sobhan would not agree.

The other was Naila in Ratnogram, a woman in her mid-thirties who already had seven children and was pregnant again with number eight. Four of these children had died in infancy, two of tetanus, one of cholera and the latest, "very small," slipped away after two days. She had also had two spontaneous abortions at very late stages of pregnancy. She looked anaemic and worn out. She had a wheezing cough the entire time we knew her and she shivered as she sat in the winter sunshine. When she discovered she was pregnant with this one, she wanted to go to the district hospital for an abortion, but her husband hit her when she brought it up. The year before she had arranged to go for a ligation, but her husband found out beforehand. He beat her severely and locked her in the house. Nor will he allow her to take the Pill.

"He just gives me a baby every year. He doesn't know how to prevent it and he is not interested," Naila wheezes.

"Don't worry," comments her sister in law. "This baby will be born and then it will die. It comes to the same thing in the end."

At this, tears start leaking zigzag down the weary folds of Naila's face.

"An abortion worries his Islamic mind, but he doesn't worry how we can manage these children or how my health is destroyed." She coughs, gasping for breath.

But Naila is a rarity — so much so that the black comedy of her sex life (he's crazy about it; she isn't; their arguments break up the night) is the subject of ribald comment, including to me. It seemed that most women were in control of their reproductive lives. This was true for both Grameen and control groups. Contraception seemed to be an area where the women's networks were more powerful than husband's rights. When we asked who decided about contraception, most women said it was decided together with their husbands. But when we asked about the process of getting information and deciding which method to use, it was almost always the woman who took the initiative, through women relatives, and then talked to her husband and got his agreement. Daria, in the control group, who has two children out on labour contracts and another two at home, and who has very little say in her household, had a copper T fitted after her last child.

I talked to my sister and mother in law and the family planning worker about the different methods. I am afraid to have a ligation, because if you are not complete after death you cannot be accepted by God. The pill gives me a headache. The family planning worker told me about the copper T, so I decided on that. I discussed with my husband, but he is not an educated man; he doesn't know much. He just said: 'If you think it is better, then you do it.' So I went to the health center and had it done.

There were several GB women and their husbands who were opposed to ligation on religious grounds, and who suffered side effects from the pill. But this seemed to be a shared belief and these women did not have to suffer annual unwanted pregnancies as a result, like Naila. One couple used the rhythm method and another condoms, both of which required the cooperation of the husband.

Several of the older GB women were opposed to the whole concept of small families. Banu, one of the most successful Grameen borrowers, is a family planner's nightmare. "Children are my prosperity," she says calmly. She is right. She has had 12 children, of whom eight survived their infancy. Her two elder daughters work in Chittagong and regularly send money home to their mother to invest. They are also putting their younger brother through college in that city. Two grown sons live at home, farm the land and do daily labour, putting their earnings into her hand. The two younger boys go diligently to school and then gather grass for the cows.

"Many children are needed for a family. I had children until I naturally stopped. My husband agrees with me."

Where there were acknowledged disagreements on the issue of family planning, it concerned the method and the timing, rather than contraception itself. There were three women in the control group who went ahead and had ligations although their husbands were opposed to it. (Not violently, like Naila's husband.) And there were several busy Grameen women who wanted to delay a third child, over their husband's protests.

Zarinah, the ambitious young woman who pushed for the purchase of a *bigha* of land during the year, is taking the pill. She has two sons. They both want a daughter, but Zarinah has too much to do right now. "He gets angry when I take the pill. He wants a daughter now." The card of pills is lying openly on the table though, in full view.

When I asked Fodzilla about contraception, her husband was there, although I had warned him about the subject matter. They have two children, a boy and a girl. The youngest is eight. "I think it's enough, but my husband wants more, so we will have one more," she says, smiling at him her wide and beautiful smile. "But not now," she continues and she takes the card of pills out of her trunk to show me. Where does she get them? *He* buys them for her, in Gopalpur.

Food Entitlements

Although we have data on the household consumption of food, we did not measure the amount of food consumed per day by individual members of the household, so we have no physical measure of discrimination in the feeding of women or their girl children. What I did try to discover through systematic questioning was whether the attitudes and practices which lie behind unequal entitlements to food were changing as a result of the increased economic contribution of Grameen women.

Food is a loaded issue in every culture; no less so in Bangladesh. For example, it is customary for a man to eat first, and to be given the best that is available, and for his wife to eat last and get the leftovers. In a food-scarce household this guarantees that the woman gets less than she needs. But I quickly got the impression that this custom was beginning to break down amongst the Grameen families, at least, and probably in general amongst the nuclear families of the poor. I was alerted to this change by some Grameen women who described their caring relationships with their husbands in terms of food. They said things like:

He always calls me to eat together with him.
We share the food equally. Although I try to give him more, he refuses to accept it.
I try to put more on his plate, but he says all should eat together and eat the same.

I thought that all these were ways of saying: "My husband loves me."

On the other hand, on any more formal occasion, like the visit of a male relative, custom ruled; the wife would never sit and eat with her husband. And once when I was talking about this to a woman in the control group, her husband scolded her:

"Don't tell sister we eat together. She will think we are shameless!"

Since the custom of women eating last is so basic to their unequal entitlement to food, I decided to systematically question the women about how the main meal of the day — the evening meal — was organised. These are the results. Of the Grameen women questioned 68% usually ate together with their husbands. In the control group 27% usually ate together with their husbands.[2]

Eating together does not mean, of course, eating the same. But it seems more likely to be the case, particularly as the sharing of the meal and pressing each other to eat more are seen as acts of love and caring on the part of *both* husband and wife.

But it is precisely because food carries this baggage of love around with it that women deny themselves food when there is not enough. The same women who admitted proudly that their husbands insisted they eat together were equally insistent that if there was not enough food she should eat less. This was not usually justified in terms of the husband's needs, but almost always in terms of the children.

> If I take more, my children will have less.
> If my children eat well it is as though I am eating myself.
> If there is not enough, who do *you* think should eat less? In our society the mother gives up her share to the children. That is our custom and it is good.

The Grameen women who did eat last were generally the older and more traditional women or they were in households where food was often insufficient. Rina, whose husband has eczema and cannot work, and whose family is one of the poorest in the GB group, told me they ate together when there was enough food. If there was not she would feed her husband and children first and get by herself on the left overs.

The most outspoken critic of this custom was Norjahan, who never faces a deficit of food and who is aggressively conscious of the contribution she has made to the family's current prosperity.

"Of course we eat together, why should I be last?" she replied to my question. "I used to eat after my husband, but this is *my* family, why should I wait?" But Norjahan also, on more formal occasions, took her place meekly in the second shift with the other women.

On this issue, as with most other matters of custom sanctioned by religion, the Grameen women did not contest the dominant ideology of the self-sacrificing wife and mother — and many argue strongly in support of it. But this particular practice of eating last, which works so clearly against the physical well being of women, has largely broken down in the Grameen group.

I also asked these women whether they thought that boys *needed* more food than girls, since such a belief would predispose them to discriminate between sons and daughters. All of the women in both the Grameen and control groups rejected this notion, with only two exceptions. Neither of these two women had any daughters. Two Grameen women and two women in the control group thought that girls should get *more,* because, like Eliza who was quoted above, they would marry and leave and should be pampered so long as they were in their childhood home.

"Boys and girls come from the same womb; they need the same food," was the answer I got from most of the sample. This turns out to be one of those silly questions. Who should know better than a poor woman in a food deficit household what are the food needs of each member of her family?

But behind this are the grim economic realities I outlined in Chapter 5. The families of landless labourers, which is most of the control group, depend on the cash wages of the household male in order to eat at all. The woman's economic contribution, in Taka, is very small despite her long hours of work; her opportunities for paid employment are extremely limited. Without access to credit or some similar resource, she cannot earn much income. Her contribution comes mainly in the form of expenditure-saving activities of various kinds. One of these is denying herself food. Although she sees this in terms of sacrificing her needs to those of her children, it is understood that her husband is not expected to make the same sacrifice, so that he has the energy to do the work on which the next day's cash earnings depend.

In the same way boys may be fed better than girls in these desperately poor households. Boys as young as eight can earn a half wage working in the fields. There are few such opportunities for girls. The family's survival depends on at least one son making it to adulthood and taking over the earning role of the father, while the daughters will be married away to other villages. A dependent mother's survival is particularly tied to her sons, since she is likely to be widowed in her fifties and will then depend on their earning power.

I am not trying to justify a system which results in rates of malnutrition and death amongst girls higher than amongst boys and which kills women in childbirth at a rate higher than most countries in the world. I am trying to disentangle the impact of poverty and the marginal earning power of women on how women divide up the food from the impact of a patriarchal ideology which demands that women sacrifice their needs to those of their husbands and families. Women in our sample continue to uphold this ideology of self sacrifice even when their economic lot improves. What they change are the practical outcomes which work against the welfare of themselves and their children.

We have seen how most Grameen women are likely to eat better because most of them are eating with their husbands, not in the second shift. Grameen women also look after themselves in pregnancy better than do women in the control group. This may be partly an outcome of the education that takes place in workshops. But it is also a signal of how these women value themselves — and get their priorities across to the husbands who do the marketing. 19 of the 24 Grameen women included in the nutritional survey said that they ate "special food" during pregnancy, usually the high protein and iron-rich foods they had been taught to value in the workshops. Only one of the control group women said that she enriched her diet during pregnancy.

Finally, the childbirth histories of the women in the sample show fewer deaths of children under one year amongst the Grameen group than the control. Although the numbers are too small to be significant, it is noteworthy than the survival rate of girl children is higher in the Grameen group.

Schooling: Changing Outlooks

"As far as they can go and as far as I can afford," Eliza says of her children's schooling, while we sit on mats in Habibah's *bari* talking about education and the marriage of their daughters.

"Talk about the real thing, not just dreams!" cautions one of her group members.

The Grameen women with whom we discussed this issue are keen to keep their children in school and can see the advantages of doing so. They dream of lives for their children without the hardship and struggle they have suffered themselves. But they are also realistic. In the rural Bangladesh context, schooling beyond primary level is expensive and has no clear payoff for the family. It is particularly problematic for girls, since they cannot marry downwards and educated boys demand larger dowries. So the women's enthusiasm for education is qualified by these realities. This is reflected in the time their children spend in school.

When we look at the education of parents in our sample of poor families, there is little difference between the Grameen families and the control group. Most of them are illiterate. The husbands tend to have slightly more education than their wives, but it is a difference of an average of one year of schooling as against an average of a third of a year amongst the women. One year in the village school, where truancy is the norm, is not enough to make anyone functionally literate.

When we look at the children, however, there is a clear difference between the Grameen children and the children of the control group. This post-Liberation generation have on the whole more education than their parents, but the Grameen children are well ahead of the children in the control group. When we take the crudest measure — those children over six years who have ever been to school — *all* of the girls in the Grameen families have had at least some schooling, compared to 60% of the girls in the control group. Most of the Grameen boys (81%) have had some schooling, compared to just over half (54%) of the control group boys.

We devised a more sensitive measure of educational attainment by taking the number of years of schooling actually completed by each child as a percentage of the number of years he could have completed, given his age. For example, a child of ten should have completed four years of schooling and be in class five. If he had done so he scored 100%. If he was still dawdling in Class 2 or had dropped out at that point, he scored 40%.

In this measure we counted only the five years of primary schooling available in the village. This means that any child of eleven or older who had completed Class Five scored 100%, regardless of whether he/she dropped out at this point or went on to secondary school. This is the realistic limit of the education of most village children, given the cost, and questionable usefulness, of sending a child to school in town.

There *were* children who schooled for longer, including one boy who completed college. This group is important in terms of what is possible for some of the families in our sample, and they will be described below. But including these few in the statistical analysis would have queered the comparison.

If we compare the number of years of schooling completed by all the relevant children, Grameen children have attended 62% of the years for which they are eligible, compared to 44% for the Control children. According to the T-test of significance this comes out at .10, which is a satisfactory level of significance. Amongst the female children, the Grameen girls score better than control group girls, but only at a .20 level of significance, mainly because of the small size of the sample. For male children, Grameen boys also score better than control group boys, at a .11 level of significance.

It is noticeable that, unlike their parents, girls in this generation in both Grameen and control groups are staying in school longer than the boys of both groups. This is likely to be related to the fact that boys can earn cash income for their families as young as eight years old, while earning opportunities for girls are even more restricted than for their mothers. Therefore, the opportunity cost of keeping girls in school is less and schooling may be seen as an alternative route to opportunity for female children. When the mothers talk about it, however, they often complain that their sons are too "naughty" to attend school. Girls are socialised to be obedient, and when they are told to go to school, they go. If a boy decides he would rather go fishing, many parents do not protest too much.

Underlying this is the recognition that education, while useful in some ways, does not lead children to any better opportunities outside the village. This was hard for us to understand at first. We come from a society, Malaysia, where education has been the route of hundreds of thousands of poor rural children into urban, middle-class jobs, pulling their families after them. We have never known a village in Malaysia where there were not several poor families who had managed to keep a bright child in school long enough to win a government scholarship to college and then university.

This is not the case in Bangladesh. A secondary education might better equip a child to run a trade or business, but it is not a passport out of the village. Even a college degree is not an automatic key to a salaried, "service-holder" job. The one young man in our sample who had completed his BA at a local college, was sitting in the village unemployed. He had worked as a supervisor in a garment factory in Dhaka and been fired for looking for a government job. There was no salaried job which did not require either payment of a huge bribe or an inside "connection," his father complained, in the context of asking us to get him a job in Malaysia.

There is a generational divide amongst the Grameen women in their attitudes to education, as in their attitudes to most social questions. Saleha, the *lokkhi* farmer in Ratnogram, has spent thousands of Taka putting this son through college in Ghatail and she was very bitter about the lack of return on that investment. But her daughters had only three or four years of schooling each before being married off at puberty.

"Daughters need some education, but not too much. If we spend a lot of Taka on the daughter's education there is no return to us, she will take it all to another household."

Habibah, the leader of the Bonopur center, is a pragmatist and her investments in education are calculated in very practical terms. Her daughter had one year's schooling in a *madrasah* and her son five years in a government school. But her horizons are changing.

> My daughter is a family woman like me, so the Koran and signing her name is enough. But my son needs Class Five so that he can read and write letters and make decisions and not get cheated. Of course, if he had more education it would be good, but Class Five is enough for the life he lives now. But my grandson, I want him to go much further, now that we can afford it.

The younger women are more ambitious for their daughters as well as their sons. Fodzilla has just shifted her nine year old daughter from the village school to a private girls' school in her father's village, so that she will get a more disciplined and better education. She wants both of her children to go as far as college, and has chosen this girls' school so that her daughter can continue her education "safely," even when she is a teenager. When I go to her house to photograph them, she has them already posed in their best clothes with bundles of schoolbooks under their arms.

Gunjara in Ratnogram is depressed when she joins us for this discussion. Her aging husband has not recovered from a bout of typhoid, and is likely to die, leaving her with three young daughters. She has the same ambitions as Fodzillah, but her hopes are fading and she turns her bitterness on me.

> If we want Taka we have to push the *ghani*. If we don't push, push, push, we don't eat. I don't want my daughters to live this kind of life. Look at you. You are an established person, you walk around respectably, you wear a watch, you sit there writing, all because you went to school. My dream is that my daughters will read, so that they can be established people and will not have to struggle like us. I want them to stay in school as long as possible, but I don't know how long. If there is a disaster, I cannot keep them in school.

One of the youngest and most successful Grameen women backs her up:

> The most valuable thing for our children is to go to school. We can work hard and struggle and make money. But if we are illiterate, even if we have Taka, we have no honour (*shomman*). A man can become a *borolok* (a landlord, a rich man), but if he is not educated, he still has no honour. We want our children to have Taka *and* respect.

Despite these ambitions, there are very few children who are schooling beyond Class Five — six in the whole sample, all from Grameen families. None of the children of the ambitious young mothers quoted above are old enough to have to make that decision. And the older mothers are profoundly anxious about the implications of keeping their daughters in school too long.

Apart from Saleha's son, the unemployed B.A., one of Banu's sons was doing Class 8 in Chittagong, supported by his two elder sisters. Kia, in her effort to get her children away from anything that smelled of mustard oil, had kept her bright elder son in school until Class Six, which helped him get an apprenticeship in a furniture workshop. Amongst the other three there was one 15 year old girl who won her battle to stay in school only with the help of her older brothers. Her father had died during the year and her mother, a Grameen member, argued that she simply could not afford to send the girl to secondary school in Ghatail. Already she was passing sleepless nights about how to raise her dowry, and how would she manage if the girl got too much education?

The Curse of Dowry

Running like a stain through all our discussions of education for girls was the fear of dowry demand. Every one of the women, young and old, mentioned it as the main constraint on further education for their daughters. Not Taka; not fear for their physical security. Dowry.

"This is actually an economic problem," explains Habibah. "If a girl goes too high in school, she has to have an educated husband and then the dowry demand is impossible for us."

This is Gunjara, who has a dream of education for her daughters:

> If we keep our daughters in school up to SSC or Intermediate, it is true that they will get a better husband. We don't want to give them to a farmer, a daily labourer. But a service holder will want a huge dowry; they will demand a Honda, a TV. I would pay if I could, but I cannot afford it. If they stay in school until they are 20, they will never be able to marry!
> If I get a good proposal, I will stop the schooling and marry her. It is better to marry than to read.

The 11th Decision of the 16 Decisions of the Grameen Bank reads: "We shall not take any dowry in our sons' wedding, neither shall we give dowry in our daughters' wedding. We shall keep our center free from the curse of dowry. We shall not practice child marriage."

There was universal agreement amongst the women in our two villages that dowry was an evil. There was also almost universal payment of it. There were no recent marriages in either the Grameen group or the control group which were performed without dowry payments, with two exceptions. The beautiful youngest daughter of a GB member married the son of a small landlord a year before we arrived in the village. Although he did not demand dowry at the time, they spent

4,000 Taka on a wedding suitable to *his* station. In the year we were there he had taken over the cultivation of their leased-in field and was demanding a watch. The other girl who was married without dowry, mainly because of her parent's poverty, returned to her parent's house during the year as a 15 year old divorcee. As far as we could tell, this was because her new husband turned out to be impotent. In our discussions with the mother's fellow center members, however, they pointed to this girl as typical of the fate of a daughter married without dowry.

Child marriage was on the decline in the village as a whole. The average age of marriage of the Grameen daughters in our sample was 15; for the control group it was 14. But this was a record of all daughters married during the parent's lifetime, including daughters of older women married 15 to 20 years before. Recent marriages were taking place when the girl was 16 to 19, except in Beparipara. Here girls used to be sent (as unpaid *ghani* pushers) to the husband's household as young as eight. Now the normal marriage age was around 14. The son of one of the GB members from Beparipara was married during the year to a 14 year old girl, getting a dowry of 10,000 Taka. Negotiations to marry his sister, then 14, for a dowry of 5,000 Taka were underway. At the same time, Norjahan and Nurul, the most prosperous Bepari family in our sample, took their eldest daughter out of school at 14 to prepare her for marriage. Norjahan told me that they were prepared to pay 7,000 Taka to get a "good boy" for their daughter. However, gossip in the *para* was that they were negotiating a 20,000 Taka dowry, plus gifts and jewellery, to get a "service-holder" son-in-law.[3]

Some of the older women still maintained that it was their religious duty to marry their daughters before puberty, because their security was too much at risk living unmarried in the world of the village. Few of the other Grameen women agreed. "Now we are modern and our daughters need time to be educated and to be properly mature before they are married. We also need time to teach them our skills of how to live a productive and economical life," was the view expressed by Fodzillah, to the general agreement of most of her fellow members.

Ever-practical Habibah added: "I married my daughter at 13, but I think now that it is not healthy. If you marry daughters too young they have many physical problems and they finish all your Taka on medicines."

Over the past decade, according to the oral family records that we collected, the age of marriage of girls has been rising — but so has the amount of dowry. The marriages of Parul's four daughters, are typical of this trend. Parul is the Bepari widow who was driven out of her house and then the village after her husband died, but returned and has consolidated her position through her use of her Grameen loans.

Her eldest was married fifteen years ago at the age of 8, with a dowry of 1,000 Taka; the second at the age of 10, with a dowry of 1,800 Taka, the third at 12, with 2,000 Taka and the youngest, just three years ago, at 15, with 3,000

Taka. But Parul is one of the poorer Grameen woman in our sample. In recent marriages of daughters in the Grameen group dowries averaged around 4,000 Taka in cash and several thousand more in gold jewellery and clothing, and the more prosperous families were paying much more.

Of the 16 Decisions which make up the social development program of the Bank, the 11th, to stay free of the curse of dowry, is the most ignored. I suggest that the reason it is ignored is the same reason that has kept more Grameen daughters alive; that keeps them more healthy; that keeps them longer in school. Grameen mothers, like all mothers, love their daughters. They want to give them easier and more comfortable lives than they have had themselves. And Grameen mothers have the resources and the power to do their best for their daughters — including investing in a dowry to get them a "good" husband. They are not prepared to risk their daughters' welfare to satisfy an abstract principle, however much they might agree with it.

The received view of the root cause of dowry and its rapid inflation in recent years is that the diminishing opportunities for women to earn income and their marginalisation as their crop processing role is taken over by machines, has made a wife more of a burden than an asset. If this is true, then the penetration of Grameen Bank into more than half the villages of Bangladesh, giving credit which allows two million women to earn income, should be undermining the practice of dowry. In addition, the Bank is energetically campaigning to eliminate dowry and is promoting dowryless marriages between the children of its members. That this has already stripped legitimacy from the practice is evident in the way the women in these two villages discussed it. But in the short-term, at least, this campaign was not having any impact on actual dowry payments in the two villages we studied. Instead, the growing prosperity of Grameen families means they are able to pay more to get better husbands for their daughters. They certainly receive more for their sons.

This conflict between the Grameen campaign and actual practice, plus the intense anxiety women feel about the marriage of their daughters, caused fireworks in each of the group discussions on this issue.

After listening to Gunjara say that she would give a Honda or a TV if she could afford it, in the passage quoted above, Alia, the former Center Chief, who has attended many workshops and is a staunch defender of Grameen Bank orthodoxy, said:

"No dowry is our 11th decision and we must follow it." (When Alia's daughter married four years ago at the age of 20, she paid a dowry of 2,500 Taka. Her two sons are about ready to get married.) All the others in the group turned on her.

"You have a son and I have a daughter, but will you give your son without dowry? No-one obeys that rule; it is just the mouth talking!" Gunjara shot out, well aware, of course, that even *with* a dowry Alia would never marry her son to a Bepari girl.

Saleha, the prosperous farmer with the unemployed BA son (she got a Grade 10 girl for him who paid 20,000 Taka in dowry) said complacently: "Having a son means getting dowry. When they have sons parents feel very proud and possessive. Whether he is educated or not he is still a son."

"Even if the son is useless and is not earning, parents are proud and make demands," adds Gunjara, rubbing in the salt.

In Bonopur also the issue of dowry rose naturally out of our discussion of girls' education. Fodzillah who expresses high hopes for her daughter's education in the face of the others fears about high dowry demands, explains her view in terms of her own experience.

"I was educated more than my husband and was skilled in handicrafts and a hard worker, that is why I married here with only a small dowry. If my daughter is also skilled and educated and a good girl, she should be able to marry without dowry."

She turns to her fellow member, Zarinah, who has two sons.

"If Zarinah's son is a good boy and she wants my daughter but she asks for 20,000 Taka that will be difficult for me. But if I offer only jewellery, because my daughter is of the best quality, then what will you say?"

"If my son is no good, I will give you what you want!" replies Zarinah coolly. "But if he is of the same quality, then I will not have to make demands. Fodzillah will give willingly."

"The government should take stern action against the taking of dowry," Fodzillah replies, miffed.

Habibah snorts. "If they did, we would all be locked up. If we do not give dowry for our daughters they will stay their whole lives in our house. Even GB members with sons will not agree to marry them without dowry. Look at M — she married her daughter without dowry and now the girl is returned back to her parents and has to work as a maidservant."

Notes

1. Bruce 1989 cites several studies to show no correlation or negative correlation between higher incomes to the male earner and the nutritional status of his children.

2. This question was asked in the context of the nutritional survey so unfortunately only the mothers of children ten and younger were included. I excluded female-headed households, where the woman eats alone or with her children. The GB sample for this question is 25 and for the control group 11.

3. The village requirements of a "good boy" are a bit more basic than the middle-class requirements of a "suitable boy" ala Vikram Seth, so I will define them in negatives. Lineage is crucial, but within that the boy should be not too old, neither physically nor mentally defective, with no notable vices, like being addicted to Housie. Parents prefer a boy with a skill or trade, but if he is a *"krishi* man" (farmer) he should have at least the prospect of inheriting land. What they don't want is the kind of landless labourer they married themselves.

Conclusion

There are women in this village who are richer than me. They have Taka, but they have no power. I know everything that goes on in our house. My husband will discuss all the work with me and when he takes goods to the haat he gives an account to me of all that is sold. I am strong because the Bank is behind me and if there is any disaster then the Bank worker and the center members will come to see me and I know I will not fall. That is why I am so brave nowadays.

— Zarinah in Bonopur

Most women are not the leaders in their families and their husbands don't tell them anything. But we are different. We take Taka from Grameen Bank and so our husbands account (hisab) to us. But other women who don't work like us and don't earn, how can they expect the money to come under their control?

— Alia in Ratnogram

Don't you dare write that our husband's only love us because of Grameen Bank Taka! My husband loved me from before. But since I became a Grameen Bank member, because I am earning and taking the loans, the whole family treats me with more respect. I have more influence and when he sells my oil he gives me an account of his sales and puts the money back in my hand.

— Gunjara in Ratnogram

Ten years of membership in Grameen Bank has worked a fundamental change in the family relationships of most of the women in our sample. This is a bold statement. Can something as simple as the provision of credit alter gender politics *fundamentally* in an environment as hostile as rural Bangladesh? The empirical answer is that it has. Twenty seven of these 40 women play an active role in all aspects of the management of their households and its budget. Their husbands discuss their economic activities with them, including the cultivation of land. Some of the women play a dominant role in negotiating leaseholds and making cultivation decisions. The key these women tie to the end of their *sari* symbolizes more than the traditional role of cashbox. They have grasped control of its contents. Banu, one of the stronger women in Ratnogram, typifies the mix of traditional concepts and the new kind of power involved — the power to refuse.

This is my house and his house. Where else would he keep the Taka except here? I wear this key around my neck. When he wants money he asks and then we discuss how much he needs. If he wants it for pleasure or to waste it on Housie or something, I will not give. But if he needs it to buy food for us or a *lunggi* for himself I will give. Then all the proceeds from the sale of our paddy or livestock come back to my hand to manage. A good wife is *lokkhi* so why should the husband not trust her to manage the money?

This kind of power is the product of a process over a decade of loan use. It is not by any means inevitable. There are 13 of the 40 GB women who are marginal in the making of decisions and who are both subordinate to and dependent on their husbands or sons. Nor could the empowerment uncovered in this study be predicted from the theoretical frameworks that seek to explain gender relations. On the contrary, academics across the board make warning noises about predicting any kind of control from the increased earnings of women.

Kabeer (1994:225) talking about the Women in Development advocacy for greater access for women to development programs, says: "while these efforts may have succeeded in generating access to income-generating projects for women, few have transformed their position within the household."

Sarah White (1992) seems to be saying that women can never escape the ideology that subordinates them. If they earn income it is subsumed within their family roles; it gives them no autonomy. Ownership of assets does not automatically confer any real control over them. If women shift out of domestic tasks or domestic space, they simply carry their lowly status out with them; new tasks do not shift power relations in the family. (Although this is not what the women themselves, in the village of Kumirpur, told her. They recognised the relationship between work that brought in cash and greater centrality in their families, P136.)

I am not a theoretician. All I have done is observe, as an experienced journalist, and describe as accurately as I can, this group of women over a year of watching them negotiate their lives. It is for the theoreticians to accommodate these real women into their constructs. All I will try to do in this conclusion is to explain why I think the contribution of GB women to their families counts, where in other contexts women's work may be both invisible and undervalued.

Nothing to Lose but His Poverty

The most obvious reason it counts is because the contribution of the GB women is just so large, so regular and so sustained. Two thirds of the GB women in our sample contribute more than half the total income of their households. Most of them take three loans a year — their general loan, an irrigation or seasonal loan and usually a group fund loan as well. They are eligible for a loan to build a house, to buy a houselot and to install a tube well. They have been borrowing and investing in productive assets for ten years, each year getting more capital and extending their activities.

In a poor household this contribution is not pin money for bangles, it is fundamental to the family's survival. The movement of the Grameen Bank families from the despised underclass of the village into the ranks of respectable middling farmers is based on it. For the men of the household to ignore this contribution would be like refusing to see the difference between a full rice store and an empty one or to pretend that the cow in the yard is invisible or the tin roof is still made of straw.

Nor is gender politics necessarily about conflict between husband and wife. We have to look at whose interests are served and whose are threatened by the progress of Grameen women in income, assets, self-confidence and influence. The landlord's wife in the *borobari* may be the clearest loser. She is often a moneylender to other women and GB women seldom need non-benevolent loans. The landlord's wife trades on the desperation of the poorest women to extract a full days work for meals alone. GB women are no longer her clients in this respect either.

The landlord himself has to pay more for daily labour (Khandker 1993) and his GB clients are busy transforming themselves into independent farmers. But that also means they are not always coming to him for advances on their wages and a great deal of the GB capital coming into the village is trickling *up* to landowners through the mechanism of leasehold and purchase of land (Gibbons forthcoming).

The earning power of GB women and their meetings in the center hut are subversive of the whole culture of dependence which subordinates village women to male providers and guardians. This is why the Grameen Bank in some areas of Bangladesh has attracted the ire of *mullahs*, moneylenders, landlords and fundamentalists. But how is the GB member's husband or son a loser in this process?

Previously, when Begum's husband, Shakeeb, ploughed a field, the figure squatting on the bund under a black umbrella, making sure he didn't stop to rest, was the landlord. Now there is no-one lurking on the bund. The field is *his* — in the sense of being leased in partnership by he and his wife. It is ploughed by their own cows. The undivided harvest belongs to the family. Begum's loans have been used for joint family enterprises to his direct benefit. When you talk to him it is clear that he does not feel marginal — they make joint decisions and his hard work is as important as Begum's capital. Begum has more influence at home; if she wants something he had better listen. If he is in a bad mood he had better not take it out on her in beatings. But in the village, *his* status has also risen. He is a farmer, not a contract labourer. Now landlords come to him and ask if he will sharecrop or lease their fields, or rent his team to do their ploughing. Is it so surprising that he treasures her, willingly acknowledges her contribution to the family and boasts that she is "the best woman in the village?"

If Grameen Bank women are empowered in the household as a result of the use of their loans, their husbands have been empowered in the world of the village, by being transformed from labourers dependent on landlords for work, into farmers or traders working for themselves.

What have they lost besides their poverty? Their wives are still at home, cooking meals and washing clothes; still doing all the domestic duties, in other words, that the patriarchal culture ordains as their natural duty. Apart from the odd husband who looks after the children while his wife is at the center meeting or off at the branch office for the day, I observed few dents in the idea that women are solely responsible for housework and childcare, and this is universally accepted by the women themselves.   The work that women do is an extension of their customary work, performed within the *bari*, and is combined with their traditional domestic roles in ways that minimize conflict with family males and village society, as well as psychological conflict within themselves.

It is important to understand, however, that in the village context, the work GB women do, even though it is mainly confined to the *bari*, gives them both considerable amounts of income and considerable self-respect. And once again, I come into head-on conflict with a number of other studies on women at work and the "household trap" (Jain 1985). Mies famous study of the lacemakers of Narsapur (1982) shows nothing could be worse than working at home. Her lacemakers are isolated and their contribution devalued by the 'real' breadwinner as 'pocketmoney' earned in their 'spare-time,' i.e. after the housework. Ever since Boserup (1970), writers on rural women in Asia have pointed out that so long as a woman remains secluded at home, in her domestic role, her real economic contribution to agricultural production will not be counted.

Against this we have to put some realities of the way production is organised in these two villages. Women are certainly secluded, in the sense of spending most of their time within the *bari*, although they are not isolated by any means. Grameen Bank women are notably more mobile than other women in the village. But they are not the exploited peripherals of the multinationals, doing piecework, like the lacemakers of Narsapur or the wire-coilers of Mexico city (Dwyer & Bruce 1988). They have the capital to invest in activities from which they get the full return. Moreover, production and reproduction are not separate here. The *bari* is a rice-mill, an oil mill, a godown, a dairy and a poultry farm.

Nothing was more striking to us, coming from modernised rice-growing areas in Malaysia, than the extent to which women are still essential to the production of paddy, the main agricultural crop, in Bangladesh. In Malaysia, huge combine harvesters munch through the standing paddy, cutting, threshing and bagging in one operation, dropping the filled bags like turds in their wake. These are thrown into a truck and taken straight to the mill. Women have been entirely eliminated from the harvest by this machine. In Bangladesh, men cut the paddy by hand and bring it, stalks and all, back to the women in the *bari*. It is their business from then on. The importance of women's processing work is acknowledged in the village, as White (1992:121) points out. But now their contribution has extended far beyond processing the crop.

There is an interesting discussion in Kabeer (1994:118-120) of farming systems in the Indian sub-continent where men and women are responsible for sequential tasks; the men plant and harvest, the women boil and husk, the men market. Since the 'critical stages' — the field work and the selling — are in the hands of men, the women's contribution disappears without a trace into the general household budget. But if we look at the context of poor, landless families in these two villages, the most 'critical stage' of all is *getting* the land. Grameen Bank women members are using their capital to get access to land to cultivate, often the first time their families have been able to do so. In addition, she is providing the capital for fertiliser and other inputs and the cows for ploughing.

It is the income from land cultivation which has pushed most of the successful GB families out of the poverty group. Land is also strongly invested with other emotions. It means food security; "eating our own paddy." It is the asset which confers the most status within the village, and turns the husband from a labourer at the mercy of the landlord, into an independent farmer. It is the crucial nature of land and the critical function of the woman's capital in getting access to it that I think underlies the very strong position that two-thirds of our sample have been able to attain in their families.

This conjunction of capital in the woman's hand and the use of it to get access to land, over which she is able to assert entitlement, has in fact overturned the material basis for male power in the rural context, what Kabeer calls the "non-negotiable" male control over "household land, capital and other valued resources" (1994:225). GB loans have made the major assets a matter for women to negotiate.

The alternative route to women's empowerment favoured by writers from Boserup to Sen, of getting education or training and escaping the household trap by 'going out to work' is not yet a realistic option in either of these villages. The only opportunities for paid employment, except for the rare CARE job for widows, are very low status forms of domestic slavery. Women who work as servants are often subject to verbal and even physical abuse, they work long hours for payment in kind and they feel ashamed, not strengthened, by what they do. Not surprisingly, GB women stop working in the *borobari* as soon as they have capital to finance work in their own *bari*, work which gives them both cash and self-respect, and is accepted and acknowledged by their husbands.

To summarise, the contribution of these Grameen Bank women counts because it is simply too large, persistent and fundamental to the survival and welfare of the family to ignore. It is visible in assets like houses, fields and cows, some of which are legally owned by the woman with the backing of the Grameen

Bank. The women have capital for self-employment which gives family members the full return on their labour. Because so much of their loan capital has gone into getting access to land, GB women have overrun an area which is traditionally male and which is critical to the material and social status of their families.

At the same time, the woman's economic activities are performed in a way that minimises conflict with custom and increases the status of the whole family, including its male members.   Her domestic burden is unchanged and her activities still serve the interests of the family. Over the decade of her membership these activities have strengthened her negotiating position until currently, most of the GB women have achieved a central, and sometimes leading, role in their families.

The Break-Down Position

So far, we have looked at how the men in the family recognise and acknowledge the woman's contribution. What may be even more important is how she values it herself. Sen (1990) in his "cooperative-conflict" model of how households operate, argues that the outcome of intra-household bargaining is better for the partner whose *perceived* contribution to the household pot is larger. As we saw in Chapter Two, GB women are not only perfectly conscious of how much they contribute, they quite frequently *overestimate* the size of their contribution.

This pride in the role of the *lokkhi* wife, the manager of the family resources, is not unique to GB women; several of the women in the control group are also confident of their value, although they tend to be older women or to have some other resource — like Kadeera's strong links to her natal family. Where most poor non-Grameen women are fatally weakened, however, is in the absence of a decent break-down position; what happens if the cooperation collapses and the family falls apart. Fear of divorce by husbands or abandonment by sons must frequently settle family arguments against the woman's interests. For example, when Rahman insisted that Daria withdraw from ASA at the point when she became eligible to take a second loan, the fact that she owned nothing and both her parents were dead made it inevitable that she would comply. She is so dependent that she simply could not survive on her own.

All the married GB women would be worse off if they were divorced by their husbands. Female dependence is structured in Bangladesh — in their exclusion from market places, from working in their own fields, in their residence in their husband's village where their position and entitlements rest on being his *bo*, and in their physical insecurity. Even the most powerful GB women would find it difficult to maintain the same levels of income without the active hands and feet of an adult male. However, those who have retained control over the loan use (30 of the 40 women) and who have managed to build up assets under their control, would survive well enough. They don't *have* to put up with abusive husbands, dictatorial mothers-in-law, or second wives.

Which explains why the GB women in our sample don't have them. Only one woman was occasionally beaten — as her husband spiralled down into one of his episodes of madness, he went through an intensely patriarchal phase when he pranced about declaiming "I am her Lord! She must obey me in every particular!" and hitting her when she protested at his wilder actions. This was symptomatic of his insanity rather than his power.

There is also the confidence expressed by Zarinah at the beginning of this chapter, that the Bank is behind her, so she cannot fall. Grameen Bank does come through for its borrowers in times of disaster, by rescheduling loans and providing emergency help of various kinds. The knowledge that they are members of, and own, an institution with the national clout of Grameen Bank fuels its member's confidence and willingness to take risks.

What also makes the position of GB women so different is that the breakdown position of GB husbands is often less rosy than that of their wives. Like other poor men in the village, if the marriage broke down a GB husband could get another wife, perhaps even a small dowry. His meals would be cooked and his *lunggi* washed. But if he divorced a center member, he would be hard put to get another GB wife. And there would go the loans, the assets in her name — and for 17 of the 40, even the house and houselot. The benefits of cooperation are strong on both sides, but, on balance, stronger for him than for her.

Of course, total breakdown is rare; it is the awareness of where it might leave you that influences the bargaining process in a marriage. We were looking at women who had already worked through the early conflicts with their husbands over loan use. But there is an interesting description in Counts (forthcoming) of a women in her first loan cycle using the threat of not taking another loan to change her husband's behaviour. A second wife, who was persuaded by her husband to use her first loan to lease in land for him to cultivate, discovers that he has taken the cut paddy to the house of his first wife. She erupts in rage and threatens to refuse a seasonal loan which they plan to use to boost the next crop. By the end of the day the paddy has arrived in her *bari*.

In our two centers, the Grameen Bank culture is already well established. In our group discussions, the women vied with each other in statements which showed how "brave" they are and how "strong" a line they take against any husbandly extravagance or waste. It is clear that their awareness of their contribution and the power that it gives them is bolstered by this kind of boasting within the group. Similarly, their husbands have had a decade to adjust to the increasing activity and assertiveness of their wives. Men like Zarinah's husband, who used to be teased and shamed by comments about his wife and her group "walking on the road like a herd of water buffaloes," now belongs to a fraternity of upwardly-mobile GB households, envied by other men in the village. With few exceptions, GB husbands freely admit the importance of their wives' contribution to this progress and praise their management competence.

The Process of Moving out of Poverty

In 1976, Professor Muhammad Yunus studied the poor women of Jobra village and thought: "If they had some capital, they could do wonders." He didn't think, as was then and still is the normal reaction of educated professionals to poverty: "If she had new technology and training she could raise her productivity. If she were literate she would change her backward attitudes. If she joined a movement she could demand her fair share." The Grameen Bank system, as elaborate as it has become, is based on a very simple confidence that poor women have survival skills, otherwise they would be dead. If you give her a loan, she has the skills and locally relevant knowledge to use it productively and a powerful determination to invest the profits in security for herself and her children.

The success of the Grameen Bank, its outreach to two million women and their faithful repayment, has vindicated Yunus's original confidence many times over. Our study of 40 GB members shows how effectively women have used this capital to pull their families out of poverty and to invest in assets to secure this progress.

It is time to pull together the various case histories scattered throughout this book and make some generalisations about how women have used their loans to pull their families out of poverty.

Although the history of actual loan use differs radically from the loan use records in the branch office, I think that most women did use their first loans for paddy husking. It is a low-risk activity with which they are familiar and it put paddy in their store which they could eat when food was short. But women rarely use all their loans for one activity — even if they husk four *maunds* of paddy between one *haat* and another, the capital they need to roll over comes to less than 1,000 Taka. They spread the risks between activities which generate cash for repayment and longer-term investment in assets. In the first loan cycles these were small assets: poultry, ducks, perhaps a calf or goats to fatten.

Barring accidents, the first couple of loan cycles gave these women some basic security — particularly food security, without which they cannot raise their heads and plan for the future. As soon as they were over that first hump, most of them set their sights on cows and land for cultivation. They began turning their husbands gradually from daily labourers to small farmers, thereby reversing the age-old process of loss of inherited land that has aggravated poverty in Bangladesh (Jansen 1987).

As soon as these GB families had capital, and particularly if they had a cow for ploughing, they became attractive to landowners as sharecroppers. They could fund the inputs that would boost the harvest, of which the landlord gets half, and they would not always be touching him for loans. But leasehold is a much better proposition to a poor family than sharecropping. If the woman can put up a lump sum to lease a field, the whole harvest comes to the family and her capital remains intact — since in Tangail a landowner must allow the leaseholder at least two harvests and must pay back the full lease price to get his land back.

Different families followed different strategies. Some, like Shakeeb and Begum, put the loans into leasehold from the very start. They are the risk takers. They rolled 500 Taka into paddy husking and sank all the rest into a lease. As Shakeeb said: "If we bought paddy only, that would make us lazy," meaning it would always be there to eat and they would not have to hussle so desperately to come up with the repayment before their leased field gave them a harvest. Several loanees, like Banu, who could rely on her husband's daily income from vegetable trading, were prepared to risk putting all their loans into a lease, knowing that they would get the full harvest instead of sharing it with a landlord. That was the strategy of the most of those who are now the most successful borrowers, usually because they already had the security of some land, like Zarinah and Habibah or some secure source of income, like Banu and Jamilah. Or like Shakeeb and Begum, who started with nothing, or Swapna, the young divorcee, they were so determined to get land that they were willing to do without for a while longer.

Others did not begin putting their loans into leasehold land until they were in their fourth or fifth cycles. For most loanees the progression has been from paddy husking and poultry, to sharecropping and cows, to leasehold, while some portion of the loan continued to be put into building up her *bari* assets in poultry and livestock and stocking paddy, both for consumption and resale. There are, of course, other patterns. Families already in a trade got themselves out of the clutches of wholesalers by using the capital to buy their own mustard oil or aluminium pots, or exchanging a rented rickshaw for one of their own. They used the capital, in other words, to get a full return on their labour. But with few exceptions, these women held back part of their loans to put into poultry and livestock and they also began to accumulate land in addition to their husband's trading business.

Once these families had achieved basic food security, additional surplus was not usually used up in consumption. Women who remembered hunger and disaster made sure of that. Houses were mended; straw roofs replaced by tin. Houselots, the production floor, were bought or extended. Livestock were purchased and housed. But above all, GB families began acquiring land. Several, including Habibah, Saleha and Azgar, and Norjahan and Nurul began to reassemble the father's landholdings by buying out the interests of sisters and other relatives. Others purchased land from fathers and brothers. But the main mechanism was leasehold, which could give a family land to cultivate, with a full return from each harvest, while the capital remained intact, for 6,000 Taka a *bigha*.

This pursuit of land was hidden, because it was against the rules of the Bank. It is very much in the interest of the husband, since it gradually freed him from daily labour and made him into an independent and respected farmer. If you believe that the acquisition of land is inimical to women's interests because it is traditionally owned in the name of the male head of household and increases her processing burden, then it is hard to explain the almost universal passion amongst the women in our sample to get access to land for their men to cultivate, and the sacrifices they are prepared to make to accumulate the capital to do so. But as I argued in earlier chapters, land is a women's issue. It puts paddy in her baskets and secures her basic food supply. A woman who cannot 'manage' enough food is not only sure to go hungry herself, she is considered to be incompetent, as cruelly unjust as this belief is. Only when she has paddy in store, can a woman lift her head from the day to day scratching for subsistence and plan for the future. It is a resource that she can turn into cash or use to give small loans. Just having a full paddy basket gives her a *feeling* of security in the unpredictable natural world of the Bangladesh village.

A woman in a household with some land makes a bigger contribution to its economy than the wife of a landless daily labourer. All the crops come into her hands for processing and storage. Her position as a busy *bari* wife, guardian of the granaries, manager of plenty, gives her much more scope to negotiate control than when she waited by the empty pot for her husband to return with his daily wages.

Finally, land is the means to an independent existence for the most threatened species of women — widows and divorcees. With control over land, a woman can secure her food supply and make an income regardless of the unkindness of husbands and the faithlessness of sons. There are few other assets, except ownership of the house and houselot, which can give her the same autonomy. Investment in land now, for married women, is their best insurance against widowhood in the future.

The Double Day

Recently, at a seminar in Dhaka, Professor Yunus was confronted by a radical feminist who argued that credit programs simply doubled the work burden of poor women, for the benefit of others in the family, leaving the woman to carry the repayment.

"Do you want me to stop giving loans to women?" Professor Yunus asked in some puzzlement.

"Yes," she replied.

When I held group discussions with some of the GB women in the last month of data collection, I put the 'burden thesis' to them and asked for their reaction. Saleha responded indignantly:

> Do they think we cannot manage our time? At night I plan what has to be done the next day. I wake very early and I do all the household work one by one. By 10 a.m. I can finish it, even cooking for the field workers. Then I do my Grameen Bank work. After ten years in GB that is my habit. It is true that before we carried two *maunds* and now we carry four *maunds*. But we are making income from this extra work.

"Yes," chipped in Alia. "Household work is our duty, but income work is better." Then a young woman, whose husband was completely landless before she joined GB, spoke up:

> Sister, listen. It is a *pleasure* to do this income work. It is because of this that Taka is coming in, and since it is mostly our Taka, we become the *matbar* (leader). Before, after I finished the housework I used to just sit around. Now I get Taka from Grameen Bank and I use it to make more Taka. I tell you it is a joy to work hard when you are making progress.

Where is the false consciousness? Here in Ratnogram or in the seminar in Dhaka?

In Bonopur, a discussion of how they manage their time turned into an exchange on the ethics of employing other women during the peak harvest season. As it turned out, it was not the ethics of hiring poorer women for 'a pot of rice' a day which was worrying them, nascent capitalists to the last woman, but whether they were justified in paying anything at all for work which they could, with superhuman effort, do themselves. Habibah finally summed up the consensus by saying: "If I can make Five taka by spending one Taka, why shouldn't I hire labourers?"

When Mahabub Hossain (1988) asked his sample of GB borrowers the main reasons for their improved economic position after joining Grameen Bank, the most important reason women gave, after the accumulation of capital, was additional employment in productive work. Two thirds of the women gave this as the primary or secondary reason, while the male borrowers more frequently cited their freedom from the clutches of moneylenders. Rushidan (1986) also found employment in income generating work to be the major impact of borrowing on women members.

Time allocation studies in Bangladesh do not show that women work longer hours than men. Kabeer argues that their work burdens are less than in cultures where women are responsible for food cultivation (Hamid 1989; Kabeer 1994:124). In very poor, landless households, women are often underemployed. This does not mean they are idle — they spend their time in expenditure saving activities like searching for edible leaves or fuel, or in work with extremely low returns, like Naima's dung sticks. When GB women get capital, this kind of work is usually displaced by self-employment with better returns. In this sense then her work load is not doubled, but reorganised, certainly to her benefit.

There is no doubt, however, that GB women who have invested in land work a lot harder than when they were landless. I think that this is a factor behind the boasting women do about their hard work. The busiest women in the village are those in small farm households, when the paddy, wheat and spice crops pile into the *bari* and all the processing is done by family members. But if the poorest women are the idlest, and that included most GB women before they joined the Bank, then there is much status attached to being busy with produce from your own land. Since this increased workload is associated with a new prosperity and particularly with a supply of food piling up in the store, it is not surprising that it is a source of pride rather than resentment amongst the GB women.

There is no comparison between what they are doing and the benefits that they derive from it and the lot of women factory workers who work a full day for a bare subsistence and then return home to face the domestic chores as well.

I think, on balance, the false consciousness was expressed in the seminar in Dhaka rather than in the discussions amongst the GB women. This strand of feminist scholarship asks important questions — who uses the loans and who gets the benefit. But their stress on the negative and their ability to find it, for instance, by conflating loan use and control so that loans used for rickshaws and land cultivation are automatically classified as appropriated by males, distorts what actually happens within families. When these researchers then go on to recommend that credit programs for women be scrapped or slowed down they do a great disservice to poor women.

The Process of Empowerment

In Chapter Two I challenged the stereotypes of rural Bangladeshi women, the passive victims, illiterate and confined, who people the academic literature. I pointed out that this singleminded focus on exploitation and misery obscures how much they are actually able to do. This is not to deny the existence of blatant discrimination against women and structures which at once exploit their labour but keep them dependent and powerless.

Imagine Norjahan more than twenty years ago when she first married Nurul. She was ten years old; he was 20. She had never been to school and rarely out of her father's village. He could count and followed his father to all the *haat* in the area. He was at home; she was in a stranger's house, an alien village. All day she pushed her father-in-law's *ghani*, as unpaid family labour. She was at the very bottom of the family pecking order.

But Norjahan did not jump into a well. Somehow she survived. Just as poverty teaches women economic survival skills, so the very oppressiveness of these patriarchal structures forces them to learn *social* survival skills as well. It would take many life histories to pinpoint how these skills develop. But it is possible from our data to outline what they are. Foremost are the skills women invest in building networks and alliances, winning the acceptance and support of in-laws and the 'kindness' of husbands, making allies of other women who have married here from the same village and maintaining the links with their own families in their natal villages. These relationships are vital to women because they are dependent, but they can also be used to negotiate their independence.

Initially, some of these strategies work against the young bride's welfare. She wins over her mother-in-law by working harder and eating less than other family members. Her dowry helps make her acceptable but it is usually swallowed up by the joint family. She ensures her welcome at her natal home by surrendering her land inheritance to her brothers.

But by the time these women are in their twenties and thirties, they are using these networks for their economic survival. Some of their strategies involve the subterfuge of the powerless. They try to keep some secret hoards of paddy or cash to feed their children when their husbands fail to come home or come back empty handed. They try to build some assets or a nest-egg of their own against the possibility of abandonment. From their networks women can know the local market prices, can buy and sell small items without their husband's knowledge, can get share-goats to fatten, can borrow and lend in a crisis and call on other women to help with childcare or paddy drying. When the center begins, women already linked in these ways form its groups.

Grameen Bank loans capitalise poor women's economic survival skills so that they can make a cash income. Many of their economic activities depend on their networks, and the income they make from their loans in turn strengthens and extends them. We saw Habibah in Bonopur oiling her networks with benevolent loans to the village Union Member as well as to an array of GB women. Nurjahan attended a nephew's wedding in her natal village during the year, giving a brass betel set to show her new status. A young member, somewhat offside with the current center chief, ensured Alia's future support by lending her money for repayment when Alia was ill. Before Begum and Shakeeb bought a second cow, they had an reciprocal arrangement with Banu to borrow her cow to make a pair for ploughing. And so on. Strong support from their own families, good relations with their in-laws in the *bari* and relationships of support outside the family give women status and respect and strengthen their position in intra-household bargaining.

Women in the village are also adept at turning the ideology, which is fundamentally hostile to women's independence, to their advantage. They make a virtue of their hard work and boast about it endlessly. I imagine that they use it with their husbands as a kind of moral club. With the GB women, this is reinforced by the culture of the Bank — "Discipline, Unity, Courage and Hard

Work" is the first of the 16 Decisions and the most popular slogan for shouting at visitors. In this way the virtue of hard work has an almost religious status. (I was coming into Bonopur with Nahar one morning and saw Fodzilla walking about a mile from her house. Later Nahar asked her where she had been going. "I went to visit a relative," she replied. "But don't tell Apa. She'll think we're not hard working.")

In Chapter 4 I discussed some of the cultural levers women could use to legitimise their creeping control over the management of the household. Their traditional role of keeping the money and assets of the family safe while the men are working 'outside' can be transformed into more than guard duty. Their ownership rights over minor livestock can be extended to major assets they acquire through their loans. The unquestioning care and obedience a son owes to a Bengali mother can be capitalised through her loans to increase the income and build up assets for the family as a whole. The concept of *lokkhi* can clothe an active, controlling, managerial woman with cultural legitimacy. If she is as successful economically as more than half of the GB women in our sample have been, it becomes both convenient and profitable for her husband to surrender the household management to her.

"He is happy to hand over all the money to me. He knows if he gives me two Taka I will make it into four," commented one of the borrowers in Ratnogram.

This then is the process by which GB women have become central in their families. Poverty and patriarchy have equipped them with both economic and social survival skills. When they get their loans they use their economic skills and their information and support networks to invest this capital and make more income. Their increased income and resources are, in turn, used to strengthen their networks and negotiate more control over the cash, the assets and the earnings of working children. Over a decade of loan use as experienced by the GB women in our sample, these processes have made a marked difference in the prosperity and security of most households and given most woman a central position within it.

The Limits of Grameen Bank

But not all of them. Six of the 40 GB families are still extremely poor in per capita income terms and 11 are better off than they used to be but still under the poverty line. When we look at those who are still floundering badly we find a combination of chronic ill health of the male breadwinner coupled with a lack of activity by his wife, so that their capital is used for emergency consumption and medical treatment. The demands of repayment on such families persuade them to borrow against future loans, so that much of their capital is used up before it arrives and there is not enough balance for investment. These women can use their access to credit to prevent them falling into complete destitution, but they are still locked into a situation which makes investment in productive assets almost impossible.

It is notable that a number of the women borrowers who are still in the poverty group are not using the loans themselves and are dependent on some other male in the household. These women are vulnerable to disaster because they are not earning themselves and because the household has only one main source of income. We found ten women of the 40 'pipelining' their loans to others, and seven of them are still in the poverty group. This overlap between poverty and powerlessness is striking. These women are making a minimal contribution to the household income — simply delivering the loans for others to invest. Like Rina, their attitudes are still dependent; they do not consider it is their business to earn the income, that is the duty of their husbands. Several of them fall under the authority of an elder male; not their husbands, with whom it is easier to negotiate a more equal relationship. Rina had her loans taken from her by her father-in-law for as long as she lived in the joint family; the father of her fellow group member appropriated all his daughter's loans for eight years. The widow Parul struggled for years to free herself from the bullying authority of her elder brother-in-law.

One can see how the structures which dictate dependence press on these women. But if we look at the group which should be most disadvantaged by *purdah* restrictions and the exploitative authority of elder males — widows and divorcees who head their own households — we find four out of six of them are doing well. These four had managed to get themselves clear out of the poverty group and three had accumulated substantial assets. They are tough women; their lives have seen some bitter struggles. But their success proves that it is possible for women on their own, if they have access to credit and some support from their center, to carve out a decent life for themselves, even in an environment which is hostile to their very existence.

Several of the women whose loans were appropriated by male relatives were not handing them over willingly, but were struggling as best they could against authority figures to whom traditionally they owed obedience and respect. Some countervailing pressure from their centers and from the staff of the Bank would have helped them in this struggle. But they did not get it, partly because the officers of the Bank are not getting accurate information about loan use from the field. Similarly, a woman like Parveen, the elderly widow now shunted unhappily between her sons, might have been encouraged from the beginning to retain more control over her loans or to have registered some of the assets bought with her capital in her own name.

Increasing numbers of Grameen Bank borrowers will become widows as they move through their forties and fifties. If the gains they have made in income and assets are to be sustained and if the control they have negotiated over their lives is to be maintained, it is important to look at how they can build their basis for independence and what Grameen Bank can do to strengthen them.

There are three measures which could help mitigate the effects of illness and widowhood on GB women. The first is a more effective loan utilisation check, particularly in the early years of the Center, when the habits of loan use are being established and women are most vulnerable to appropriation. Bank workers have to be trained to recognise women who are pipelining their loans without control over the proceeds, and especially those who are being exploited by some male authority figure outside the nuclear household. Motivation work in the center should emphasis the borrower's own income earning efforts and the need to retain ownership and control of assets bought with her loans. Currently, even the 16 Decisions are silent on this issue.

The second is to make the loan use more transparent. The monthly collection sheets kept at the branch offices of Ghatail and Shajanpur have a column for recording the loan use. Most of them have 'paddy husking' written at the top, followed by a column of ditto marks. This custom has continued with the seasonal loan. If an accurate record were kept of assets purchased and land leased in or purchased with the GB loans, it would be possible to insist that these assets are kept in the name of the woman borrower. Leasehold agreements, for example, are sometimes verbal agreements, but there seems to be a trend in these villages for them to be written down and stamped, although there is no legal registration at the land court. It is within the power of center and bank to insist that leasehold arrangements financed by seasonal and general loans be stamped agreements in the woman's name and that land purchases be registered in her name. While legal protection is never complete protection, making it a requirement and including it in motivation work with the centers, would strengthen the woman's hand in the face of pressure from relatives, particularly when she becomes a widow.

The third measure is the health scheme currently being tested in a few branches in the Tangail and Dhaka Zones. If this scheme can be extended to all branches of the Bank, it will prevent many deaths, like the TB which killed Sofiah's husband and made her a widow in her early thirties. For other families, it will lower the cost of treatment and provide a trusted source of advice, so that they will be less likely to have to sell their assets. This is particularly important because the assets which are likely to be sold first are the assets in livestock and leasehold land which are held by the women.

The Strength of the Center

I have been at pains to demythologise the actual operations of the Grameen Bank at village level. I pointed out that the main meaning of the center to the women in our sample is as a window for credit to pursue their individual self-interest, firmly rooted in their primary loyalties to their families. I do not see it as a collective movement or a sisterhood. The social development programme, as embodied in the 16 Decisions, is an important source of information and motivation. But this document is far from being a woman's charter. It says nothing about domestic violence, arbitrary divorce, claiming of inheritance rights, ownership of assets or the elimination of discrimination against girl children. Its concern is with the women's better functioning as mothers and household managers and so it reinforces the culture of maternal altruism which persuades women to sink their own interests in the good of the family.

The women themselves strongly support these ideals and they are clearly functional for the Bank, since their discipline and self-restraint (women don't blow their profits in the tea shops or haunt the Housie parks) help ensure their repayment and the reinvestment of their profits.

I have tried to show that GB women effect change more like termites, hollowing out structures quietly from within, rather than pushing them over. There is no doubt that most of them have been successful in protecting their individual interests within the family. The strongest advocate of hard work and self-sacrifice — Norjahan — is also the woman who indignantly refuses to eat last and keeps a silk *sari* in her trunk. GB women look after themselves much better during pregnancy than do control group women and they are much more likely to see an MBBS doctor when they are ill.

When the peddler who sells scented soap turned up one morning in Ratnogram, I noticed that all these maternal altruists turned out in force, giggling a little at their self-indulgence, but buying — while Naima, from our control group, sat glowering over her dung sticks, without the means to do the same.

But I do not want to carry this debunking to the opposite extreme. Membership of group and center certainly has an impact on GB women. There is no doubt that ten years of attending meetings, articulating loan proposals, dealing with male bank workers and walking to town to visit the branch office, has given women an awareness and self-confidence in addition to the self-esteem they get from their economic contribution. Through its rituals and slogans and the activism of its members, the Grameen Bank has created its own culture in the village and has changed attitudes on gender issues. This came through when we administered our first questionnaire on decision making. Although the results had not much relation with reality, the *ideal* of joint decision making was strongly held by the GB women, in contrast to the women in the control group, where a substantial number still accepted the complete authority of their husbands.

That there is a definite "trickle-out" effect from the presence of Grameen Bank in the village is shown in several studies which compare a Grameen Bank sample with both non-GB women in a Grameen Bank village and non-GB women in a non-GB village. The Schuler-Hashemi study (1994) shows that non-GB members in GB villages are more mobile, more active income earners, less likely to be beaten by their husbands and slightly more involved in major family decisions than are non-members in villages with no Grameen Bank presence. Contraceptive use is higher in Grameen Bank villages across the board than in non-Grameen Bank villages. These findings indicate that the activities of GB members and their organisation into groups and centers is changing ideology and practice in the villages where they operate, with an equalising effect on gender relations.

It is not that ideology has thrown a blanket over the achievements of GB women, hiding them or moulding their meaning into something domestic and peripheral, as scholars like Sarah White would argue. I think the GB women, by their activities, have incrementally shifted attitudes in the village so that all women have benefitted.

In Chapter 7, I pointed out that although Grameen Bank is overwhelmingly a bank for women, its staff is almost entirely male. At various times during the year of data collection, after encounters with some of its more chauvinist officers, I wondered how any organisation so skewed against its female staff, could possibly empower poor women. But that is to misunderstand how GB works with its members. Grameen Bank supplies the credit, through a structure at village level that the women themselves can understand and operate; *the women use the credit to empower themselves.*

The groups and centers are small and organised so that the women learn to run them themselves. They know the rules and how the hierarchy works, and, by and large, this is an organisation which follows its own rules. In the two centers under study, after a decade, the women felt they *owned* their centers. They solved their own problems, often without reference to the branch office, but they knew how to demand attention from the branch manager and outflank the bank worker when their interests were threatened.

Given that this is a structure which they have learned to operate, and which also serves as a very efficient delivery mechanism for credit, it liberates women to use their skills to do the best they can for themselves and their families. And we have seen how well that works on many levels. GB families have increased their incomes and built up their assets and more than half have escaped from the poverty group altogether. But its impact is more than economic. GB women have moved from the margins to the center of their families. They are more mobile and have more confidence and awareness, not only in the *bari* but in the world outside of it. They and their children are better fed and better housed. And they have used their power over the household budget to make sure that their children are healthier, better educated and likely to lead easier lives than they have themselves.

Epilogue

Some 18 months later, in September, 1994, I walk through the fresh green of young *amon* paddy (planted late because the rains were very late) which surrounds the village of Ratnogram. The first person I see, walking out of a lane leading from Beparipara, is Kia, in a bright *sari*, laughing with excitement at our return.

We go straight to Gunjara's house. Fulu, her husband, who contracted typhoid during the year of data collection and was bedridden when we left, has died. Gunjara, a round-faced beauty only 18 months before, seems to have shrunk. All the light is gone out of her face. But she has survived. Before Fulu died he gifted to her 10 decimals of land as well as the 15 decimals he had already registered in the names of his three daughters. She owns the house and the five decimals on which it stands, and, no, the stepsons have not tried to drive her out.

This is the woman who told me that her dream was to educate her daughters, "so that they can be established people and will not have to struggle like us." That dream has faded. Her eldest daughter, now 12, has been sent to the house of a relative in Tangail, to 'help out.' The second has suffered a series of eye infections and has dropped out of school.

In the past year, with both general and seasonal loans, Gunjara has got 16,000 Taka in capital. She has bought two rickshaw vans and leased in another *bigha* of paddy land. She rents out the vans to two male relatives and operates the land herself with hired labour.

"We can eat. I can cover the repayments. I can bring up my daughters. I can manage. Everything is O.K.," she says quietly, sitting in the darkness of her house and looking at the ground. Then she adds: "My husband has gone. Love has gone. And nothing is O.K."

1993 was the year of a giant leap in loan disbursement in Tangail Zone. The seasonal loan, which matched and sometimes exceeded the general loan, more than doubled total disbursement in 1993. More than 50 *crore* Taka was disbursed in the new seasonal loans. This growth in disbursement made Tangail the second most profitable of the 11 zones in Grameen Bank; it expects a profit of around ten *crore* in 1994.

I knew that the stronger women in the Ratnogram center could easily absorb this new infusion of capital. But I was very doubtful whether the weaker members could cope with the doubled burden of repayment. I was wrong. Everywhere I went in Ratnogram there were signs of increased prosperity — and new zinc and cement-pillared houses. Norjahan's house had sprouted a verandah and an extra room. Saleha, the *lokkhi* farmer, had built a roomy house and installed her graduate son, still unemployed, in the old one. A newly dug pond, stocked with *rui* fish, wafted a cool breeze through her windows. Most of the center members had put their seasonal loans into acquiring leasehold land and had got good harvests in the 1993 *amon* and '94 *irri* seasons.

It seemed that far from sending weak members under with the weight of repayment, the seasonal loans had given them a new start. Even Rina. In the place of her stick and straw hut, into which were crowded her sick husband and four children in the past, I was amazed to see a very large house, its roof and walls made of sheets of tin. Inside was a wide wooden bed, over which Rina has sewn a flounce of *sari*. On the platform at the other end of the house are several sacks of rice. Rina is beaming with houseproud satisfaction.

When we were here in 1992 Rina's husband had excema and never held a job for more than a couple of months. She was living from one week to the next borrowing from relatives against her general loan, so that all her capital was literally eaten up before she received it. Just before we left she got a seasonal loan and gave part of it to her brother in return for 100 Taka a week to cover the repayment.

With the repayment on that loan covered and her husband back at work as a clerk in a rice mill, Rina did not have to borrow in 1993. When she got her next general loan the capital was intact. She leased in 15 decimals, which eased her anxiety about food, and put the rest into livestock. The results are making a row outside as we talk. There are six goats and enough ducks and hens to give 60 Taka worth of eggs each week, Rina says. Her husband is on constant medication, which costs them several hundred Taka a month, but they are making enough income to cover that cost too. Rina's desperate scramble of borrowing against future loans to feed her family and keep up her repayments seems to be over.

When she got her next seasonal loan, this time 8,000 Taka, she again pipelined most of it to her brother. But she kept enough to buy more goats and he covered repayment on the whole sum. In effect, she is charging him 60% interest. With her latest general loan she bought a large stock of *irri* rice, when the price was low. They eat some of it and sell some when she is short of cash. Because the *amon* planting is late and the harvest will be less than normal, the price of rice is rising steadily and she is making good money on the resale.

Far from drowning her, the seasonal loan gave Rina a lump sum of capital that she used as a springboard to start over. When I visit another three GB members in Ratnogram who were struggling well below the poverty line in

1992-93, the same process is evident. Large airy houses stand proudly on the spot where we used to sit inside a huddle of straw and jute sticks. Each household used the seasonal loan to lease in paddy land — a *bigha* or more, which has secured their food supply and gives them a lump sum in cash from the sale of the surplus at harvest time. Only Aloda, whose husband is mad and is now physically ill as well, is still in desperate straits.

Kia has leased in half an acre and her eldest son, who was working in a furniture shop, is back at home cultivating it and doing daily labor. She is very excited to see me and full of wild plans. She will take a family loan[1] and set up a furniture shop for her son, because the place where he worked has closed. The 40 decimals Kia had leased in when we left have been given back "so that I can buy two *bigha* from my father." This is one of Kia's stories. Two *bigha* would cost over 60,000 Taka and, anyway, her father does not own any land. But I am too pleased to see her and there are too many people crowded into her house to confront her with these embarrassing facts. I think I can see where that money went. Her husband, who was cured of TB in 1990, fell sick again this year and x-rays have found another spot on his lung. That diagnosis, in a hospital in Modhupur, in the next *upazila*, must have cost a bundle of Taka, and a cure will cost them a lot more.

Parul, the widow with three daughters who resisted efforts to throw her out of the village nearly two decades ago, is still in her tiny house. But she has two rickshaws now and no trouble with repayment. She has even managed to get back at last the ten decimals of land her husband left her, which she leased out several years ago.

I check the monthly collection sheets at the branch office — not a single default on either the general or seasonal loans in this center for the past year, despite the fact that most members are now carrying a weekly repayment of between 250 to 400 Taka. We sit in Kia's house with a whole gang of members and talk about how they manage it.

> *Nah*! It's not too big a burden. We invest the seasonal loan in lease-in land, so we get the harvest from that. Some of us have bought rickshaw-vans and each one brings in 100 Taka a week rental. When we take the general loan we invest half in some business and we keep half to help with repayment. Sister, things are much better now than when you were here.

So they are rolling some of one loan to help pay another. Like so many of the things they do, it is against the rules and it works.

There have been lots of marriages since we left; new brides are pulled shyly from their houses to be introduced. And some of my favourites — the 14 and 15 year old girls the same age as my daughter — have already gone to the villages of new husbands. One GB woman, whose husband is frequently ill with a resistant form of malaria, married her 15 year old this year.

"It would have been better to keep her in school another year or so, but I am afraid of some scandal. I am most afraid my husband will die. I wanted it settled," she said. She paid 10,000 Taka in dowry, using both seasonal and general loans, an unusually high dowry because the girl's leg is severely scarred by a burn. But the money did not go to the boy. It bought a piece of land in his village, but in the girl's name.

This is the way that Grameen Bank women effect change, I thought. Not by overturning anything, but inch by inch, pushing out their boundaries, altering the norms to their advantage. Maybe the 11th Decision of the Bank, which bans dowry, and which hardly anyone follows, should be changed to: "I will not give dowry to my son-in-law, but instead I will give my daughter the means to earn her own income."

Aina, Norjahan's bright-faced daughter is also married, but she is here visiting her parents. She radiates happiness and a new self-confidence. Women her mother's age are now joking with her as one of themselves. Her husband is almost as young as she is, 18 to her 16 years. "Close in age, close in love," remarks Kia sagely. He runs a small grocery shop near the bazaar in Ghatail town and Aina tells me how she "extracts" every last detail of his business from him when he comes home — to approving laughs of the Grameen women who are standing around us.

One of the Grameen Bank staff who is with us and who has never been to this village before begins a heavy lecture against child marriage. I find myself, oddly enough, stiffening almost as much as Norjahan herself. A college girl that we know in this village was kidnapped from her house last month by a gang of 15 men, paid for their work by a rejected suitor. She was rescued, but her future is in tatters. Who are we to make these pre-packed judgments, I think, in the face of Aina's obvious well-being and the real threats to girls' security?

The center in Ratnogram is more unified now, the GB women inform me. In 1993, the center chief who had been using the interest payments to bail out members in her faction was replaced by Kia, so a Bepari finally got a shot at leadership. This year Alia, who had been center chief many years before, was back in control. Alia, the poet, has composed another song, which she sings to us in a voice a little more cracked than last time, but still haunting. Alia, the diplomat, has pulled the center back together again.

Her very real understanding and commitment to the ideology of the Grameen Bank lies behind the most encouraging development I discovered on my return visit to Ratnogram. Center 42 has expanded from six groups to eight, ten new members. They didn't really select themselves, according to best GB practice. Alia selected them. But, although at least two of them are her relatives, her choice is sound. I know most of them. They are hard working, enterprising — and very poor. Five of them are former members of our control group.

Naima, whose husband Barek suffered from gastric ulcer and whose son went to another house on a labour contract at the age of eight, is now a GB member. Just in time. When we left they had just managed to scrape together enough savings to lease in 3 decimals of land. They managed to hold on to that acquisition for less than a year. In the rainy season their roof leaked so badly and their children got so sick that they returned the land in order to put a tin roof on their tiny house.

Daria, who told me in 1992 how hard it was to have her children working, and ill treated, in the houses of landlords, has both her eldest children home again. She got her first GB loan a month ago. She stocked paddy, bought goats and paid the inputs for the acre of land her husband is sharecropping this season. She has already gained a promise from her father-in-law to register part of the houselot in her name so that she can build a GB house.

Kadeera, the most successful, dominant and enterprising of the women in the Ratnogram control group, has dropped her ASA membership to join Grameen Bank. She wants more loans and bigger loans than ASA can provide, she admits. Her first loan will be for 'paddy husking' she says in the center meeting, with an embarrassed laugh. The others see the disbelief on my face and laugh too. It is obvious what she will do. Her husband is still sharecropping the Khan's land. She will move him into the more productive business of cultivating leasehold.

The fidelity to the original objectives of Grameen Bank in this selection of new members is in stark contrast to what is happening in Bonopur. Although the center is filling its empty places, none of our control group have managed to get in.

I go back to visit Roshonara, the young widow in our control group with two young sons. She has managed to get back the land her husband leased out before he died and is cultivating it herself with the help of her eldest son. Both the boys are back in school, keen now to get an education after an unhappy stint washing dishes in a tea shop in Gopalpur. There are two new goats in her *bari* and a flock of chickens and ducks. All this she has achieved through farming her small piece of land, working at the *boroba*ri during the harvest season and some help from her brother. But when she went to see if she could get a place in the Grameen Bank center, Habibah was dismissive. So she approached the Bank worker, who said, according to Roshonara:

"You have no husband. What can you do? Wait until your sons are big and then you can join the Grameen Bank."

The seasonal loan has had a big impact here, as in Ratnogram. Most of it has gone into leasehold. Zarinah and Zahir, who dared to both build a house and buy a *bigha* of land in the last two months of 1992, have bought another *bigha*, as well as getting back the land they leased out to finance the first purchase.

But, unlike Ratnogram, not all members have benefited from this loan. Two have gone under. Sofiah, the widow who tried and gave up on running a grocery shop, and who tried half a dozen other ways of earning an income the year we were here, has been married off to a man in his seventies and has left the village — leaving behind her a large debt to the Bank.

And Rohimah, the gentle widow who brought up her sons by domestic labour and then started all over again and brought up two grandchildren, no longer even has a place to sleep. I can hardly recognise her *bari*. Where one grandson used to live is a large tin-shed house, reverberating with singing and clapping. A new BRAC school, a very hopeful development for this village. But Rohimah's house has broken walls standing open to the sky. The roof has gone. She is squatting, shivering in her old blue *sari* on this hot day, inside a small hut that belongs to Aziz, the other grandson. She has been sick for two months, she tells us. She has no food, no saline for her diarrhoea. She is nearly three months in arrears. Where is Aziz? What happened to the rickshaw he was driving? What did you do with your seasonal loan?

She has been very weak for more than a year and cooking for Aziz was increasingly difficult. So although he was barely 17, she found a wife for him. When she got her seasonal loan her sons pressured her to buy the 10 decimals which adjoins the houselot — in Aziz' name. Her repayment went up to 220 Taka per week. What with the food, the repayment and the demands of a new wife, Aziz could hardly manage. Then the rickshaw was damaged in an accident and there was no money for repairs. They sold it and for a few weeks that money covered the repayments. Aziz went back to the unremunerative broken glass business. Then she sold the tin roof off her house to meet the repayments and she sleeps here and there, in whatever *bari* will tolerate her for the night. The last two months she has been ill and has stopped attending the center meetings. No-one from the center has come to find out what is wrong and nor, she claims, has the Bank worker.

On my way to see the center boss, Habibah, I am stopped by a woman I got to know well, although she does not appear in this book. "I'm at my wits end," she says. "I only have five more payments before I can get my new loan. But my vegetable harvest is finished and I don't have Taka to make my payment at tomorrow's meeting."

I go to Habibah's *bari*, and she tells me blandly that there are no arrears in her center and no-one is having any trouble handling the doubled repayment. She herself is now cultivating 7.5 *bigha*. No, she didn't take a seasonal loan. She doesn't need that kind of money. She is waiting for a family loan of 50,000 Taka so that she can buy more land.[1]

It was Habibah's skill and leadership in rehabilitating defaulting members that put this center back on its feet in 1987-88. But whatever tolerance she once had for the weak and poor, she has lost it. When she selects new members they are women like herself. Not only are these the kind of people she respects; they are also the kind who can buy their place in the center by paying off the arrears of defaulters who have dropped out.

The bamboo center hut in her *bari* has been replaced by a new center hut with zinc walls and roof. It would be stretching things to imagine that some of these zinc sheets came from Rohimah's roof, but they don't signal much fidelity to the 14th Decision of the Grameen Bank: "If anyone is in difficulty we shall help her."

When the afternoon rain stops I make the visit I have been dreading all day. To Sobhan's *bari*, the man with two wives and six malnourished children, whose eight year old son, Faruq, had kwashiorkor and was on the point of death when we left.

Faruq is very much alive. He comes running in and poses with a shy smile for our camerawoman. His mother tells me that the Union Member, with whom we left money, gave her eggs, milk, fish and vitamins daily until the boy recovered. At that point, I wander off into the banana grove to hide my tears, thinking of my own son. Moriom, the younger wife, goes into her house and starts an unearthly howling. It was *her* son, three year old Fazlul, who died. The child on her hip, who was born while we were in the village and is now two years old, looks acutely wasted. So does the youngest child of the other wife. It isn't enough to dole out charity to one. The mothers must have the means to help them all.

In both Bonopur and Ratnogram the influx of seasonal loans into the leasehold market has driven up the leasehold price. In 1992 the going rate in both villages was around 200 Taka per decimal, or between 6,000 to 7,000 per *bigha*. In mid 1994 it is around 8,000 Taka per *bigha*. In Ratnogram, most poor families are now GB members. But in Bonopur, the majority of poor families in this large village are not GB members and have little chance of joining. (The branch office had a plan to start a new center here in 1993, but nothing has come of it.) So the rise in the price of leasehold has made it harder for non-GB poor to get access to agricultural land.

Like most established areas in Grameen Bank, both Shajanpur and Ghatail Branches are still expanding, but at a much slower pace than before. The Ghatail area, for example, in which the village of Ratnogram is located, grew by 28% in membership in 1993. This has slowed to an annual growth rate of 12% in 1994. Profits, however, because of the upsurge in seasonal and housing loans, doubled in 1993 and are expected to double again in 1994, from 7.8 million Taka to more than 14 million. This means in most of the Tangail Zone that the poor who remain outside the Bank have little chance of getting in, despite a rapid increase in Bank profits.

There is a downpour on the morning of our last day — the farmers shovelling water into their fields to save the *amon* crop can relax. Then the sun comes out with a brilliant, washed light that makes the photographer ecstatic. It is hot, with a quick breeze that carries a promise of autumn. This is the photographer's day. Nahar and I sit about gossiping, enjoying ourselves. We end up in Rina's *bari*, snapping children, snapping ducks. Photograph her by the pond, I suggest, it's more natural. Dumb idea. As soon as the ducks hit the water they sail off for the other side, leaving Rina hooting uselessly. Her son dives in to herd them back again, and succeeds, to the cheers of the gathered crowd.

One after another the children jump into the big pond, shouting and splashing. Then, to my astonishment, in goes Alia, the center chief, ducking and gamboling with the children like a young girl. With a leap Rina follows her, her *sari* billowing up behind her. Off in one corner is Alia's ancient husband, having his bath. Alia swims up to him and they stand in the water side by side, stiff as two posts, while the photographer takes their picture. Then Alia gives a little giggle and starts rubbing her husband's back.

"Humph!" snorts Banu, who lost the power struggle when Alia became center chief. "Washing with no soap!"

The photographer keeps snapping, while the crowd erupts in laughter and comment.

Note

1. This is another new loan of up to 50,000 Taka given through the GB member to the husband and/or sons to cultivate land or engage in any business. So far, it is being given very selectively only to old branches with no arrears, centres with perfect repayment records for three years, and only to borrowers who are already economically successful, have labour power in the family and an economic opportunity to exploit. So far, no family loans have been given in either the Ghatail or Shajanpur Branches, nor are they likely to be under these rules.

Alia (scandalously) rubbing her ancient husband's back in the Musjidpara pond on our last day in Ratnogram.
Photo Credit: Nurjahan Chaklader

Appendix 1: Methodology

Our objective was to select long term borrowers in order to look at the impact on continued access to credit on income and empowerment. There were two zones where Grameen Bank had been operating for more than 10 years: Chittagong, where it began in 1986 as an action research project, and Tangail, where it began operations in 1989. Some 19 of the 24 Branches which have been disbursing loans since 1980 or earlier are in the Tangail Zone. This is also the crucible in which the Grameen Bank approach was fully developed and refined, so this is where we decided to look for the relevant centers.

We decided that the two senior researchers (David and I) could cover two centers in different Branches and different villages to lessen the risk of anything peculiarly local affecting the results. However, we ruled out large-scale sample survey methods as being too superficial to get the information we wanted. We wanted women's centers, of course, and we looked for conditions that would be fairly typical of rural Bangladesh: not too close to a large urban center, primarily dependent on double-cropped paddy for income; mainly Muslim; with at least half its population landless and no more or less prone to disaster than most of Bangladesh.

The first criteria did not leave us with much choice. Most of the centers first established in the Tangail Zone had been male centers. Only two branches had fairly old female centers and were also reasonably typical of rural Bangladesh conditions: Ghatail and Shajanpur. These branches also differed from each other in important ways. Shajanpur was more isolated than Ghatail, being well off the main trunk road north and about three hours by bus from Tangail. Ghatail was on the main trunk road and about one and a half hours by bus from Tangail. We thought that loanees in Ghatail branch would have more access to markets and therefore might have been able to make more profitable use of their loans.

Second, Ghatail branch was one of the best in the area for repayment and profitability — it had never had a repayment crisis and had been profitable for several years. Shajanpur had been one of the worst branches in the Bank. It had almost been closed down when its repayment rate dropped to 17% in 1987 during the great repayment crisis in Tangail. Although the branch had recovered it had still not made a profit by the end of 1991. We thought the performance of the two branches probably reflected the performance of their loanees. We therefore expected that the impact of GB loans would be greater in Ghatail than in Shajanpur.

Within these two branches we then went looking for female centers which were neither the best nor the worst, but average in performance and where the loanees had been borrowing for at least eight years. These criteria again severely limited our choice.

Finally we settled on two centers; Center 42 in Ratnogram and Center 36 in Bonopur. As Center 36 had only 17 members who had borrowed at least eight times, however, three more were chosen from Center 35 in the next village. This gave us 20 women borrowers from Ratnogram in Ghatail Branch and 20 from Bonopur and its neighbour in the Shajanpur Branch, all of whom had borrowed at least eight times.

From each village we then selected 12 households as a control group. We did a quick census of each village and through interviews established their land ownership and occupation ten years earlier, selecting those who had been qualified to join Grameen Bank in 1980, but had not done so. We had to reform this control group of 24 households several times so that the household size and ages of head of household and spouse were similar to that of the Grameen Bank member sample. The final control group was still slightly younger than the Grameen group (the husbands had an average age of 44.2 years compared to the Grameen husbands of 46.6 and the wives were 37.7 years old on average compared to the Grameen members at 39 years). The households of the control group were also slightly smaller; 0.5 persons smaller. These differences were not large enough to affect the comparability of the samples.

This sampling is the basis for the with-without Grameen Bank comparison. All 64 households were poor 10 to 12 years ago. In 1992 both the Grameen and control groups were at a similar point in the life-cycle of rural households in Bangladesh and had roughly the same opportunities in elapsed time to acquire productive assets. Average household labour supply was about equal. Therefore, current major differences in terms of household income and productive assets and in the empowerment of the adult women of the household should be due to access to credit by the Grameen group over the previous ten years.

Data Collection

Quantitative data were collected on the composition of the household, employment of its members, ownership and access to productive assets and current income and expenditure including lending and borrowing. This data was collected by two interviewers, one for each village, in opening and closing inventories and in weekly interviews throughout the year, to cover for seasonal variations. In these weekly interviews, the women respondents were also asked about their mobility during that week, visits to the household, any crisis, including illness, which had occurred and how they had been handled. The interviewers kept weekly diaries in which they recorded any extraordinary events.

During the first two months of data collection I took charge of supervising the opening inventories and weekly interviews in Ratnogram, while David did the same in Bonopur. As we became more familiar with each family, these weekly interviews were extended to obtain more qualitative data on decisions as they were made, on the woman's economic contributions and how the household budget was managed.

In April, we left the research team on the ground and returned to Malaysia for six months, receiving their data reports monthly by post and responding with our queries in the same way, a very slow and unsatisfactory procedure. By our return in November, however, we had a wealth of weekly data to use as a basis for the next four months of in-depth qualitative interviewing.

While the regular weekly data collection continued, I worked with an interpreter on those issues related to empowerment: the processes of decision making and crisis management, health issues, the nutrition of children and the dynamic of groups and centers. In our last month I held a series of group discussions amongst, unfortunately, only Grameen members, on some of the social issues which I knew to be relevant to these women.

At the same time, David was collecting more detailed information on important economic issues, like access to land, crops planted and their yields. He used this opportunity to cross-check some of the information I had received with the husbands of the respondents.

In looking at this data one needs to be aware that 1992 was a better than normal year for Tangail. Although the rains were a bit late, most villagers got a bumper *amon* crop because of the absence of flooding. Because the Grameen group operated much more land than the control group, this probably exaggerated the income differences between them, although access to more land can be regarded as one of the direct results of the Grameen group's access to credit.

Appendix 2:
Childrens' Growth

We measured the heights, weights and middle upper arm circumference of all the children in both Grameen Bank and control groups ten years and younger. There were 64 of them. We did not measure the children under 12 months because it was not possible to get birth weights and we thought that nutritional deficiencies would not show in any significant way until the child was taking solid food as well as breast milk. We calculated heights and weights for age and weight for height against the international reference standard (the NCHS) used by the Bangladesh Bureau of Statistics (BBS) in its nutritional survey of 1989-90.

Although the NCHS is a supposedly culture-free international measure, Bangladeshi children on the whole perform dismally on it. So we thought it necessary to compare the sample families with the average heights and weights of the whole population as recorded in the BBS 1989-90 Survey, so that these children could be seen in the context of their Bangladeshi peers. These anthropomorphic measures are designed to identify various forms of Protein Energy Malnutrition (PEM).

These measurements were simple to do and a source of great amusement to the children. What was more difficult was establishing their exact ages. We found that their mothers usually remembered accurately the month or season in which the child was born. Since Bangladesh has six distinct seasons, each lasting only two months, this made it possible to fix the birth month fairly accurately. Fixing the birth year was more of a problem. But mothers concerned with the survival of their children have sharp memories of natural disasters and could recall the age and condition of each child in relation to these times of danger. Tangail was hit by a disastrous flood in 1988 and the neighbouring village to Bonopur was hit by a tornado in 1990. These freaks of nature enabled us to fix the ages of the children under five with reasonable accuracy. We are less sure of the older children, although most women knew the spacing between each child, so that we could figure the ages from those of their younger brothers and sisters.

We calculated the heights and weights of each child as a percentage of the NCHS reference heights and weights for that age group, and then again as a percentage of the Bangladesh mean. Then we took an average of these percentages for the total in the GB and control samples.

When we look at the heights of Grameen Bank children compared to children in the control group, GB children are slightly taller but the difference is so small as to be insignificant. The differences in weight, indicating more current impact of better nutrition, are larger. However, when we broke down these figures, we found stronger differences within the younger age groups. If we look at the children from the age of one to the age of five, the children of the Grameen families are a little taller and quite a bit heavier than the children of the control group. These are the children born to mothers who were already on their fourth or fifth loan cycle and had been putting increases in income into improving the food eaten by their families as well as into more immediate and systematic treatment of illness.

When set against the NCHS reference median of **height for age**, the mean of the Grameen children aged one to five years is 91% of the standard. In other words they are a bit short by international standards, but not so short as to be classified as stunted. They just miss. Set against the Bangladeshi average for the whole population, however, the Grameen children are slightly taller than the national average. They measure 102% of the Bangladeshi mean.

Children in the control group measure on average only 88% of the NCHS reference heights. In other words the majority are stunted. They are also slightly shorter than the average Bangladeshi; their mean height was 99% of the national average.

Height for age is more a measure of chronic and long term malnutrition since it reflects the gradual growth of bones and skeleton. Children who are less than 90% of the reference height are classified as *stunted*.

When we look at the results on the **weight for height** measures, the Grameen children also perform better on this measure of current nutrition. Children can lose and gain weight quite rapidly, but even if starved they cannot lose height. So the measure of weight for height indicates acute and current malnutrition. It is also the most accurate measurement, given that we may be wrong about some of the ages. Children who are less than 80% of the reference median of weight for height are classified as *wasted*, meaning they have lost fat and tissue off their bones. The Grameen Bank children average 90% of the NCHS reference, which means they are normal, but only just. The results are a bit skewed by the four year old twins of a Grameen member, whose husband is mentally ill and whose per capita income is the lowest in the sample. These two girls reach only 79% of the reference.

The control group children measure 85% of the reference weight for height; they are wasted by this classification. The control group reaches 93% of the Bangladeshi mean of weight to height. The Grameen children are 99% of this mean.

Weight for age: Weight for age is a more general, nonlinear measure of how underweight is the child compared to the reference median. We grouped these children under the Gomez classification as normal, or as suffering from first, second or third degree malnutrition.

Table A.1 Height and Weight for Age

	Height			Weight	
	% Reference	% B'desh Mean		% Ref.	% B'desh Mean
GB Total	89.3	98.8	72.4	97.4	
Control Total	88.3	97.1	68.6	89.9	
GB Under 6 Yrs.	90.8	101.9	76	103.3	
Control Under 6	88	99.4	68.3	93.8	

The Gomez classification:
* 90% or more of the reference weight — normal
* 89.9% to 75% of reference — first degree malnutrition
* 74.9% to 60% of reference — second degree malnutrition
* Below 60% of reference — third degree malnutrition.

According to the BBS survey of 1989-90, the average Bangladeshi child is so seriously **underweight** as to suffer from second degree malnutrition by the Gomez classification. Our small group of Grameen children are also underweight by this norm, but less so than the national average. The Grameen children weighed only 76% of the NCHS reference weights. In comparison with their Bangladeshi peers, however, the majority are heavier. They measure 103% of the national average. By the Gomez classification they suffer from first degree rather than second degree malnutrition.

The control group children can only be described as skinny. They measure a mere 68% of the NCHS reference weights; which means that the average child suffers from second degree malnutrition. They are also more seriously underweight than the average Bangladeshi child, measuring only 94% of the national mean.

We did not find the middle upper arm circumference (MUAC) to be a sensitive measurement for the majority of the children. It did, however, indicate extremes in our sample. BBS uses a measurement of 12.5 or less as an indicator of serious malnourishment and one of between 12.5 to 13.4 as a borderline case. There were only four children in our sample of 68 with MUAC of 12.5 or less. One was dying of kwashiorkor; there were two two year olds who could barely stand unaided; and a girl who was recovering from a long bout of diarrhoea, the only Grameen child amongst this sad group.

Appendix 3:
The Sixteen Decisions

1   We shall follow and advance the four principles of Grameen Bank — Discipline, Unity, Courage and Hard Work — in all walks of our lives
2   Prosperity we shall bring to our families
3   We shall not live in dilapidated houses. We shall repair our houses and work towards constructing new houses as soon as possible
4   We shall grow vegetabes all year round. We shall eat plenty of them and sell the surplus
5   During the plantation season we shall plant as many seedlings as possible
6   We shall plan to keep our families small. We shall minimize our expenditures. We shall look after our health
7   We shall educate our children and ensure that we can earn to pay for their education
8   We shall always keep our children and their environment clean
9   We shall build and use pit-latrines
10 We shall drink water from tubwells. If it is not available, we shall boil water or use alum
11 We shall not take dowry at our son's weddings, nor shall we give any dowry at our daughter's weddings. We shall keep our center free from the curse of dowry. We shall not practice child marriage
12 We shall not inflict injustice on anyone, nor shall we allow anyone else to do so
13 We shall collectively undertake larger investments for higher incomes
14 We shall always be ready to help each other. If anyone is in difficulty we shall help him or her
15 If we come to know of any breach of discipline in any center, we shall go there and help restore discipline
16 We shall introduce physical exercises in all of our centers. We shall take part in all social activities collectively

Note: These Sixteen Decisions were formulated in a national workshop of 100 women center chiefs in March, 1984, and form the social development programme of the Grameen Bank. All members are expected to memorise and implement these decisions.

Glossary

amon	main season paddy harvested November-December
apa	sister; term of respect for non-kin women
aus	early summer paddy, harvested September
bari	home; homestead; a courtyard surrounded by the houses of close kin
begun	brinjal/eggplant
Bepari	mustard-making and trading caste, fairly low down the scale.
bigha	approximately one third of an acre; 30 decimals
biri	local cigarette
bo	wife
boro	winter dry-season paddy, harvested May-June
borobari	lit: big *bari*; landlord's house.
borolok	landlord; rich person
bota	a curved knife used for all cutting work, whether chicken, bamboo or cloth
bumihin	landless; poor person
burka	all-enveloping garment, including hood for the head and flap to cover face, worn by women going outside in order to keep strict *purdah*
choki	large wooden platform-bed
Choitro	Bengali month from mid-March to mid-April. Hot, dry and dusty.
dai	traditional village midwife
dheki	wooden mallet for husking paddy, mounted on a wooden beam and operated with the foot
dhoby	washerman; laundry
dhormo-ma	a religious relationship like a godmother
dol	village faction or patron-client cluster; group
doy	yoghurt, usually sweet
Eid	festival marking the end of the fasting month of Ramadan. Actually *Eid -ul-Fitri*. The other *Eid-ul-Azha* is known as *Korbani*
ghani	stone mill for grinding mustard seed, turned with wooden arms loaded with stones and working on a pivot
ghor jamai	marriage where husband settles in his wife's parent's *bari*; literally "house son-in-law," which gives the prejorative flavour
gusti	patrilineal kin group
haat	weekly or bi-weekly markets, some specialised like cow *haat*, *sari haat*

hisab	counting
hujor	spiritual healer
huturi	unqualified doctor; quack
irri	winter, or *boro* paddy crop, named for the International Rice Research Institute in the Philippines, which developed the "green revolution" package which made winter cropping possible in irrigated fields
Kartik	Bengali month from mid-September to mid-November. The pre-harvest hungry month
khas land	government-owned land
khata	patchwork quilt assembled from old *lunggi* and *sari* too worn to wear
khobiraj	herbal healer using homeopathic methods
Korbani	*Eid-al-Azha,* the festival of sacrifice which ends the season of pilgrimage to Mecca, celebrated by slaughtering an animal and distributing the meat to the poor
lau	marrow; usually grown over the roof of the house
lokkhi	having the qualities of Lakshmi, goddess of grain and plenty
lunggi	male garment; tube of cloth tied around waist; *sarung* in Southeast Asia
matbar	village leader
maund	measurement of paddy; 37.25 kilos
Muharam	the Muslim New Year
mullah	religious scholar or teacher
murri	puffed rice, essential during the fasting month for breaking fast
paan	*betel,* an addictive nut rolled in leaf with lime and chewed
para	section of a village; neighbourhood
pitta	winter cakes, often made from special rice flour and eaten hot
poisha	unit of currency; the smallest coin
punjabi	in the village context, a long tunic for men worn on formal occasions
purdah	seclusion of women from outsiders; dress which veils her from the gaze of strangers
roti	unleavened bread rolled into a round and baked on a griddle
sari	long piece of cloth wound around the body, worn universally by married women
service-holder	someone with a salaried occupation
shaak	spinach
shalish	village court or hearing attended only by men and presided over by the *matbar*
shomman	honour, respect
sim	beans
taka	unit of Bangladeshi currency. 40 Taka = US$1, during 1992
talak	the repudiation of a wife by a husband; three are required for final divorce
Thana	sub-division of an upazila; police station
utuli	squatters, lacking even a houseplot
Upazila	sub-district
waris	inherited; belonging to the patrimony

Bibliography

Abecassis, David. 1990. *Identity, Islam and Human Development in Rural Bangladesh.* Dhaka: University Press Ltd.

Arens, Jenneke and Jos Van Beurden. 1977. *Jhagrapur: Poor Peasants and Women in a Village in Bangladesh.* New Delhi: Orient Longman.

Bangladesh Bureau of Statistics. 1991. *Report of the Child Nutritional Status Survey, 1989-90.* Dhaka.

Beneria, L. and Sen, G. 1981. "Accumulation, Reproduction and Women's Role in Economic Development: Boserup Revisited." *Signs* Volume 7.

Berger, M. 1989. "Giving Women Credit: The Strengths and Limitations of Credit as a Tool for Alleviating Poverty." *World Development* Volume 17:7.

Berninghausen, Jutta and Birgit Kerstan. 1992. *Forging New Paths: Feminist Social Methodology and Rural Women in Java.* London: Zed Books.

Blanchet, Therese. 1984. *Meanings and Rituals of Birth in Rural Bangladesh.* Dhaka: University Press Limited.

Boserup, E. 1970. *Women's Role in Economic Development.* New York: St Martin's Press.

BRAC. 1980. *The Net: Power Structure in Ten Villages.* Dhaka: BRAC Publications.

Bruce, J. 1989. "Homes Divided." *World Development* Volume 17:7.

Chen, Martha Alter. 1985. *A Quiet Revolution: Women in Transition in Rural Bangladesh.* Cambridge, Ma.: Schenkman Publishing House.

Chowdhury, A. M. R., Mahmood, M. and F.H.Abed. 1991. "Credit for the Rural Poor — the Case of BRAC in Bangladesh." *Small Enterprise Development* Volume 2:3.

Counts, Alex. mimeo. *Give Us Credit.* Random House forthcoming.

Dwyer, D. and Bruce, J. eds. 1988. *A Home Divided: Women and Income in the Third World.* Standford: Standford University Press.

FAXNET (now *Credit for the Poor.)* Quarterly newsletter of Credit and Savings for the Hard-Core Poor (CASHPOR) Network. Seremban, Malaysia.

Folbre, N. 1986. "Hearts and Spades: Paradigms of Household Economics." *World Development* Volume 14:2.

Fuglesang, Andreas and Chandler, Dale. 1988. *Participation As Process — What Can We Learn From Grameen Bank Bangladesh.* Dhaka: Grameen Bank with Norwegian Ministry of Development Cooperation.

————— and ————— . 1993. *Participation as Process — Process as Growth.* Dhaka: Grameen Bank.

Gardener, Katy. 1991. *Songs at the River's Edge: Stories from a Bangladesh Village.* London: Virago Press.

Getubig, I. ed. 1993. *Overcoming Poverty Through Credit*, Kuala Lumpur: Asian Pacific Development Center.

Gibbons, David S. and Sukor Kasim. 1990. *Banking on the Rural Poor*. Kuala Lumpur: Center for Policy Research/Asian Pacific Development Center.

Gibbons, David S. ed. 1992. Revised 1994. *The Grameen Reader*. Dhaka: Grameen Bank.

Goetz, Anne-Marie and Rina Sen Gupta. "Who Takes The Credit? Gender, Power and Control over Loan Use in Rural Credit Programmes Bangladesh." forthcoming in *World Development*.

Grameen Bank. *Annual Report, 1989*. Dhaka: Grameen Bank.

Hamid, S. 1989. *Women's Non-Market Work and GDP Accounting: The Case of Bangladesh*. Dhaka: Bangladesh Institute of Development Studies.

Harriss, Barbara. 1992. "The Intra-Family Distribution of Hunger in South Asia." in Sen A.K. ed., *The Political Economy of Hunger, Volume 1*.

Hartmann, B and Boyce, J. 1983. *A Quiet Violence: View From a Bangladesh Village*. London: Zed Books.

Hashemi, Syed M. 1994. "Disparate Responses to Men's and Women's Health Problems: Evidence from Rural Bangladesh." mimeo. Dhaka: Development Research Center.

Haque, Trina. 1989. *Women and the Informal Credit Market in Bangladesh*. Dhaka: Bangladesh Institute of Development Studies.

Holcombe, Susan. 1995. *Managing to Empower: The Grameen Bank's Experience of Poverty Alleviation*. London: Zed Books.

Hossain, Hameeda, Cole P. Dodge and F. H. Abed eds. 1992. *From Crisis to Development: Coping with Disasters in Bangladesh*. Dhaka: University Press Limited.

Hossain, Mahabub. 1988. *Credit for Alleviation of Rural Poverty: The Grameen Bank in Bangladesh*, Dhaka: International Food Policy Research Institute with Bangladesh Institute of Development Studies.

————. ed. 1990 "Special Issue on Poverty in Bangladesh." *Bangladesh Studies* Volume XVIII, No 3.

———— and Rita Afsar. 1989. *Credit for Women's Involvement in Economic Activities in Rural Bangladesh*. Dhaka: Bangladesh Institute of Development Studies.

Hossain, M. 1987. *The Assault That Failed: A Profile of Absolute Poverty in Six Villages of Bangladesh*. Geneva: UNRISD.

Hossain, Mosharaff. 1991. *Agriculture in Bangladesh: Performance, Problems and Prospects*. Dhaka: University Press Limited.

Huq, A. Ameerul. ed. 1978. *Exploitation and the Rural Poor*. Dhaka: BRAC Publications.

Huq M. and M. Sultan. 1991. "Informality in Development: The Poor as Entrepreneurs in Bangladesh." in A.L. Chickering and M. Salahdine eds. *The Silent Revolution: The Informal Sector in Five Asian and Near-Eastern Countries*. San Francisco: International Center for Economic Growth.

Jain, D. and N. Banerjee eds. 1985. *Tyranny of the Household*. New Delhi: Shakti Books.

Jansen, E. G. 1987. *Rural Bangladesh: Competition for Scarce Resources*. Dhaka: University Press Limited.

Kabeer, Naila. 1989a. "Monitoring Poverty as if Gender Mattered: A Methodology for Rural Bangladesh." Sussex: Institute for Development Studies Discussion Paper.

————. 1989b. "The Quest for National Identity: Women, Islam and the State in Bangladesh." Sussex: Institute for Development Studies Discussion Paper.

————. 1994. *Reversed Realities: Gender Hierarchies in Development Thought.* New Delhi: Kali For Women.

Kamal, Ghulam Mustafa, Mohammad Bazlur Rahman and A.R.M. Ahmedul Ghani. 1992. *Impact of Credit Program on the Reproductive Behaviour of Grameen Bank Women Beneficaries.* Dhaka: National Institute of Population Research and Training.

Khan, Shakeeb Adnan. 1989. *The State and Village Society: The Political Economy of Agricultural Development in Bangladesh.* Dhaka: University Press Limited.

Khandker, Shahidur R., and others. 1995. *Grameen Bank: Performance and Sustainability.* Washington D.C.: World Bank.

Kramsjo, Bosse and Geoffrey D. Wood. 1992. *Breaking the Chains.* Dhaka: University Press Limited.

Meis, M. 1982. *The Lacemakers of Narsapur: Indian Housewives Produce for the World Market.* Geneva:ILO Report.

Mihar, Ainon Nahar. 1994. *In Quest of Empowerment: The Grameen Bank Impact on Women's Power and Status.* Dhaka: University Press Limited.

Mannan, M. A. 1989. *Status of Women in Bangladesh: Equality of Rights — Theory and Practice.* Dhaka: Bangladesh Institute of Development Studies.

————. 1990. *Mother and Child Health in Bangladesh: Evidence From Field Data.* Dhaka: Bangladesh Institute of Development Studies.

North-South Institute. 1985. *Rural Poverty in Bangladesh: A Report to the Likeminded Group.* Ottawa.

————. 1990. *Rural Poverty in Bangladesh: A Report to the Likeminded Group. 1990.* Dhaka: University Press Limited.

Ong, Aihwa. 1987. *Spirits of Resistance and Capitalist Discipline: Factory Women in Malaysia.* New York: State University of New York Press.

Osmani, S. R. 1989. "Limits to the Alleviation of Poverty Through Non-Farm Credit." *The Bangladesh Development Studies* Volume XVII:4.

————. 1990. *Food Deprivation and Undernutrition in Rural Bangladesh.* Helsinki: WIDER.

Quasem, M. A. 1991. "Limits to the Alleviation of Poverty Through Non-Farm Credit: A Comment." *The Bangladesh Development Studies* Volume XIX:3.

Rahman, Atiur. 1986a. *Consciousness-Raising Efforts of Grameen Bank.* Dhaka: Bangladesh Institute of Development Studies.

————. 1986b. *Impact of Grameen Bank Intervention on the Rural Power Structure.* Dhaka: Bangladesh Institute of Development Studies.

————. 1989a. *Impact of Grameen Bank on the Nutritional Status of the Rural Poor.* Dhaka: Bangladesh Institute of Development Studies.

————. 1989b. *Housing for the Rural Poor: The Grameen Bank Experience.* Dhaka: Bangladesh Institute of Development Studies.

————. 1989. *Human Responses to Natural Hazards: The Hope Lies in Networking.* Dhaka: Bangladesh Institute of Development Studies.

Rahman, Hossain Zillur ed. 1991. *Rethinking Poverty: Dimensions, Process, Options.* Poverty Trends Study. Dhaka: Bangladesh Institute of Development Studies.

Rahman, Rushidan I. 1986. *Impact of the Grameen Bank on the Situation of Poor Rural Women.* Dhaka: Bangladesh Institute of Development Studies.

Ray, Jayanta Kumar. 1987. *To Chase a Miracle: A Study of the Grameen Bank of Bangladesh.*Dhaka: University Press Limited.

Safilios-Rothschild, C. 1991. "Gender and Rural Poverty in Asia: Implications for Agricultural Project Design and Implementation." *Asia-Pacific Journal of Rural Development* Volume 1:1

Schuler, Sidney Ruth and Syed M. Hashemi. 1994. "Credit Programs, Women's Empowerment and Contraceptive Use in Rural Bangladesh. *Studies in Family Planning* Volume 25:2.

Sen, A. K. 1990. "Gender and Cooperative Conflicts." in Tinker, I., ed., *Persistent Inequalities.* Oxford: Oxford University Press.

Sen, Binayak. 1989. *Moneylenders and Informal Financial Markets: Insights from Hoar Areas of Rural Bangladesh.* Dhaka: Bangladesh Institute of Development Studies.

Sennauer, B. 1990 "The Impact of the Value of Women's Time on Food and Nutrition." in Tinker, I., ed., *Persistent Inequalities.* Oxford: Oxford University Press.

Shams, M. Khalid. 1992. *Designing Effective Credit Delivery System for the Poor: The Grameen Bank Experience.* Dhaka: Grameen Bank.

Shehabuddin, Rahmuna. 1992. *The Impact of Grameen Bank in Bangladesh.* Dhaka: Grameen Bank.

Sobhan, Rehman. Coordinator. *Report of the Task Forces on Bangladesh: Development Strategies for the 1990s: Policies for Development.* Dhaka: University Press Ltd.

Tinker, I. ed. 1990. *Persistent Inequalities: Women and World Development.* Oxford: Oxford University Press.

Von Pishke, J.D. 1989. *Finance at the Frontier: Debt Capacity and the Role of Credit in Developing the Prvate Economy.* Washington D.C. World Bank.

Westergaard, Kirsten. 1983. *Pauperization and Rural Women in Bangladesh: A Case Study.* Dhaka: BARD.

White, S. C. 1992. *Arguing With the Crocodile: Gender and Class in Bangladesh.* London: Zed Books.

Wood, Geoffrey D. 1994. *Bangladesh: Whose Ideas, Whose Interests?* Dhaka: University Press Limited.

World Bank. 1990. *Bangladesh: Strategy Paper on Women in Development.* Washington D.C: World Bank.

Yaron, Jacob. 1992. *Successful Rural Finance Institutions.* Washington D.C.: World Bank.

Yunus, Muhammad. 1984 "On Reaching the Poor." in Gibbons ed. 1994. *The Grameen Reader.* Dhaka: Grameen Bank.

———— . 1986. "Grameen Bank As I See It." in Gibbons ed. 1994.

———— . 1987. "Grameen Bank: The First Decade." in Gibbons ed. 1994.

———— . 1989. "Credit for Self-Employment, A Fundamental Human Right." in Gibbons ed. 1994.

———— . 1991. *Grameen Bank: Experiences and Reflections.* Dhaka: Grameen Bank.

———— . ed. 1987. *Jorimon and Others: Faces of Poverty.* Dhaka: University Press Ltd.

Index

About the Book and Author

For two decades, the Grameen Bank of Bangladesh has successfully administered a unique program that lends small sums to poor women for income generation. This is the first empirical study to examine the long-term influence of these loans on the borrowers, and it demonstrates that credit alone can fundamentally change the lives of poor women— even in the absence of other aid programs and in an environment distinctly hostile to women's autonomy. Helen Todd spent a year in two villages in Bangladesh following the lives of women who have been borrowing from the Grameen Bank for a decade. She focuses on the day-to-day processes of how they generate money from their tiny loans, what they do with the resulting income, and how much control they retain over it.

In stark contrast with nonmembers, most Grameen women emerge from this study as strong individuals, successfully battling for positions of power in their families and for respect in their villages. Moreover, the Grameen women's gains have been sustainable, since most of them have invested in access to land. Through the vivid stories of individual women, Todd paints a picture of women empowering themselves with the crucial ingredient of continued access to credit over the course of a decade.

Helen Todd is a Malaysian journalist who edits *Credit for the Poor*, the newsletter of the CASHPOR network of Grameen Bank replicators in Asia.